THE NEW ATHEISTS

THE NEW ATHEISTS

THE TWILIGHT OF REASON AND THE WAR ON RELIGION

Tina Beattie

DARTON·LONGMAN+TODD

First published in Great Britain in 2007 by
Darton, Longman and Todd Ltd
1 Spencer Court
140–142 Wandsworth High Street
London SW18 4JJ

ISBN–10   0–232–52712–1
ISBN–13   978–0–232–52712–4

A catalogue record for this book is available
from the British Library.

Designed and produced by Sandie Boccacci
Phototypeset in 11/14pt Bembo
Printed and bound in Great Britain by
CPI Antony Rowe, Chippenham

Contents

Contents

Acknowledgements

Every book emerges out of a community of conversations, influences and ideas, and it would not be possible to name all the students, friends and colleagues who have shaped my thinking during the course of writing this. Like many other theologians, I owe a debt of gratitude to Richard Dawkins for reawakening public interest in God more effectively than any preacher could have done. Special thanks must go to Brendan Walsh, Claudine Nightingale, Helen Porter and the team at Darton, Longman and Todd. They have been a joy to work with, and I cannot thank them enough for the exceptional quality of their editorial support. Rebecca de Saintonge, close friend and literary critic, waded through an early draft with a keen eye for obfuscations and exaggerations. Emma Brown's doctoral research has been a valuable resource, and her influence is clear in chapter two.

My family have been there for me, as always. This book is for them, and particularly for Dave, for his kindness as well as his love. Readers will discover why that matters.

Dust

We are made of dust, we are
Flying on every wind,
Blown to the back of the earth,
Stormed at, broken, defiled.
We are people of dust
But dust with a living mind.

Dust with a spirit, grace
Goes to the end of the earth,
Follows the dark act, the thought
Lying, wounding, distraught,
We are dust from our birth
But in that dust is wrought

A place for visions, a hope
That reaches beyond the stars,
Conjures and pauses the seas,
Dust discovers our own
Proud, torn destinies.
Yes, we are dust to the bone.

Elizabeth Jennings

Dust

INTRODUCTION

Forty years ago, there was a widespread belief that religion was a spent force in the Western democracies, having been confined to the private sphere and destined to be eliminated altogether by the forces of science, reason and secularism. However, in the last three decades religion has been catapulted back into public consciousness, not least by acts of violence, extremism and various forms of fundamentalism. This has generated considerable public debate about the potentially harmful effects of religious faith. Is it irrational to believe in God? Is religion simply so much mumbo-jumbo? Does religion justify violence? Does it turn good people into fanatics and extremists?

One reaction to the growing influence of religion has been the emergence of an anti-religious movement known as the 'new atheism', sometimes also known as 'militant atheism'. The new atheism is spearheaded by the popular science writer Richard Dawkins, whose book *The God Delusion*[1] went straight to the top of the bestseller lists in Britain and America when it was published in 2006. Christopher Hitchens' book, *God Is Not Great*,[2] has achieved similar levels of success since its publication in 2007, and other books promoting atheism by Sam Harris and Daniel C. Dennett have also enjoyed considerable popularity.[3] A number of religious writers, mainly Christian theologians and scientists, have published books defending the compatibility between faith and the demands of science and reason. The theologian Alister McGrath and the Director of the Human Genome Project, Francis Collins, have both written about how they converted from atheism to

Christianity as a result of their involvement in science.[4]

My main aim in this book is not to defend religion against the new atheists, nor is it to deny the problem of religious extremism and its growing political influence. If this book says relatively little about the dangers of certain forms of religion, it is because I think the recent atheist bestsellers have identified these very well, and there is no need for me to repeat their arguments here. But to suggest that religion can be universally defined and condemned by referring to various forms of extremism which have flourished in late modernity is to give a distorted and reductive account of a much more complex and diverse human phenomenon. Those who have sought to present a more positive view of religion so far have tended to come from a fairly conservative Christian perspective. As a result, the debate is too narrowly focused on questions of rationality and belief, and it fails to take account of the many different challenges posed to both Western secularism and religious traditions by those whose voices are excluded from the conversation. I seek to broaden the discussion by situating it in a wider social and historical context. If we are to understand the role that religion plays in people's lives, then we need to be more attentive to the many different ways in which religious and cultural narratives act as vehicles of meaning for those who inhabit them.

The new atheism and the liberal *zeitgeist*

Dawkins has been promoting his brand of scientific atheism for a number of years. His main argument is that, after Darwin's theory of evolution and in the light of modern science, it is no longer rational to believe in God, and any educated person who continues to do so is guilty of wilful ignorance. Moreover, he argues that religion has been responsible for most of the violence in the world throughout history, and that it has a corrupting influence on values and ethics. He has recently claimed that to bring children up with any sense of religious identity is tantamount to a form of child abuse.

In the aftermath of the 9/11 attack on America, Dawkins

declared his commitment to a more militant form of atheism, and he was soon joined by a number of other public figures who interpreted 9/11 as a clarion call to defend the values of Western secular liberalism against the rising tides of religious fanaticism. For example, in an article in *The Guardian* newspaper in 2002, the novelist Martin Amis wrote:

> Since it is no longer permissible to disparage any single faith or creed, let us start disparaging all of them. To be clear: an ideology is a belief system with an inadequate basis in reality; a religion is a belief system with no basis in reality whatever. Religious belief is without reason and without dignity, and its record is near-universally dreadful.[5]

Amis's description of all religion as irrational, unreal and immoral offers a neat summing up of claims which are made in one form or another by all the new atheists.

In the preface to *The God Delusion*, Dawkins declares that his intention is to convert religious believers to atheism by helping them to overcome their 'childhood indoctrination'[6] in order 'to break free of the vice of religion altogether'.[7] As the Simonyi Professor of Public Understanding of Science at Oxford University, Dawkins would seem ideally placed to launch this militant campaign on behalf of scientific atheism. He was, after all, voted as one of the world's top three intellectuals by *Prospect* magazine. However, reviewing *The God Delusion* for *Prospect*, Andrew Brown describes it as 'Incurious, dogmatic, rambling and self-contradictory'. He observes, 'It has been obvious for years that Richard Dawkins had a fat book in him, but who would have thought him capable of writing one this bad?'[8]

Yet if some critics have condemned *The God Delusion* as an exercise in shoddy polemics, there are many others who clearly do not share this perception. In their book sales and public audiences, the new atheists have attracted a large following and they clearly speak for a significant number of British and American people. In March 2007, an audience of more than 2000 attended a debate in London on the proposition, 'We'd be better off without religion', with Dawkins, AC Grayling and Hitchens defending the proposal, and Rabbi Julia Neuberger, Roger Scruton and Nigel Spivey opposing it. Those giving the case for religion were moderate and thoughtful in their arguments, while Grayling, Dawkins and Hitchens were repetitive, anecdotal and occasionally confrontational – Hitchens heckled the rabbi while she was speaking. In a glowing review of Hitchens' book, *God is Not Great*, Dawkins recalls that, when they were preparing for this event, Grayling observed that 'Hitch will spray AK47 ammo at the enemy in characteristic style'.[9] Nevertheless, the Dawkins side won the debate when a vote was taken at the end, which suggests that this form of atheism has captured the liberal *zeitgeist*, so that the quality of the arguments matters less than the ability to tap into the mind-set of a particular sector of the British and American public.

The ideas represented by the new atheists therefore demand to be taken seriously, whatever the deficiencies in their style and arguments. However, we need to find a different form of engagement between custodians of knowledge in the world's religious traditions, and the more recent claims to intellectual authority by advocates of various forms of scientific materialism and atheist rationalism. We must resist the impoverishment of public discourse on matters of religion which has come about not only (or maybe not even) because of the threat of religious fanaticism in all its many forms, but also because of a no less virulent secular fanaticism which has taken hold of the intellectual classes. The wholesale condemnation of religion is an ideology which, like all ideologies, involves considerable distortion of history and a lack of the kind of insight which would invite a more nuanced approach to the role played by religion in different contexts. All forms of belief, including atheism, are a product of their social and historical environments. If we are to explore the ways in which ideas and beliefs function in society and in relation to one another, we have to understand those environments and the place of particular beliefs within them in terms of their cultural, ethical and political influence.

Contextualising the debate

The new atheism is primarily a British and American phenomenon. Critics argue that it is simply a distorted version of Christianity, since it is a form of rebellion which is defined by and dependent upon that which it rejects. Philosopher John Gray describes it as 'a Christian heresy that differs from earlier heresies chiefly in its intellectual crudity.'[10] A professor of theology (Denys Turner) tells of how he makes a bet with his atheist students that, if they can tell him why they do not believe in God, he will tell them which Christian denomination they were brought up in. He says he usually wins the bet.

Hitchens writes that 'my particular atheism is a Protestant atheism',[11] and this description would fit all the new atheists. While continental atheisms are often informed by Jewish and Catholic perspectives and place a strong emphasis on language and symbolism, the new atheism is the product of a post-Protestant intellectual environment associated with white conservative men (WASPs, to use an American expression), and primarily concerned with questions of evidence, proof and rationality. In his review of Dawkins' book, Terry Eagleton describes Dawkins as displaying 'a very English brand of common sense that believes mostly in what it can touch, weigh and taste'.[12] The new atheists are uniformly condemning in their treatment of religion, but their primary targets are Islamist extremism and American Christian fundamentalism, and it is helpful to bear this in mind when considering their arguments.

In America there has long been an intellectual confrontation between evolutionary scientists and Christian creationists, who reject the theory of evolution in favour of a literal interpretation of the creation story in the Book of Genesis.[13] The latter have acquired growing political influence in recent years, and there is good reason for liberal thinkers to be concerned about their attempt to hijack the American educational and political system. However, creationism is a fringe movement in Britain which is so small as to be politically insignificant. Notwithstanding the hostility of a small handful of atheists and the creationist tendencies of an even smaller handful of educationalists such as the wealthy philanthropist Peter Vardy, Britain has a different religious history and culture from that of the United States. America is a relatively young nation, founded on secular ideals underpinned by a deistic notion of God (that is, an impersonal creator rather than the personal God of some religious traditions), with a religious identity primarily influenced by Protestant Christianity. Britain, like the rest of Europe, has a longer, more complicated and more bloody religious history, and it has also developed a more thoroughly secularised political ethos – although it is important not to underestimate the ongoing influence of the Church of England as an established state religion.

A survey undertaken by researchers at the University of Minnesota in 2006 identified atheists as America's most distrusted minority, who attracted more hostility than Muslims, gays and lesbians or recent immigrants.[14] Whereas a confession of atheism might still damage those seeking office in American public life, British politicians are viewed with suspicion if they give the impression of allowing their personal religious beliefs to inform their political decisions. Tony Blair was the most overtly Christian prime minister in modern times, but his then press secretary, Alastair Campbell, sought to deflect any reference to Blair's religion when he told a television interviewer, 'We don't do God.' Although Prime Minister Gordon Brown shares his predecessor's Christian faith, he too has been careful to distance his political position from his religious convictions. Blair might have been George W. Bush's ally in the war in Iraq, but his speeches were markedly free from the religious rhetoric which has been a common feature of Bush's public utterances. All this means that attempts by British atheists such as Dawkins to portray themselves as daring radicals in their embrace of atheism are a little far-fetched. Atheism in Britain simply does not create the kind of controversy that it does in America. To attempt to stir up an intellectual confrontation by suggesting otherwise is mischievous, and risks undermining the liberal consensus which we enjoy in this country on such issues at a time when we should be doing everything that we can to strengthen that consensus.

Representing religion – who speaks for whom?

In considering the social and political context of debates about religion, we also need to attend to questions of power, gender and representation. Who speaks for whom, whose voices are privileged and whose voices are silenced when a small and influential (but not necessarily knowledgeable) minority claims the authority to pass judgement on the beliefs of the majority of the world's people? Dennett writes:

> It is high time that we subject religion as a global phenomenon to the most intensive multidisciplinary research we can muster, calling on the best minds on the planet. Why? Because religion is too important for us to remain ignorant about. It affects not just our social, political, and economic conflicts, but the very meanings we find in our lives. For many people, probably a majority of the people on Earth, nothing matters more than religion. For this very reason, it is imperative that we learn as much as we can about it.[15]

This is not an appeal to study thousands of years of literature, art, philosophy and scripture in the world's religious traditions to discover what wisdom they might still have to offer, or to better enable an understanding of their followers' cultures and beliefs. Rather, it is an appeal to bring scientific objectivity to bear on a condition which afflicts 'a majority of the people on Earth', but which only those who are free from its grip are capable of analysing. This means that religious believers are treated not as feeling, thinking human beings but as objects of study by a highly unsympathetic Western elite which sets out to destroy those beliefs by 'breaking the spell', to use Dennett's expression, or by releasing them from a 'delusion', to use Dawkins' expression.

The high-profile atheists who have so far engineered this

confrontation between religion and scientific rationalism offer scant engagement with modern religious scholarship. Dennett describes scholars of religion as 'second-rate colleagues' of scientists,[16] and he makes the astonishing claim that there is an 'absence of information about religion'.[17] I presume that this is because his definition of 'information' is restricted to that which agrees with his theory that religion is nothing more than a quirk of natural selection, a cultural contagion spread by memes, and a Freudian illusion. Lifetimes of study have been spent on the texts and languages of religious traditions, while across the fields of anthropology, sociology, psychology, history and philosophy as well as theology a significant body of scholarship has accumulated around the study of religions. New atheists such as Dawkins and Dennett sweep all this aside in favour of outdated religious theories associated with nineteenth-century thinkers such as James Frazer and William James, whom no serious scholar of religion would cite uncritically today.

In their representation of religion, these popular authors owe their success partly to the fact that, in a media-driven culture, the opinions of the famous often count for more than the thoughtful analyses of those who have studied a subject and are aware of its complexities and ambiguities. Public debate thus becomes domi-nated by celebrities rather than scholars or, in the case of Dawkins, by scholars turned celebrities. For example, after his earlier polemic against religion, Amis wrote a much longer piece for *The Observer* newspaper titled 'The Age of Horrorism'.[18] Amis may be a good novelist, but he is no expert when it comes to religion. The essay offers some incisive observations, including a diagnosis of the age of terror as 'the age of boredom', which he describes as 'the global confrontation with the dependent mind'. But the essay is unfocused, self-contradictory and at times almost incoherent in its treatment of religion, with the author seeming unable to decide whether his target is Islam in general, the radical form of Islam known as Islamism, or all religion everywhere. The piece was surely given extensive space in a quality Sunday newspaper not on the basis of its merit but because it was written by a famous novelist.

Theologians such as Keith Ward and Alister McGrath have sought to challenge the new atheists on their own territory, by offering robust defences of the rationality of Christian beliefs about God.[19] However, although they are considerably more knowledgeable about their subject than the new atheists, they still tend to focus on the preoccupations of a minority of predominantly male Western thinkers which, as I suggested above, fail to take into account the many different questions raised by those who have so far been excluded from the debate. They also generally fail to take seriously enough the real dangers inherent in new forms of fundamentalism and extremism which are becoming more common in all religions, including Christianity. These pose a particular challenge to women who remain in those religions through choice or because they have no alternative.

Men of science vs. men of God

I write from what Dawkins describes as 'the ditzily unreal intersection of theology and feminism',[20] which might be something of a double whammy as far as he is concerned. I approach the new atheism with different arguments than those offered by my male colleagues who have so far entered the fray. I have at times been bemused by the complacency with which some of them have hurried to the defence of God, with barely a murmur of acknowledgement that the discipline to which they belong may have been partly responsible for creating the 'God' which Amis, Dawkins and Hitchens reject. John Cornwell assumes the *persona* of the Almighty to respond to Dawkins in a letter published in *The Sunday Times*, signed by 'God'. The letter ends with the ominous words, 'you have not heard the last of Me.'[21] That version of God who signs Himself off with a capital 'M' and makes a veiled threat before vanishing is part of the problem, not part of the solution.

There is something a little comic, if not a little wearisome, about this perennial stag-fight between men of Big Ideas, with male theologians rushing to defend the same pitch that they have fought over for centuries, which is now being colonised by men of

Science rather than men of God. For an example of the testosterone-charged nature of this debate, I recommend Johann Hari's review of Hitchens' book, *God Is Not Great*, in the *Independent* newspaper. Hari begins with the observation that

> The legion enemies of Christopher Hitchens have long argued that he has declined into a premature alcoholic senility where he can only belch and flail incoherently. This dazzling howl against religion will bitterly, brutally, disappoint them. It shows Hitchens can still intellectually get it up – and how.[22]

A reader who reviewed Keith Ward's book, *Is Religion Dangerous?*, on the Amazon UK website, described it as 'a smart, ballsy book'.

Scientists have taken over from Christian theologians the belief that they are custodians of the one and only truth, and such beliefs always mask imperialising tendencies which risk colonising different ways of interpreting the world. Singular and exclusive concepts of truth stifle plurality and difference, sifting the wondrous and irreducible diversity of our experience of the world into narrow grids and dogmas. Too often, these justify the silencing and ultimately the destruction of those who offer different versions of truth or reality. This is as true of atheist versions of absolute truth as it is of any religious version. Stalin and Mao were no respecters of difference and plurality.

In its war on religion, scientific rationalism constitutes the latest phase in the West's long history of domination by which it has sought to defeat every form of difference, including religious difference. The vast majority of the world's religious believers belong among non-Western cultures, and they include many millions of women whose views are seldom represented by their scholarly elites. This means that we need to cultivate a much greater awareness of both the limits and the oppressive effects of a debate dominated by the opinions of a small clique of white English-speaking men staging a mock battle about rationality and God, which fails to address the most significant humanitarian questions of our time. This includes the many different roles played by religion in sustaining and generating hope, meaning and creativity, without which we would be less than the humans we are.

The myths we live by

To be human is to live an interpreted life. It is to inhabit an imagined world which enables us to make sense of our experiences and to lend coherence and meaning to our lives. We are a story-telling species whose capacity for imagination, memory and language makes us unique among all the many evolved life forms which share our space on planet earth. The word 'religion' cannot be defined with any precision, but it refers to that particular genre of enacted stories – the vast majority, in fact – which are informed by a sense of transcendence and which seek meaning beyond the material facts of our biological existence. It refers loosely to an inclusive but elusive landscape of culture, theology and philosophy, art, history, politics, myth and devotion. The fact that this landscape of ideas and their forms of expression is not readily susceptible to scientific scrutiny, rationalisation and proof does not render it false or unreal. It simply means that we must change the focus of the lens if we are to understand its contours and questions.

Paraphrasing a parable told by the astronomer Arthur Eddington, Francis Collins writes about a man who decided to study deep-sea life using a net with a mesh-size of three inches: 'After catching many wild and wonderful creatures from the depths, the man concluded that there are no deep-sea fish that are smaller than three inches in length!' Collins goes on to suggest that, 'If we are using the scientific net to catch our particular version of truth, we should not be surprised that it does not catch the evidence of spirit.'[23] By broadening the scope of the encounter between science and religion, I am fishing for meanings which so far have slipped through the net. These meanings are as likely to be found in popular culture, social institutions and the arts as in science, philosophy and theology, and by weaving these different dimensions into our net of understanding, we may 'catch' considerably more meanings than we would in a net with fewer strands.

But we also need to recognise that scientific understanding itself is not outside the myths we live by. It is a delusion to think that science offers an objective, value-free position from which to evaluate all claims of truth and meaning. The philosopher Mary Midgley argues that evolution has become a powerful quasi-religious myth by which atheists such as Dawkins confer meaning on the world. She refers to the 'cosmic mythology'[24] associated with the theory of evolution, arguing that it is 'not just an inert piece of theoretical science. It is, and cannot help being, also a powerful folk-tale about human origins.'[25] Like any myth, scientific rationalism shapes our view of the world, but it also has the capacity to delude its followers with its utopian promises and claims to knowledge beyond the scope of its own authority.

Religious narratives are our responses to the vast questions which science will never be able to answer. 'Why is there something rather than nothing?' 'What does it mean to find ourselves as reasoning beings in a finite world, capable of imagining such concepts as God, infinity, goodness and truth?' 'How do we situate ourselves as creatures of language, feeling and consciousness in a world of such vulnerability and beauty, such anguish and tragedy, with the capacity to imagine both eternity and our own infinitesimal space of existence in the grand scale of the cosmos?' These are questions about meaning rather than cause. Science may well be able to answer many of our questions about causality, but it is one thing to ask what caused the world, and quite another to ask what it means.

Dawkins demands proof of God's existence, for only that which we can prove beyond reasonable doubt is worthy of belief. But the word 'God' does not denote a 'thing' whose existence we can prove, any more than we can prove the 'existence' of love, beauty, compassion or hope. I cannot prove that my husband loves me, nor can I prove that Mozart's music is sublime, Michelangelo's *Pièta* is beautiful and Nelson Mandela is good, but even so, I am not irrational or deluded when I say that I believe all these things to be true. Indeed, our capacity to believe in intangible truths such as goodness, love and beauty is the source of our most creative human endeavours, including those associated with religion. The evolutionary biologist and Christian Joan Roughgarden writes, 'to me God is an experience, not an idea.'[26] The language we use is never adequate to describe our glimpses of eternity, but this does not mean that we are deluded or deceived if we use the word 'God' in seeking to interpret our experiences of transcendence. It just means that there is an innermost responsivity to our way of being in the world which translates poorly into explanation and interpretation, and is highly resistant to demands for proof or rationalisation.

Nevertheless, we also live in an age when all our stories about the world are in a state of flux and transformation. Religious or not, we are negotiating our way through constantly changing social, scientific and spiritual landscapes. Perhaps never before has human knowledge been assailed on so many different fronts at the same time, always with the awareness that unimaginable destruction might lurk just beyond the horizon in the form of nuclear holocaust or environmental catastrophe.

The crisis in knowledge

In the midst of global political turmoil, we are experiencing a dramatic upheaval in values, beliefs and ideas. For religious believers, there is a growing challenge across a range of frontiers, from cultural and religious relativism to scientific atheism. The boundaries which separated science, theology and philosophy are themselves dissolving in the face of scientific discoveries which call into question our whole understanding of a world divided between mind and body, the material and the immaterial. Contrary to our long dualistic tradition in the West which clearly distinguishes between mind and matter, body and spirit, quantum physics is revealing to us that matter itself emerges out of a state of numinous mystery in which there is neither something nor nothing. Our natural environment becomes more wondrous but also more vulnerable the more we discover, calling us to a transformed relationship between culture and nature. This requires a transformation in scientific as well as philosophical understanding. Thomas Kuhn famously argued that 'normal science' operates within established paradigms which limit its capacity for discovery and innovation. It takes a crisis to create a new paradigm, and to bring about a scientific revolution which demands an entirely new way of organising and interpreting knowledge.[27]

The word 'crisis' is derived from the Greek *krisis*, which refers to a time of risk and opportunity. A *krisis* is a turning point, not something to be feared but something which brings about a change in our ways of knowing and being in the world. It is also a time of discovery, when knowledge must yield before wonder, newness and mystery. Discovery is what happens when thought seeks to liberate itself from knowledge, when we look at the world as if for the first time through the eyes of the child or the mystic and allow ourselves to be astonished by its wonder. This requires of us a new approach to questions of wisdom and understanding, in which the modern scientific mind-set must yield to more holistic ways of being and knowing.

As the shadows grow deeper in the twilight of modernity, we need to abandon aggressive forms of intellectual and political confrontation governed by sterile concepts of rationality and necessity, in order to discover new modes of dialogue and engagement capable of respecting the common humanity which we all share. This poses a significant challenge to the world's religious believers, but it poses a no less significant challenge to the emergent cult of new atheism. This is beginning to show all the hallmarks of some of the twentieth century's most destructive ideologies in its intolerance of difference and its labelling of its enemies with the language of malevolence, vermin and pestilence. For example, Dawkins uses the highly contested theory of 'memes' to argue that religion is like a virus, acting as a form of contagion which replicates itself in culture in much the same way that genes replicate themselves in biological organisms.[28] Grayling, another new atheist who has recently become more militant in his anti-religious writings, describes religion as 'one of the worst toxins poisoning human affairs'.[29] Hitchens compares religious believers with the plague-carrying rats in Albert Camus's novel, *The Plague*, waiting in the sewers to spread the pestilence of religious belief among new and unsuspecting generations.[30] Nobody with an awareness of twentieth-century political ideology should fail to be disturbed by this kind of rhetoric. Before the Nazis killed the Jews, they labelled them as vermin. Before the Rwandan genocide, Hutus referred to their Tutsi neighbours as 'cockroaches'.

With its emphasis on violence and division, the new atheism is a pessimistic and potentially dangerous creed. By focusing only on the negative, it fails to take account of the positive role played by religions and of the many ways in which our era of communications technology and globalisation provides unprecedented opportunities for voyages of discovery across religious and cultural boundaries. If our world is not to be sucked into a vortex of violence without end, we need to cultivate our human capacity for encounter and dialogue sustained by a spirit of good will towards the other in all his or her irreducible difference and diversity.

The wisdom of kindness

We should not allow the very real challenges we face to blind us to the fact that human beings are probably more united in understanding, language and values today than at any time in history. This brings with it questions of neo-imperialism, economic exploitation and global domination by the world's powerful nations, but it also brings with it the possibility of widespread social and political transformation at grassroots level. If we are to take advantage of this opportunity, then we need to listen to the stories which others tell about the world, and to explore how we can all find a space of co-habitation and flourishing on this beautiful and threatened planet. We have no hope of understanding our fellow human beings unless we are willing to embark upon the struggle of trying to understand those whose views of the world may be very different from our own. Unless we seek such understanding, we are condemned to ever greater violence and tyranny arising out of the clash between dominant and powerful majorities, and alienated and desperate minorities.

If we are to preserve our modern liberal culture and its intellec-tual traditions, we also need to rediscover the forgotten virtues of civility, courtesy and respect in the ways in which we conduct our public debates, for it is dismal to see some of our most popular thinkers descending to the level of the gutter press in their polemics. Not long after the publication of *The God Delusion*, I asked Keith Ward if Dawkins and he were actually good buddies when they met in the common rooms of Oxford University. He told me cautiously that they had always got on very well on a per-sonal level. Then he paused and said, 'I'm not sure I could feel the same now.' I asked him why not, and he told me that he believed Dawkins had betrayed everything that the Western intellectual tradition stands for, with its privileging of informed scholarship based on the study of texts. Something in the way he spoke gave me a brief glimpse into what might be at stake in this confronta-tion, and it left me with a lump in my throat. For a moment, what I was witnessing was not masculine hubris, but the grief of a serious scholar who feels that one of his colleagues has committed an act of intellectual vandalism against all that is worth believing in and fighting for in Western literacy and culture. I may find Ward's approach too narrow in its privileging of texts and ration-ality, but he represents a form of scholarly integrity which we may never recover if we allow it to be corrupted by self-publicising academics who sacrifice the demands of serious scholarship in favour of popularising polemics.

Nevertheless, Western theologians have historically been as blinkered as the scientists who have replaced them, for the scope of their knowledge has been limited by their cultural assumptions and prejudices, including those of gender. So let the men fight about God if they want to. My concern is not with debates about God but with creation and nature, with language and meaning, with people, and with kindness. The quest for God is inseparable from all the muddled human realities which these words describe. Together, we struggle in the space of our own mystery with all its opportunities and threats, and science and faith are part of that struggle. On the subject of kindness, I am in sympathy with a character in A. C. Grayling's play, *On Religion*, when she says, 'kindness, that's the big one, not love … [I]t's probably the more boring – definitely – kindness – because it's calm and considerate and hesitant and certainly the more difficult one to do.'[31]

The chapters which follow form a series of essays which can be read as a connecting argument, but which can also be read individually for those interested in particular topics. I have used broad brushstrokes because I have wanted to cover a wide range of issues without burdening the reader with excessive detail, and the book can be read without reference to endnotes. However, for those who want to explore any of the ideas in greater depth, I have provided fairly extensive references to enable them to do so. In the first two chapters I look more closely at what we mean by 'science' and 'religion', in the context of nineteenth-century developments in Western thought. In the third and fourth chapters, I consider the legacy of the Enlightenment and our modern Western values with regard to ethics, poverty and war. The next two chapters explore questions of religion, natural law, intelligent design theory and rationality in the shaping of Western ideas. In the penultimate chapter I discuss the emergence of religious fundamentalisms and different forms of identity politics associated with postmodernism. In the final chapter, I reflect upon questions of creativity, imagination and the arts in relation to faith. I ask if we might rediscover a sense of transcendence through literature and the arts, as forms of communication and truth-telling which enable us to go beyond the combative rhetoric of a culture fuelled by competition and aggression, to a more courteous and respectful exchange of ideas.

Chapter 1

THE INVENTION OF SCIENCE

There is a tendency today to refer to science and religion as if we know what we are talking about, often in ways which present these as opposing and irreconcilable claims to knowledge. But both of these words have a long history of different meanings, and only in the nineteenth century did they acquire something like the meanings they have today. Their place in our modern vocabulary is inseparable from a late nineteenth and early twentieth century world-view in which imperialism and scientific rationalism went hand in hand. While European nations were on an adventure to conquer the world and to superimpose Western civilisation on 'savage' and 'darkened' cultures, European thinkers were on a no less ambitious venture to conquer the human mind and super-impose their version of science and reason on the dark intellectual legacy of religion and superstition. The era of three of the most influential modern men of science – Darwin (1809–82), Marx (1818–83) and Freud (1856–1939) – broadly coincided with the era of European expansionism in Africa and India. The fact that these three thinkers in quite different fields were all regarded as scientists is evidence of the growing prestige of scientific knowledge towards the end of the nineteenth century.

To understand the impact of *The Origin of Species* and the on-going struggle between evolutionary science and religion, we need to situate Darwin in a wider context with regard to the changing relationship between theology and science in Victorian England. Science emerged as a profession in its own right in the second half of the nineteenth century, and this brought some members of the scientific community into direct conflict with the clerics and theologians who had previously ruled the academic and moral roost of English public life.[1]

Militant science and the struggle for power

At the beginning of the nineteenth century, science had been the pursuit of more or less skilled amateurs, many of whom understood their work in terms of natural theology. Indeed, the word 'science', from the Latin *scientia*, meaning knowledge, has for most of Western intellectual history been a generic word to describe all forms of knowledge. Thus, in medieval Europe, theology was known as the queen of the sciences, because it was the form of knowledge which informed all others. When science was concerned with the study of the laws of nature and the material world, it was known as natural philosophy. Only in the middle of the nineteenth century did the word acquire the narrower meaning we are familiar with today. The word 'scientist' was first used by Revd William Whewell in 1834, but it became popular towards the end of the century, when scientists had begun to displace the authority of theologians and clergymen. From this perspective, the nineteenth-century conflict between science and religion was not only a struggle between religious and scientific ways of explaining the world, it was more importantly a power struggle between men of science and men of God, most of them socially conservative members of the English ruling classes.

This power struggle meant that it was not in the interests of scientists to make any concessions to their religious counterparts. The triumph of science over theology required the total discrediting of theological knowledge. The emergence of new scientific societies, and the tightening up of rules of membership of the Royal Society in 1847, represented the successful attempt by scientists to dissociate themselves from the natural theologians and clergymen with whom they had once been closely identified. Scientists who sought a more conciliatory approach to theology were often ridiculed. For example, the Roman Catholic biologist

St George Jackson Mivart famously tried to reconcile aspects of evolutionary theory with the teachings of the Catholic Church, which earned him the contempt of his scientific peers. Although his endeavours to reconcile science and faith were initially well received by the Catholic Church, his liberalism brought him into increasing conflict with its hierarchy. After a bitter struggle, he was excommunicated in 1900 and died a few months later, 'the tragic outcast of science and faith'.[2] Responding to Mivart's attempt to reconcile science and Catholicism, T. H. Huxley warned that 'no one should imagine that "he is, or can be, both a true son of the Church and a loyal soldier of science."'[3] Elsewhere, Huxley triumphantly observed that 'Extinguished theologians lie about the cradle of every science as the strangled snakes beside that of Hercules'.[4]

Huxley, whom the science historian James Moore describes as 'the self-styled "gladiator-general" of evolutionary science',[5] was one of several militant scientific voices seeking a confrontation with religion,[6] and looking for ammunition to use against Christianity. For example, it is now widely acknowledged that the flat earth theory is a nineteenth-century fabrication which attracted a small but persistent following of biblical fundamentalists, but which was also seized upon by scientists in their war against religion.[7] Western philosophers and theologians have been 'globularists', to use Christine Garwood's expression, since the time of the ancient Greeks. When, 'in fourteen hundred and ninety two, Columbus sailed the ocean blue', nobody feared that he might sail off the edge of the world. This is a Victorian myth which has been uncritically repeated by scientists and historians, to demonstrate the ignorance of religion compared with science. The evolutionary biologist and popular science writer, Stephen Jay Gould, describes it as part of the late-nineteenth-century 'construction of the model of warfare between science and religion as a guiding theme of Western history.'[8]

The assault of militant scientists on the Christian bastions of professional and academic life coincided with a widespread religious revival which extended from Britain and parts of Europe to

America, and which was manifest in different ways in the Nonconformist, Anglican and Catholic churches. Catholics had gained a degree of acceptance in British public life with a number of legislative changes in the late eighteenth and early nineteenth centuries, but England was still deeply anti-Catholic. Some of this prejudice was fuelled by the authoritarianism and anti-modernism of the Catholic Church under Pope Pius IX, whose 1864 *Syllabus of Errors* was a denunciation of many of the values that the liberal and progressive classes were beginning to hold dear. All this re-inforced scientists' belief that they were locked in a battle for truth against the forces of religious intolerance and superstition.

However, it is important to recognise that, in the nineteenth century as much as in our own time, the conflict between science and religion involved a minority of extremists in both camps. The overall picture is far less antagonistic than the metaphor of warfare suggests. Recent research by historians reveals a more complex debate between scientists and Christian believers over the implica-tions of the theory of evolution. Moore argues that the adoption of military metaphors by early defenders of evolution in their struggle against theology has become a self-fulfilling prophecy which distorts the historical picture. Moore writes:

> There was not a polarisation of 'science' and 'religion' as the idea of opposed armies implies but a large number of learned men, some scientists, some theologians, some indistinguish-able, and almost all of them very religious, who experienced various differences among themselves ... Nor, finally, was there the kind of antagonism pictured in the discharge of weaponry but rather a much more subdued overall reaction to the *Origin of Species* than is generally supposed and a gen-uine amiability in the relations of those who are customarily believed to have been at battle.[9]

With respect to the post-Darwinian controversies, Moore argues that 'the military metaphor perverts historical understanding with violence and inhumanity' and he appeals for interpretations which are 'non-violent and humane'.[10]

Writing in 1979, Moore could not have anticipated the most recent declaration of war by scientists on religion, with Dawkins now in the role of 'gladiator-general', and the ranks being swelled by a growing number of supporters.

Darwin and Christianity

Darwin's *The Origin of Species* was first published in 1859 under the full title, *On the Origin of Species by Means of Natural Selection, or the Preservation of Favoured Races in the Struggle for Life.* In 1871, Darwin published *The Descent of Man, and Selection in Relation to Sex*, in which he applied his idea of natural selection more closely to human races and societies. The theory of evolution was not new – the French naturalist Jean-Baptiste Lamarck (1744–1829) had developed a now discredited theory of the hereditary nature of evolution before Darwin – but by introducing the theory of natural selection to describe how species evolve over time through a random process of elimination and survival, Darwin provided an explanation which had eluded earlier thinkers.

Darwin had intended to become a clergyman before his voyages on the *Beagle*, and he seems to have been ambivalent about the extent to which his theory offered an essentially mechanistic and random view of life. The main challenge to his Christian faith arose more from the death of his beloved nine-year-old daughter Annie in 1850 than from his theory of evolution. Thereafter he described himself as agnostic but he denied that he was an atheist. There are times in *The Origin of Species* when he seems to invest the theory of evolution with an almost mystical sense of awe and purpose, as in the closing paragraph:

> There is grandeur in this view of life, with its several powers, having been originally breathed into a few forms or into one; and that, whilst this planet has gone cycling on according to the fixed law of gravity, from so simple a beginning endless forms most beautiful and most wonderful have been, and are being, evolved.[11]

The Origin of Species was published in six editions during Darwin's lifetime, and each time he introduced changes. In the second edition, he amended the closing paragraph to read 'having been originally breathed *by the Creator* into a few forms or into one' (my italics). This may have been to appease his religious critics, but it is possible that Darwin remained affected by his early Christian faith throughout his life, so that it may never have been entirely eradicated by his theory of evolution.

The most famous account of the Christian reaction to Darwin's theory of natural selection is the legendary confrontation between Huxley and the bishop of Oxford, Samuel Wilberforce (1805–73), at a meeting of the British Association in Oxford in 1860, where Huxley presented a paper in defence of Darwin. This debate has been widely reported – and misreported. Here is a first-hand account by Mrs Isabella Sidgwick, written long after the event and published in *Macmillan's Magazine* in October 1898:

> Then the Bishop rose, and in a light scoffing tone, florid and fluent he assured us there was nothing in the idea of evolution; rock-pigeons were what rock-pigeons had always been. Then, turning to his antagonist with a smiling insolence, he begged to know, was it through his grandfather or his grandmother that he claimed his descent from a monkey? On this Mr Huxley slowly and deliberately arose. A slight tall figure stern and pale, very quiet and very grave, he stood before us, and spoke those tremendous words – words which no one seems sure of now, nor I think, could remember just after they were spoken, for their meaning took away our breath, though it left us in no doubt as to what it was. He was not ashamed to have a monkey for his ancestor; but he would be ashamed to be connected with a man who used great gifts to obscure the truth.[12]

The exaggerated significance of the Huxley/Wilberforce debate has created the mistaken idea that Darwinism met with widespread Christian opposition from the beginning. However, just as in our own time there are many Christians who see no conflict between the theory of evolution and their Christian faith, so in the nineteenth century, the opinions of a thoughtful majority risk being overlooked if we focus only on the conflict between militant scientists and biblical literalists.[13]

Darwin challenged Christian thinking not primarily because his theory called into question literal readings of the story of creation in Genesis – most educated Christians did not read the Bible literally, and German historical biblical criticism was increasingly influential in the English context in which Darwin worked. Rather, the theory of natural selection was incompatible with a natural theology which saw each species as individually created and hierarchically ordered by God, according to a benevolent and purposeful design. The ways in which this sense of order pervaded the understanding of society as well as nature is clear in the popular Anglican hymn, 'All Things Bright and Beautiful', written in 1848 by Cecil F. Alexander. Not only does this hymn celebrate God's creation of 'Each little flower that opens, Each little bird that sings', it also affirms God's ordering of the social classes:

> The rich man in his castle,
> The poor man at his gate,
> God made them, high or lowly,
> And order'd their estate.

The idea that the vast diversity of life-forms had evolved from a shared origin as a result of a directionless and brutal struggle for survival threatened this Christian belief in an orderly and meaningful universe. It called into question the idea that social and natural hierarchies were divinely ordained, and it could potentially have posed a radical challenge to the Victorian *status quo*. However, while some interpreters tried to give a socialist or feminist spin to Darwin's theory, ultimately it has always been used more to serve the interests of a ruling male elite than to challenge social, racial and sexual hierarchies. Indeed, social Darwinism was used to justify some of the most grotesquely supremacist racial ideologies of the twentieth century, including Nazism.

Darwinism, politics and sex

There is much debate about the extent to which Darwin was aware of the political implications of his theory. Among those who take a critical view of his politics, his biographers Adrian Desmond and James Moore write that 'his notebooks make plain that competition, free trade, imperialism, racial extermination, and sexual inequality were written into the equation from the start – "Darwinism" was always intended to explain human society.'[14] The term 'social Darwinism' only became widespread in the twentieth century, but it is a concept which predates Darwin. It refers to the application of evolutionary theory to explain the development of superior and inferior cultures and races. Its sources include the demographer and economist best known for his views on population control, Thomas Malthus (1766–1834), the political theorist Herbert Spencer (1820–1903), and Darwin's relative Francis Galton (1822–1911). Galton was inspired by *The Origin of Species* to develop the theory of eugenics – the idea that the quality of a society can be improved through encouraging the educated classes to have more children and inhibiting the reproductive capacities of the lower classes. The phrase 'survival of the fittest' was first used not by Darwin but by Spencer, and it only appears in later editions of *The Origin of Species*.

Despite these various influences, it is Darwin's name that attaches to a social theory which lent scientific respectability to racist ideologies and to different forms of social engineering, including the widespread popularity of eugenics in the early twentieth century, culminating in Nazism. Like many great thinkers, Darwin cannot be held responsible for the ways in which his ideas have been used to justify repugnant social practices, but his own relationship to social Darwinism remains ambiguous.

Darwin was a Whig who supported the abolition of slavery and welcomed the Great Reform Act of 1832 which made British government more democratic, but he took little active interest in politics. Despite his liberal views and his opposition to the more extreme racial theories of his time – for example, the idea that different races belong to different species – he was a man of his time who viewed both non-European cultures and women with an inherent sense of Victorian male superiority. When he developed the social implications of his theory of natural selection in *The Descent of Man*, Darwin explained that the inferiority of women to men could be attributed to natural selection. The evolutionary struggle for survival favoured those men who, in their rivalry for women, showed greater intellectual skills as well as physical strength. While 'Woman seems to differ from man in mental disposition, chiefly in her greater tenderness and less selfishness',[15] men's intellectual and physical superiority is evident:

> The chief distinction in the intellectual powers of the two sexes is shewn by man's attaining to a higher eminence, in whatever he takes up, than can woman – whether requiring deep thought, reason, or imagination, or merely the use of the senses and hands ... We may also infer, from the law of the deviation from averages ... that if men are capable of a decided pre-eminence over women in many subjects, the average of mental power in man must be above that of woman.[16]

The fact that 'man has ultimately become superior to woman' in the evolutionary struggle has, however, been modified because 'the law of the equal transmission of characters to both sexes prevails with mammals'.[17] Had it not been for this fortunate fact, Darwin thought it 'probable that man would have become as superior in mental endowment to woman, as the peacock is in ornamental plumage to the peahen.'[18]

Sarah Blaffer Hrdy, an anthropologist and evolutionary scientist, has shown how romantic ideas of femininity and motherhood skewed the interpretation of evolutionary science. She argues that

> It was no accident that first moralists and then Victorian evolutionists looked to nature to justify assigning to female animals the same qualities that patriarchal cultures have

almost always ascribed to 'good' mothers (nurturing and passive). Women were assumed to be 'naturally' what patriarchal cultures would socialize them to be: modest, compliant, non-competitive, and sexually reserved.[19]

Joan Roughgarden, an evolutionary biologist, also argues that Darwin's understanding of the rules of natural selection was distorted by Victorian sexual stereotypes, not least in the suggestion that 'social life in animals consist[s] of discreetly discerning damsels seeking horny, handsome, healthy warriors'.[20] She argues that there is far greater sexual diversity in the natural world and among humans than Darwin's cultural bias allowed him to recognise.

As both these critics point out, Darwin was simply reflecting views which were common for his time. However, this demonstrates how even a scientific theory as apparently radical as the theory of evolution is interpreted through the lenses of culture and society, so that science never transcends the social contexts in which it is produced. In the end, Darwin's theory of evolution consolidated rather than undermined the power of men like himself in a world which was becoming increasingly dominated by the British ruling classes.

While Darwin was developing his theory and reflecting on its possible reception by his scientific and religious peers, he was shocked to learn that another scientist – Alfred Russell Wallace (1823–1913) – had developed a theory of evolution almost identical to his own. Unlike Darwin, Wallace was not an educated and affluent Englishman but a self-taught Welshman from a poor background. He was a socialist with radical views about politics, science and religion. He insisted that human consciousness transcended the evolutionary process, so that he saw a less radical difference between more and less civilised societies than Darwin did. Wallace embraced spiritualism in later life, which made him unpopular among his scientific peers. Although he was one of the most eminent scientists of his time, his legacy has been overshadowed by that of Darwin.

Some would argue that the story of Darwin and Wallace serves to illustrate the extent to which nineteenth-century science was a profession of privileged and influential men, who took over from their clerical forebears the mantle of society's custodians of knowledge. Wallace may have been one of the last of the great amateur scientists motivated not by professional ambition but by a passionate curiosity and love for the art of science, whose discoveries arose from an untamed vision suffused by childlike wonder at the world, its peoples, and its mysteries.

Society, religion and science – the challenge of Karl Marx

Marx posed a more profound and far-reaching challenge to the *status quo* than Darwin, with the publication of his revolutionary tract *The Communist Manifesto* in 1848 – eleven years before the publication of *The Origin of Species*. Marx's later work was influenced by Darwin's theory, which he admired, although not without criticism. He sent a copy of *Das Kapital* to Darwin when it was published in 1867 as a sign of his appreciation, although the claim that he wanted to dedicate the book to Darwin but Darwin politely declined has been disproven.[21]

Marx adopted an evolutionary perspective to explain the historical influence of economics on social structures. He saw social history as essentially an economic struggle between the different classes in the gradual evolution of society from peasantry and feudalism to capitalism and industrialisation and finally to communism, which would represent the ultimate achievement of society's development. However, the capitalist system was held in place by religion, which placated the working classes by reconciling them to their suffering and offering consolation with the promise of an illusory hereafter. His explanation of the function of religion has been widely quoted:

> The wretchedness of *religion* is at once an *expression* of and a *protest* against real wretchedness. Religion is the sigh of the oppressed creature, the heart of a heartless world, and the soul of soulless conditions. It is the *opium* of the people.[22]

Marx saw this as an inversion of reality which cultivated false consciousness among the masses, making them docile and subservient to the ruling classes. This is why he described the critique of religion as 'the prerequisite of every critique'.[23] Only through liberation from the distorted vision offered by religion would the oppressed majority recognise the reality of their situation and be empowered to stage a revolution against the system of bourgeois capitalism. Although Marx wrote little directly on women, he saw the family and the subjugation of women as part of the system of private property and exploitation associated with capitalism. Similarly with race, his insistence that the only significant differences between human beings were class differences associated with capitalism meant that his theory was intrinsically more socially egalitarian than that of Darwin.

Like Darwin and later Freud, Marx put forward a less benign view of the human story than his Christian predecessors. For pre-modern thinkers such as Thomas Aquinas, and still today in the Catholic natural law tradition, society is given by God for the well-being of the human species, and it is ordered according to God's precepts. There are many forms of just society, but each of them is capable of cultivating institutions and laws which enhance human flourishing.[24] Marx's view of capitalist societies as exploitative and morally corrupted ideologies sustained by the false consciousness of religion ran deeply counter to a Christian world-view which had more or less sanctified the prevailing *status quo* since Christianity's incorporation into the Roman empire in the fourth century. There have in Christian history been many revolutions, reformations and movements which might rival Marx in their social critique, but none has caught the political imagination quite as Marx did – perhaps because institutionalised Christianity, like all established religions, has functioned mainly as a conservative force in society. It has as effectively suppressed or domesticated its own internal rebellions and uprisings as it has resisted and survived those from the outside.

Throughout the twentieth century, Marxist atheism was, with

considerable justification, seen as the great enemy of the Christian faith. One of the reasons why the Catholic Church was not more robust in its condemnation of Nazism was because they shared a common enemy in Bolshevism. Yet from the beginning Marx has had an influence on Catholic thought. In 1891, Pope Leo XIII published his encyclical *Rerum Novarum*, which constitutes the beginning of a body of ideas that is today known as Catholic social teaching.[25] Although rejecting communism and defending the right to private property, *Rerum Novarum* also called for justice for the working classes. Some of the social encyclicals written after the Second Vatican Council (1962–65) express a Catholic ethos which shows more sympathy to liberal socialism than to advanced capitalism. This is particularly evident in the Catholic Church's critique of the absolute right of property and its insistence upon the obligations of the rich towards the poor, not as acts of charity but as fundamental duties incumbent upon nations and political and economic institutions as well as individuals. In the late 1960s, the emergence of liberation theology in Latin America represented an attempt at a synthesis between Catholic theology and Marxism. Although the Vatican has tried to repress liberation theology, it continues to influence much religious thought and practice, and has spread far beyond the bounds of Latin American Catholicism to different religious and political cultures.[26]

The darkness within – Freud, faith and the unconscious

The third great scientific thinker who transformed Western society was Sigmund Freud. A generation after Darwin had developed his theory of evolution, Freud embarked on a similar undertaking with regard to the evolution of human consciousness. Freud was working in an environment in which Darwin's ideas had achieved widespread influence.[27] Science had also acquired considerable prestige, and Freud was determined that psychoanalysis should be recognised as a science. Although it started out as a theory of the development of individual consciousness, Freud's later works such as *Totem and Taboo*, *Moses and Monotheism* and *The Future of an Illusion* extended the scope of psychoanalysis to offer a universal explanation for the origins and development of society. Like the consciousness of the infant child, he argued that collective human consciousness comes into being in an oedipal world of murderous desire and guilt focused on the parental relationship. The gradual progress from polytheism to Jewish and Christian monotheism is the story of the evolution of human consciousness, from the sense of inhabiting a world ruled first by the chaos of nature, then by the caprice of the ancient deities, and finally by the moral order of the God of monotheism. Freud argued that psychoanalysis provided an explanation which did away with the need for any God at all, proving that religion was a sustaining illusion which could be replaced by the more rational insights of science, which represented the pinnacle of progress.

Like Darwin, Freud took a lofty view of men like himself – men of civilisation and reason who were far above the ordinary and uneducated masses, and who were inherently superior to women. In his writings on women, Freud argued that they were psycho-logically poorly equipped to cope with the demands of civil-isation, as a result of which they suffered from chronic moral underdevelopment and premature ageing. *The Future of an Illusion* ends with a confident assertion of science's capacity to provide the answer to all of life's questions: 'our science is no illusion. But an illusion it would be to suppose that what science cannot give us we can get elsewhere.'[28]

Freudian psychoanalysis, with its controversial focus on the sex drives, touched on some of the deepest taboos and fears of soci-eties shaped by Christianity's highly ambivalent if not thoroughly repressive attitude towards human sexuality, but the reception of Freud's theory varied widely in different cultural contexts.[29] For example, his ideas received an immediate welcome among the Spanish intelligentsia and they quickly became popular in the United States, but they met with a hostile reception in his native Austria and were slow to gain acceptance in England. Within a few years of Freud's visit to the States in 1909, psychoanalytic theory had acquired widespread influence, although in a less radical form than he himself was happy with. All this demonstrates once again that scientific theories do not exist as objective ideas in a cultural vacuum. They are products of their time and place, and the ways in which they are received, interpreted and developed is to a large extent determined by their cultural contexts.

Darwin, Marx and Freud – evaluating the legacy

Darwin, Marx and Freud are something of a paradox insofar as they were radical thinkers but also conservative men in terms of their social relationships and lifestyles. Even Marx, who offered the most far-reaching social critique of the three and who experienced significant financial hardship when living in London with his wife and family, nevertheless aspired to the bourgeois living standards of his time, with the economic support of his friend and collaborator, Friedrich Engels. But together these three opened up Western awareness to new possibilities about the kind of species we are, the kind of consciousness we live by and the kind of societies we inhabit, and their influence continues to shape the ways in which we view the world and our place within it. Although they were men of the Enlightenment with their confidence in science and reason and their belief in progress, they also marked the beginning of the end of the Enlightenment by calling into question some of its fundamental assumptions.

Thanks to Freud, we doubt not only the reliability of the world around us, but the reliability of our own consciousness and desires. We know that we are buffeted by unacknowledged influences, by the hauntings of childhood and unhealed wounds of the psyche. Whereas once Descartes could confidently assert, 'I think therefore I am', we lack his confidence in our ability to know our own thoughts. Freud has helped us to acknowledge the hidden depths of the unconscious which threaten the Cartesian I.

Inseparable from this is the influence Marx has had on our understanding of history. The emergence of history as an academic discipline dates to the nineteenth century and is part of that century's widespread quest for objective, factual and verifiable knowledge. Yet Marx makes it impossible for us to read history as a truthful and factual account of the past, by drawing our attention to the extent to which the telling of history is always shaped by political and economic forces. A Marxist perspective invites recognition that history is re-written by the victors, and it demands that we analyse the untold stories and listen to the silenced voices in order to discover the histories of the world's oppressed and subjugated peoples. We must learn to read history against the grain, and even then we will never know the whole story. To Marx we owe our suspicion of history, and our awareness that it is more a story of power struggles than a transparent account of what happened and when.

Today, we are rightly critical of aspects of Freudian and Marxist thought. Freud's theory of psychoanalysis may not be quite as universal or as all-embracing as he believed it to be. Feminist critics have shown how he suffered from a mental block with regard to the psychological development of women, even although his psychoanalytic theory was developed largely as a result of his encounters with women patients. His claims to be a scientist have been challenged by the French psychoanalyst Jacques Lacan (1901–81), who argues that psychoanalysis is more a theory of language than a science. Many have questioned what they perceive as Freud's over-emphasis on the role of the sex drives in directing human development, beginning with his erstwhile disciple and later critic, Carl Jung (1875–1961). So, while Freud's influence continues, he is no longer enthroned as the great master of the mind, if he ever was.

With Marx too, the collapse of communism saw the end of Marxism's political influence, at least for the time being. However valid his critique of capitalism might be, only the most dogged old Marxist would still claim that Marx was strictly speaking a scientist. Like Freud's later theories about civilisation and society, Marx's historical materialism developed a transcendent perspective in its later stages, leading to Utopian claims which made it sound quasi-religious. Having moved beyond Marx, we recognise now that economic analysis is only one limited way of understanding the different forces and influences on society, and it is reductive to believe that all history can be understood in terms of the class struggle. So again, Marx continues to inform our understanding of the world, but he is no longer the master of history the way he might have been in some social science faculties of the 1960s and 1970s.

Only Darwin has escaped this relativising influence. While these other great thinkers and myth-makers of the nineteenth and early twentieth centuries have found their niche in a wider landscape, Darwin's acolytes still speak with all the unassailable confidence of those nineteenth-century men of science and empire. Darwin's theory of evolution has been modified, not least by evolutionary geneticists such as Dawkins who locate the struggle for survival at the level of genes rather than within organisms or species as a whole. Others, such as Stephen Jay Gould, have proposed a more radical critique of Darwin by arguing that life forms have become less rather than more complex through the process of evolution.[30] Darwin's ideas, like those of Freud and Marx, might have become a less dominant feature in the landscape of science and society, had it not been for the emergence of creationism in the early twentieth century. If we want to understand why evolutionary scientists have become locked in a ferocious battle of ideas with Christianity, then we have to situate the debate not in the context of the nineteenth-century encounter between Darwinism and Christianity, but in the twentieth-century conflict between evolutionary science and Christian creationism.

Atheism, science and creationism

As I suggested in the Introduction, the current confrontation between science and religion must be understood within a particular context – namely, the clash between American educationalists who teach theories of evolution and American Christian fundamentalists who promote creationism and reject evolution. This is the original meaning of the word 'fundamentalist'. It was first used with reference to American evangelicals' insistence on the literal truth of the Bible in the early twentieth century over and against the theory of evolution, although it has since acquired wider significance.

This clash between evolutionists and fundamentalists can be traced back to the 1920s, when some Southern states passed statutes forbidding the teaching of evolution. In Dayton, Tennessee in 1925, the American Civil Liberties Union instigated a famous test case in which a young physics teacher, John Scopes, agreed to stand trial to test the constitutionality of the anti-evolution law in defending his teaching of evolution. After a complex and protracted trial, Scopes was found guilty but his conviction was overturned on a technicality. The result was considerable legal ambiguity regarding the teaching of evolution in some American states until 1968, when a teacher from Arkansas, Susan Epperson, took her case to the Supreme Court and the prohibition against promoting evolution was declared unconstitutional because it violated the First Amendment.[31]

The impact of creationism on British education has been nowhere near as significant as in the United States. Although the growing influence of conservative evangelical Christianity should not be underestimated, it still forms only a small part of Britain's broad religious and cultural landscape. Even in America, there is growing support among Christian congregations for 'Evolution Sunday', as a way of affirming the theory of evolution over and against creationists and intelligent design theorists. (I shall discuss the idea of intelligent design in Chapter 5.)

The British Humanist Association (BHA) has taken up a campaign against the teaching of creationism, prompted by concerns that it was part of the curriculum in at least one of the recently established academies sponsored by the Christian evangelical and wealthy car dealer, Peter Vardy. On 12 February 2003, more than 40 academics, scientists and writers signed a letter to the British Prime Minister and the Home Secretary, organised by the BHA, calling for Darwin's birthday to be made a public holiday. The short letter includes the argument that, 'At a time when creationism appears to be gaining ground in English schools, the public celebration of Charles Darwin's contribution to modern science could send out a clear message of support for scientific thinking.'[32] The claim that creationism is 'gaining ground in English schools' is exaggerated, but it is right to be vigilant and many religious people would support this initiative by the BHA. However, the BHA has become something of a showcase for militant atheism, in a way which raises questions about its commitment to liberal and open societies informed by humanist values.

The BHA describes its vision as 'a world without religious privilege or discrimination, where people are free to live good lives on the basis of reason, experience and shared human values.'[33] Many religious believers would support that ideal, but there is an implicit suggestion in much of the Association's campaigning material that 'reason, experience and shared human values' are the exclusive preserve of atheist humanism and not of its religious equivalents. Polly Toynbee is the current President of the BHA, and its Vice Presidents include two of Britain's best-known scientific atheists, Dawkins and Lewis Wolpert. In accepting her appointment as President, Toynbee described 'religious fanaticism' as 'the clear and present danger all round the world.' She went on to say that

> We need to oppose religious zealotry by promoting the positive and liberating case for believing life on earth is precious because the here and now is all there is and our destiny is in our own hands. Mankind itself has all the innate moral strength it needs, without inventing divine reward and wrath.
>
> Humanism is tolerant of all beliefs, so long as they oppress no-one else, including weak members of their own communities, and so long as they seek no special privileges from the state. The Humanist view of life is progressive and optimistic, in awe of human potential, living without fear of judgement and death, finding enough purpose and meaning in life, love and leaving a good legacy.[34]

These are worthy ideals, although in this era of fading hopes some might wonder what evidence there is to justify a 'progressive and optimistic' view of life. But those who seek a more humane and just global order cannot escape the fact that, for the majority of the world's people, values of justice and care for the vulnerable are rooted in religious rather than atheist ideals. Religious fanaticism is not the only 'clear and present danger' in our world. The greatest dangers confronting humankind are still those ancient enemies of war, poverty, ignorance and disease. These create the breeding grounds in which religious extremism flourishes, because people who have been betrayed by the world's political and economic systems often seek refuge in the alternatives offered by religion. It is often said that the most dangerous person in the world is the person with nothing to lose. The more people in our world who have nothing to lose, the greater the danger of extremism is likely to become.

If we are committed to struggling against religious fanaticism, and if we really do stand 'in awe of human potential', then we need to cultivate a much more intelligent debate about the role religion plays in nurturing that human potential through its shaping of ideas and through the hope and meaning it gives to many millions of lives. Western ideas about religion are still informed by those same nineteenth-century attitudes which led to a mock battle between science and religion – a battle which masks a much richer and more diverse engagement between the two. With this in mind, I want to consider the ways in which the modern concept of religion developed alongside that of science in nineteenth-century Western thought.

Chapter 2

THE MAN OF SCIENCE AND HIS RELIGIOUS OTHERS

In the late nineteenth century, the scientific world-view which had been developing in Western thought for some 400 years finally came into its own. This affected all areas of knowledge, including religion. The word 'religion' comes from the Latin *religio*. It is difficult to know precisely what the word meant in its initial usage, but it referred in various ways to the rituals and cults of the Roman empire and the duties associated with these. Early Christians adopted the word to reflect upon their own practices and beliefs as opposed to those of other religions, but still in a way which had a variety of meanings through different Christian eras. In the nineteenth century, the category of religion came to be more narrowly understood as referring to all those aspects of human behaviour and belief which had been bracketed out of a scientific world-view. The emergence of religion as a modern term of reference and an object of study must be understood in that context.[1]

While the Roman Catholic Church remained more or less marginal with regard to modern revolutions in knowledge until the Second Vatican Council in the 1960s, many Protestant scholars eagerly embraced modernity. In the area of biblical studies, there was a shift from reading the Bible as a source of divine revelation and truth, to reading it as a collection of historical documents which could be analysed and studied like any other texts. Known as the 'higher criticism', this movement flourished in German academic circles in the early nineteenth century and gradually gained a widespread following among British biblical scholars as well. In theology, natural theologians were eager to demonstrate that belief in God was compatible with new scientific theories such as the theory of evolution. Sometimes this went hand in hand with the Christian idea of a personal creator God, but often it appealed to deistic arguments which adopted a mechanistic view of creation. The world was designed by God to function in accordance with the laws of nature, but God did not directly intervene thereafter.

These nineteenth-century developments in biblical studies and natural theology were attempts to reconcile Christianity with scientific modernity, by men who were believing Christians. However, alongside these transformations within Christianity, the growing prestige of science gave rise to new academic disciplines among scholars who sought to distance themselves from any personal religious beliefs in order to lend scientific objectivity to their claims. This was, as I mentioned in the last chapter, an era in which European exploration and colonisation were leading to encounters with different cultures which presented new opportunities for scientific study. It was in this milieu that the various branches of anthropology came into their own right, and it was these early anthropologists and ethnologists who developed the idea of religion as we understand it today.

Religion as the man of science's 'other'

Feminists and critical theorists argue that the idea of the modern man of reason which developed during the seventeenth and eighteenth centuries resulted in the construction of the 'other' as the locus of all those forces and entities which threaten the identity of the masculine 'I'. The idea of the other has become something of an academic cliché, but it is still useful for my argument with regard to the relationship between religion and science. The other is usually understood as the repressed and silenced opposite of the dominant subject, so that the relationship between the two is not one of genuine difference but of positive and negative significance. So, for instance, when woman is described as the other of man, this suggests that male identity is secured by projecting onto the female characteristics such as passivity, emotion and dependence, which do not belong within the self-image of the active, rational, independent male. Thus, woman is not a subject in her own right, but the negation of man.[2] Similar dualisms can be found in the representation of racial and cultural differences and also, I am suggesting, in the representation of religion by atheist scientists. In each case, the language of difference masks a hierarchy of relationships between the identity of the subject, and the non-identity of its 'other'. So, in the case of religion, atheist thinkers are respectful of subtle differences in their own identities, beliefs and values, while grouping together vast undifferentiated masses of humanity under the label 'religion', in a way which eliminates difference and diversity. The term 'deconstruction' associated with postmodern thinkers such as Jacques Derrida[3] seeks to destabilise the certainty of Western ethics and knowledge by calling into question the relationship between these oppositional pairings, in order to show how their hierarchical meanings sustain social and sexual inequalities.

In this chapter and the next, I want to consider this idea of the 'other' in terms of nature, female sexuality, race and religion, as the others of science. We shall see that all of these were constructed as dark and irrational powers which had to be mastered in the interests of science, reason and progress. They were all perceived as a threat to the project of scientific rationalism and its values and beliefs, vested in the identity of the autonomous male European subject with whom it was identified.

In considering the debate between science and religion in terms of the other, it is important to separate out theology from religion. Western science and Christian theology are intimately related in the intellectual debates of modernity, because they belong within the same historical and cultural milieu, an idea I discuss more fully in Chapter 6. But for Victorian scientists as well as theologians, the religious other was an object of study, ripe for conversion by the often combined forces of Christianity and progress, but with nothing to offer in return by way of truth or understanding. These scholars were often poorly equipped to understand the religious ideas and practices of non-Western cultures, because their concept of religion was primarily informed by a Protestant Christian model which placed a strong emphasis on individual faith, scripture, and morality. In the religious milieu of Victorian England, for example, the morally austere patriarchal God of evangelical Protestantism would have been understood as quite separate from continental Catholicism with its Marian devotions and cultic rituals. The latter was certainly religious, but many would not have regarded it as godly. England's men of science may have bickered with their theological colleagues, but most of them would have shared a mutual antipathy to the religious antics of Catholics as well as those of pagans and savages.

Popular concepts of religion – including those of the new atheists – still tend to follow this Protestant model. One of the sources for Daniel Dennett's book, *Breaking the Spell*, is William James (1842–1910), the American philosopher and psychologist of religion. Dennett quotes James's definition of religion as 'the feelings, acts, and experiences of individual men in their solitude, so far as they apprehend themselves to stand in relation to whatever they may consider the divine'.[4] This may describe a certain kind of Christian theism or deism, but many religions have little to do with this kind of solitary one-to-one relationship with the divine. Although they might encourage solitude as a form of spiritual practice, religions are primarily collective expressions of social narratives and traditions which are not necessarily associated with the kind of individualistic belief to which James refers. The widespread tendency by people to describe themselves as 'spiritual but not religious' is also an expression of this individualistic ethos, which has now mutated from a Christian to a secular identity. It implies that individual spirituality is a good and desirable quality, but to identify oneself with the beliefs and practices of a religious tradition is to sign up to backward and repressive ideas which are at odds with our modern Western values.

A few years ago, England football manager Glenn Hoddle

expressed his belief that disabled people were experiencing the effects of bad *karma* from a previous life. From a Hindu perspective, this would have been a perfectly reasonable thing to say and it would have caused barely a ripple of dissent. However, it caused such a public outcry in Britain that Hoddle was sacked. It was a revealing example of how long-held religious values based on a very particular world-view continue to shape the public sphere, long after visible displays of religious belief and practice have faded into insignificance. Britain and America are Christian nations with a strongly Protestant tradition, and anyone brought up in such an environment is likely to be shaped by that tradition, unless he or she has had a specifically different religious upbringing.

These cultural assumptions about religion still mask considerable prejudice and ignorance with regard to non-Christian religions. For example, Britain has a large Hindu population which, during the Hoddle scandal, suddenly found one of its core beliefs on the receiving end of widespread public condemnation and outrage. We are witnessing similar phenomena today, when people who may never have met a Muslim person or read a book about Islam still have strong and often highly negative opinions about Islam and Muslims. These are often informed by the tabloid press, but Islamophobia has a subtle influence on the media at every level. The Pakistani diplomat and scholar of Islam, Akbar S. Ahmed, argues that 'Nothing in history has threatened Muslims like the Western media'.[5] Underlying all this is a deeply rooted belief that white Westerners are at the top of the social and evolutionary scale, and any manifestation of difference in values, beliefs or lifestyles is a sign of inferiority or barbarism.

Evolution and the concept of religion

Everywhere they looked, those nineteenth-century scholars of religion saw evidence of an evolutionary law which put them above every other race and culture. White Western men were at the top of the ladder, from where they sought to study the lesser developed of their species by observing their rituals and beliefs.

For example, the pioneering English anthropologist, Edward Burnett Tylor (1832–1917), was interested in so-called 'primitive religion' as an example of the early stages of intellectual development. He wrote of the need 'to obtain a means of measurement' in ethnological research in order to find 'something like a definite line along which to reckon progress and retrogression in civilisation'. This involved grading civilisation according to the achievements of educated Europeans and Americans:

> The educated world of Europe and America practically settles a standard by simply placing its own nations at one end of the social series and savage tribes at the other, arranging the rest of mankind between these limits according as they correspond more closely to savage or to cultured life.[6]

For Tyler, the ultimate purpose of ethnography was not simply to study these primitive religious cultures, but to eliminate all traces of them from modern culture in the name of science and progress. He wrote that

> where barbaric hordes groped blindly, cultured men can often move onward with a clear view. It is a harsher, and at times even painful, office of ethnography to expose the remains of crude old cultures which have passed into harmful superstition, and to mark these out for destruction … [A]ctive at once in aiding progress and in removing hindrance, the science of culture is essentially a reformer's science.[7]

To what extent is the war of scientific atheism against religion a continuation of this endeavour to purge 'cultured' society of the influence of 'barbaric hordes'? What might the consequences be for those many educated Western citizens who do not accept that their religious faith is a vestige of primal savagery, let alone for those who do not even have the protection of Western citizenship?

James Frazer, the best-known and one of the most widely quoted of these early scholars of religion, also adhered to this ranking of religions in terms of evolutionary development. He believed that the task of anthropology was to benefit 'all mankind' by 'enabling us to follow the long march, the slow and toilsome ascent, of humanity from savagery to civilisation.'[8] Like Tylor, Frazer believed that the comparative study of religion had a moral as well as a scientific objective, for it could 'become a powerful instrument to expedite progress if it lays bare certain weak spots in the foundations on which modern society is built'.[9] He acknowledged that this involved doing violence to ancient hopes and beliefs, but it was a task demanded by the pursuit of truth:

> It is indeed a melancholy and in some respects thankless task to strike at the foundations of beliefs in which, as in a strong tower, the hopes and aspirations of humanity through long ages have sought a refuge from the storm and stress of life. Yet sooner or later it is inevitable that the battery of the comparative method should breach these venerable walls, mantled over with ivy and mosses and wild flowers of a thousand tender and sacred associations. At present we are only dragging the guns into position: they have hardly yet begun to speak … Whatever comes of it, wherever it leads, we must follow the truth alone. It is our guiding star.[10]

I suggested in the Introduction that today no serious scholar would cite Frazer as an authoritative source on religions, which is not to deny the considerable literary merit of *The Golden Bough*. Frazer was the archetypal armchair scholar – the composition of his vast opus on religions did not involve any field-work. Yet Frazer is one of the few religious studies scholars cited by Dawkins and, while he mocks the religious beliefs described in *The Golden Bough*, Dawkins does not question its author's credentials.

Dawkins grumbles about how he grudgingly attended a conference in Cambridge sponsored by the Templeton Foundation, only to find himself accused of having a nineteenth-century worldview. He goes on to say, 'to call an argument nineteenth-century is not the same as explaining what is wrong with it.'[11] Well, I'm explaining here what's wrong with it, when it relates to religion and its origins.

In their uncritical engagement with outmoded theories of religion, the new atheists have hardly moved on from that imperial world in which cultures dominated by a white male elite remain caught up in a territorial battle of colonisation and conquest. Believing that they had attained to the highest level of knowledge and civilisation, those early scientists sought an objective vantage point from which to study and categorise the 'inferior' races and tribes they were discovering through Europe's, and particularly Britain's, imperial adventures. If we want to understand how 'religion' functions in the world according to Dawkins, then we need to situate him in the context of those nineteenth-century scholars who perceived themselves as beacons of progress in a world of seething ignorance and barbarism. Like them, the new atheists labour under the delusion of their own superior knowledge, from the perspective of an evolutionary ideology which clouds their judgement and distorts their understanding as surely as any religious world-view might.

The significance of religious differences

The nineteenth-century invention of the concept of religion meant the grouping together of a diversity of cultural practices vaguely associated with religious beliefs. The conviction that science offered a set of universal laws by which all human life could be categorised hierarchically in terms of progress, evolution and civilisation meant forcing a wide range of cultural phenomena into a narrow set of definitions and categories defined as religion. For example, the word 'Hinduism' was first used by the British to describe the vast spiritual and cultic landscape of Indian society, and scholars still debate to what extent it is accurate to describe Hinduism as a religion at all. The fact that 'religion' has been used to cover such a range of practices and ideas means that every scholarly attempt to come up with a workable definition has failed. This is either because it is so broad that it encompasses everything from football to Marxism, or because it is so narrow that it excludes belief systems such as Buddhism and Confucianism which do not necessarily appeal to a divine origin or source of revelation.

If we are to understand anything about religion, then we have to undertake the painstaking task of going beyond the idea of 'religion', to a greater appreciation of the diverse cultures, identities and histories which make up different traditions. These give rise to vastly different views of the cosmos and our place within it. Even if we set aside the almost infinite plurality of indigenous religions and oral traditions, the so-called world religions such as Buddhism, Christianity, Confucianism, Hinduism, Islam, Judaism and Sikhism all manifest commonalities and differences within and across boundaries of time, place and culture. We cannot hope to understand the human story and its endeavours without some awareness of these complexities.

The three so-called Abrahamic religions of Judaism, Christianity and Islam share the same creation myth – the *Qur'an* includes a version of the story of Genesis. They are all monotheistic religions which affirm both intimacy and difference in the relationship between God and creation. However close the relationship between God and the soul might be, it does not dissolve into undifferentiated oneness. All three religions have a linear understanding of time, in which the cosmos moves in a chronological trajectory from its creation by God to its ultimate destiny. Eastern religions include polytheistic, monotheistic and monistic concepts, in which there may be one or many gods, and in which the ultimate reality may or may not be distinct from creation and the soul, depending on which philosophical school or devotional practice one is referring to. The cosmos is understood in terms of cyclical time, governed by the laws of *karma*, and revolving through vast aeons of creation and destruction, death and rebirth. The Abrahamic religions affirm the reality of the material world. Buddhism and some forms of Hinduism see the material world as illusory, and in Buddhism the attachment to this illusion is the cause of all suffering.

It is hard to overestimate the profound impact these different beliefs have on values, relationships and social institutions. This potted survey is guilty of vast generalisations which fail to represent the multitude of differences nestling within every religious tradition. The attempt to use 'religion' in a generic sense eradicates these differences so that we develop a distorted understanding of the diversity of human cultures in their historical and geographical contexts and in their social, political and domestic dimensions.

Whether or not we are biologically orientated towards religious belief, as some recent studies suggest (see Chapter 8), religion in one form or another has been the organising centre of all cultures until the rise of atheism in modern Western society – and many would argue that the new atheism is simply another religious variant.[12] Since the nineteenth century Western thinkers have been labouring under a serious delusion about the nature and role of religion in human experience. We Westerners will continue to treat our fellow human beings in other cultures and traditions with contemptuous arrogance, unless we come to a more mature understanding of religion in its many forms and functions.

There is something profoundly misanthropic in the belief that modern Western science has shown all religious believers to be deluded savages at best and immoral bigots at worst. Christopher Hitchens writes that religion 'comes from the bawling and fearful infancy of our species, and is a babyish attempt to meet our inescapable demand for knowledge (as well as for comfort, reassurance, and other infantile needs).'[13] He repeatedly makes the claim that religion is 'manufactured' or 'manmade', as if lurking out of sight throughout the entire human story there have been Machiavellian powers at work, compelling humanity, 'on pain of extremely agonizing consequences, to pay the exorbitant tithes and taxes that raised the imposing edifices of religion.'[14] This might describe the historical functioning of many religious institutions, but it does not explain the origins or wider social functions of religion.

The truth about religion is more elusive, complex and intriguing than these formulaic dismissals can account for. Indeed, there may be no one truth about religious origins. Religions arise in the creative matrix of our shared human quest to express an awareness of something beyond our mortal, material lives. Religions are collective dramas enacted on the world's stage, which mutate and develop as they encounter one another and adapt to different cultural and historical environments. The capacity of religions for cross-fertilisation and syncretism is likely to increase as global communications facilitate encounters among different cultures. This suggests that religion is likely to become more rather than less dynamic and diverse, with considerable potential not only for new forms of religious extremism, but also for the emergence of new religious visions which weave together ancient wisdom and modern science. Indeed, it is a hallmark of any living tradition that it is able to adapt and survive, just as species are, and all the world religions are today in a phase of quite remarkable adaptation in response to the challenges of modernity and global communications. That is why they are also all home to various forms of fundamentalism and conservatism among those who resist the inevitability of change, but we'll consider these questions more in Chapter 7.

In our justifiable critique of the perverted creeds and cults which increasingly dominate the modern religious landscape, we should not lose sight of these ancient and living traditions which shape the human story. They bear all the hallmarks of our humanity, including the best and the worst of which our species is capable, because they are nothing more than the stories we inhabit as thinking, creative beings. They are the imprints which we place upon the soft and pliable material of our lives, in order to mark the time and place of our existence with meaning and hope.

Religion, the supernatural and belief in God

The confusion surrounding various debates about religion arises partly from the tendency to equate belief in God with religion, as Dawkins frequently does in *The God Delusion*. But many people who believe in God are not religious, and those who manifest the most intense religiosity may have little faith in God. For example, Dawkins is perplexed by the Christianity of the Astronomer Royal and President of the Royal Society, Martin Rees, who describes himself as an 'unbelieving Anglican ... out of loyalty to the tribe'.[15] Religion has always been as much about different forms of tribal loyalty as it has been about belief in God. While it may be true that religious authorities and scholars in different traditions have a great deal to say about God, particularly in the Christian theological tradition, it is probably no less true to say that, for many of the world's 2.1 billion Christians, Christianity is more about tribal loyalty, tradition and culture than faith in God the Father, God the Son and God the Holy Spirit or wholeheartedly signing up to the Nicene Creed. In other words, religion can arguably survive just as readily without belief in God as belief in God can survive without religion, despite Dennett's claim that 'a religion without *God* or *gods* is like a vertebrate without a backbone.'[16] In the 2001 British census, nearly 72 per cent of people claimed to be Christian, although in another poll only 35 per cent of British people claimed to believe in God (compared with 73 per cent in the United States), and only 6 per cent of the population attends church regularly.[17] Buddhism is not associated with belief in God, but its followers are often flamboyantly religious in their practices and devotions. The relationship between belief in God, religious affiliation and religious observance is complex, and to confuse them the way Dawkins does is evidence of woolly thinking, not of scientific rigour.

Dawkins acknowledges that he is dealing primarily with Christianity in *The God Delusion* (although his target is just as often Islam), but that does not prevent him from using 'religion' as a catch-all phrase to describe everything which does not fit within his scientific world-view. By the same measure, he goes to considerable lengths to deny that those who share his scientific world-view could possibly be religious or believe in God, even when their writings offer evidence to the contrary. When dealing with ambiguities in the positions of scientists such as Einstein, he conjures these away by a metaphorical sleight of hand. He is willing to concede that Einstein was a pantheist, but that's because 'Pantheism is sexed-up atheism'.[18] He insists that, when scientists such as Einstein and Stephen Hawking use the word 'God', they are using it 'in a purely metaphorical, poetic sense.'[19] When Einstein defines religiousness as a sense of 'something that our mind cannot grasp and whose beauty and sublimity reaches us only indirectly and as a feeble reflection',[20] Dawkins argues that, to use the word 'religion' to describe this kind of experience is 'destructively misleading because, for the vast majority of people, "religion" implies "supernatural".'[21] But this begs the question of what we mean by 'supernatural', and Dawkins' use of the word is misleading.

During the Reformation and the Enlightenment, nature came to be understood in a mechanistic sense as bereft of any capacity for divine grace or revelation. (I explore this suggestion further in the next chapter.) In order to appreciate the significance of this, we have to recognise that 'nature' is a cultural construct. When we speak of nature, we are using language to describe the world around us with all its species, life forms and landscapes. But nature is a concept whose meaning changes with different perceptions and ways of looking at the world. This means that 'supernatural' is also a concept which has different meanings, for it refers to phenomena or experiences which do not seem to fit within our particular expectations of what nature is or should be. The term 'supernatural' therefore depends on a certain concept of what 'natural' is. For many people who are less determinedly material-ist than Dawkins, there may be an indeterminate region which is neither strictly natural nor strictly supernatural. A red rose may be natural, but when I am given one by the person I love, I experi-ence a range of emotions, memories and associations which endow that rose with symbolic significance and make it in some sense 'supernatural'. It transcends its natural, biological functions to communicate something in the realm of beauty, hope and love.

In their most closed and authoritarian versions, religions seek to close down this capacity of the natural world to glow with trans-cendent hope which is beyond any human control. But the mystical and poetic aspects of religious traditions offer sublime examples of the capacity of the religious imagination to see, with

William Blake, 'a world in a grain of sand and a heaven in a wildflower'. Much modern religious faith owes more to this harmonious interweaving of nature and grace, or the natural and the supernatural, than it does to the kind of superstitious beliefs about deities, spooks, demons and miracles that are implied in Dawkins' use of the word 'supernatural'. Indeed, the entertainment industry and popular culture have provided a far more hospitable home to every kind of spiritual fantasy and demonic nightmare than most modern religions.

Dawkins frequently confuses the supernatural with religion, as when he discusses the religion of the obstetrician Robert Winston, whom he describes as 'a respected pillar of British Jewry'.[22] In a television interview, Winston told Dawkins that 'he didn't really believe in anything supernatural.' Dawkins continues:

> When I pressed him, he said he found that Judaism provided a good discipline to help him structure his life and lead a good one. Perhaps it does; but that, of course, has not the smallest bearing on the truth value of any of its supernatural claims. There are many intellectual atheists who proudly call themselves Jews and observe Jewish rites, perhaps out of loyalty to an ancient tradition or to murdered relatives, but also because of a confused and confusing willingness to label as 'religion' the pantheistic reverence which most of us share with its most distinguished exponent, Albert Einstein.[23]

This quotation suggests that the confusion lies more in Dawkins' mind than in Winston's religious observances. Many Jewish people would interpret their beliefs in the terms Dawkins describes, and these are not pantheistic according to any accepted meaning of the word. If Judaism is a religion, it is not based primarily on an appeal to interior faith or on supernatural claims but on one's willing-ness to live in conformity to the shared observances, rituals and values of the Jewish community. But reading Dawkins' attempts to define religion is rather like reading Humpty Dumpty speaking to Alice in Lewis Carroll's *Alice Through the Looking Glass*: "'When *I* use a word", Humpty Dumpty said, in rather a scornful tone, "it means just what I choose it to mean – neither more nor less."'[24]

Christopher Hitchens is similarly manipulative in his discussion of the religious beliefs of others. While he readily imputes quasi-religious motives to the atheist political regimes of the twentieth century, he is highly reluctant to acknowledge the role played by religion in the lives of great Christian visionaries such as Dietrich Bonhoeffer and Martin Luther King. In the case of Bonhoeffer, Hitchens attributes his willingness to die in resisting the Nazis to 'an admirable but nebulous humanism'.[25] Because King quoted the Bible in 'metaphors and allegories',[26] rather than literally acting out its violent rhetoric, Hitchens concludes that 'In no real as opposed to nominal sense … was he a Christian.'[27] One cannot possibly have an intelligent debate with this kind of polemic, for Hitchens is so defiantly obtuse in his representation of scripture and its role in the Christian life that there is no point of entry into a sensible and informed discussion. Rather than acknowledging that it might be Christianity itself which inspires a few individuals to risk their lives in the service of others – often in defiance of religious authorities – Hitchens dismisses examples of Nazi resisters such as Bonhoeffer and Martin Niemoller because 'the chance that they did so on orders from any priesthood is statistically almost negligible.'[28] If one is going to define Christians exclusively in terms of those who take the Bible literally, who model their behaviour on the warring tribes of the first millennium BC, and who only act on orders from priests, then Christianity does indeed become a religion of fanatics and murderers which would include hardly any of the Church's greatest saints and martyrs, let alone the vast majority of ordinary believers. In other words, we are arguing about straw dogs in a way which tells us a great deal about Hitchens' prejudices, but very little about the motives and practices of religious believers.

This contemptuous dismissal of the religious beliefs of others in the name of an all-encompassing secularism can be traced back to its nineteenth-century antecedents. The nineteenth-century battle for hearts and minds had a triangular shape: Western men of science versus Western men of God, with the religious 'other' forming a silent object of study, debate and conversion – endlessly spoken about but never invited to speak. Today, the new atheists are as hostile towards theologians as the most militant Victorian scientists were, but the battle lines are still drawn between two protagonists – Christian men of God and Western men of science – in a way which reflects little of the plurality and diversity of other world-views. In the nineteenth century, the religious other was made up of all those 'barbarians' and 'savages' who littered the imperial globe with their presence. Today, it is Islam which constitutes the religious other, and it is still represented as a barbaric force to be conquered and civilised by the imperial powers of reason and progress.

This new confrontation is taking shape as the era of the Enlightenment draws to a close, and we cannot yet glimpse what will take its place. In the nineteenth century, those who put their faith in science and progress had some justification for doing so, for it may indeed have seemed that Western society stood at the pinnacle of our human aspirations towards civilisation, peace and knowledge. But as we look back over the legacy of the last 400 years, through the blood and ashes of humanity's most violent century, the Enlightenment and its promises have lost their lustre. Only the new atheists continue to nail their colours to the mast of progress, and in this they have much in common with the religious bigots they oppose. Like all fundamentalists, they rigidly defend a set of beliefs against the muddle and mess of human life with all its ambiguities, promises and failures, even when those beliefs have been radically undermined by the evidence of history.

In 1990, the theologian and biochemist Arthur Peacocke wrote somewhat prematurely that

> The last trumpet in the so-called warfare of science and religion has long since become silent and those engaged in both enterprises have today, I think, acquired a new humility – not least because they have come to recognize both the limitations of their presumed knowledge and the dire, indeed evil, social consequences of ultra-dogmatic, over-confident, im-

perialistic applications of half-truths about their respective quests. For example, the intellectual descendants of the Enlightenment have long castigated religion, with justification, for the wars fought in its name, only to find themselves to have sired in twentieth-century nuclear physics the possibility of global, rather than local, holocaust.[29]

One searches in vain amidst the writings of the new atheists for any evidence of this humility in the face of science's as well as religion's dangers. Rather, there is currently an act of historical revisionism at work, in the revival of the language of scientific militancy and in the projection by atheist rationalists of all the twentieth century's humanly engineered catastrophes and threats into the sphere of religion, in a way which leaves some scientists dangerously deluded about the risks and failings of their own profession.

Hegel famously wrote that 'the owl of Minerva spreads her wings only with the falling of the dusk.' He meant that philosophical wisdom understands history only with hindsight. Truth is always retrospective. For thinkers such as Dawkins, and indeed for Hegel himself, history is progressive and forward-looking. Human beings are advancing in knowledge and in moral understanding, and for the new atheists the defeat of religion by scientific rationalism is part of that progress, so long as we remain on guard against the potential of religion to overwhelm the forces of reason. I have argued in the last two chapters that this view is informed by a nineteenth-century concept of evolution, which is inseparable from an imperial world-view with all its inbuilt assumptions about the racial, cultural and sexual superiority of white Western men over all others.

This idea of Western intellectual and cultural supremacy had a long gestation, but its modern flourishing can be traced back to the Enlightenment, which sparked a dramatic revolution in Western philosophy, politics and culture. Today, dusk is falling on the Enlightenment era, not least because of the emergence of a plurality of religious and cultural narratives which challenge the hegemony of the Western intellectual tradition. With this in mind, I want to widen the historical lens to consider the impact of the last 400 years of Western thought on our modern values.

Richard Dawkins declares himself 'thrilled to be alive at a time when humanity is pushing against the limits of understanding. Even better, we may eventually discover that there are no limits.'[30] Is this optimism justified, or do we need to re-evaluate the ways in which our so-called enlightened culture has blinded modern Westerners to the human misery which proliferates in the shadows of our obsession with progress?

Chapter 3

THE ENLIGHTENMENT AND ITS AFTERMATH

The Enlightenment is a broad term which refers to a range of political and intellectual transformations in European and American society in the eighteenth century. It also sometimes includes the so-called Age of Reason in the seventeenth century, and this in turn can be traced back to the sixteenth century, when Copernicus (1473–1543) first challenged the Christian belief that the earth was at the centre of universe. Not only did this involve a dramatic transformation in Christian cosmology, but perhaps more importantly it set in motion a gradual shift away from the authority of religion to the authority of science in the production of knowledge. History never divides up into tidy categories, but if we are to understand the emergence of scientific rationalism in the nineteenth century, we have to locate it in the context of this long revolution in European thought from a religious to a scientific world-view. In political terms, the Enlightenment signalled the end of the conjoined power of Christianity and the European monarchies, the birth of Western democracy and the rise of the modern nation state. It paved the way for the nineteenth-century triumph of science over religion, and it still provides the foundations for the scientific rationalism of today's new atheists.[1]

Knowledge and power

The rise of science brought about a transformation in the West's understanding of the relationship between nature and culture, in a way which has had far-reaching implications for social, sexual and economic relationships. In the pre-modern Christian world, the study of nature was a path to discovery and insight about the will of God, the inherent harmony of the cosmos and the place of the human within it. Humans understood themselves as organically united with the rest of nature, so that nature was not an enemy to be defeated but a potential source of revelation and grace, as well as an awesome and threatening power. The individual existed not as a rational entity set over and against nature and other humans, but as a social animal. This created a sense of continuity with other life forms and a sense of interdependence within whichever community he or she belonged to. Human nature, although wounded by sin, retained some of the original goodness of creation. Because of this, the human mind was graced with the capacity to recognise God's will in the laws and relationships of the natural world, in social institutions and laws, and in our own natural desires and inclinations governed by conscience.

The Reformation introduced a darker concept of nature with its belief that original sin had utterly corrupted human nature and destroyed our natural ability to experience any revelation of God in the material world. Stripped of its revelatory power, nature came to be understood as the opposite of grace, rather than as a manifestation of the grace of creation. Grace became an entirely supernatural concept, accessible only through the revelation of God in Christ, and divorced from the divine presence in the material world. This dis-gracing of nature paved the way for the emergence of a scientific perspective which set reason over and against nature, so that even our own human nature with its desires and instincts became an enemy to be conquered. In Tennyson's widely quoted words, nature was 'red in tooth and claw', and the main function of civilised society was to resist the savagery of nature.

Although such ideas have never been entirely lacking from Christianity, they gained new potency with the emergence of scientific reasoning. The eclipse of medieval Christianity and the privileging of more individualistic forms of faith led to the development of a sense of individual identity and moral duty over communal responsibility based on ties of faith and kin. Society would in future be held together by the social contract rather than by the duties and responsibilities of community, and reason would replace revelation as the source of morality and truth. Each man would be free to exercise his freedom as a citizen under the law in a way that was only limited by the imperative not to impinge upon the freedom of other male citizens.

This could be described in terms of another Copernican revolution. If Copernicus created a crisis in knowledge by displacing the Christian belief that the earth and therefore humankind stood at the centre of the universe, the Enlightenment reinstated 'man' – not now the species but the autonomous individual – as the only reliable source of knowledge. From the time of Descartes onwards, truth would be discovered not through prayerful intellectual reflection on God's universe, but through an increasing emphasis on the power of reason to order and control the material world. This meant a gradual change in the function of knowledge itself, and in the relationship between knowledge and power.[2] Whereas human knowledge had once been dependent upon and accountable to the wisdom and power of God, now it became in itself the only source of truth and power. To know something was to acquire power over it, and the more 'man' knew about nature, the more he was able to control it. This led to Francis Bacon's well-known claim that 'Knowledge is power.' We have seen in the last two chapters that this would eventually translate into a form of knowledge which gave Western man political and economic power over vast regions of the world, shored up by his belief that he alone had attained to the peak of progress, science and reason. I want to explore the implications of this more fully, by considering how a scientific world-view continues to hold sway over the Western imagination, to the detriment of other, more holistic ways of knowing.

Witches, slaves and the man of reason

A significant aspect of the triumph of reason over nature was that it also represented the triumph of the man of reason over his feminised and threatening 'other', represented both by the female sex and by the power of nature.[3] The idea that the female sex is a deadly threat to men is by no means confined to Western thought. In Christianity it is a virulent theme which runs through the texts of theology because of the association of Eve with temptation, sin and death in the Book of Genesis. However, this idea gained new potency with the emergence of scientific rationalism, when female sexuality became a metaphor for the dark, unruly forces of nature which man had to control in his pursuit of progress. When the man of reason set out to conquer nature, this included the conquest of the female sex. It also included the conquest of foreign territory and the enslavement of hundreds of thousands of human beings, in the drive to acquire ever more raw materials and cheap labour to fuel the rise of capitalism, which went hand in hand with the modern pursuit of science and progress.

Popular opinion often cites the burning of witches as evidence of pre-modern Christian barbarism, but recent studies suggest a more complex history in which the rise of science is implicated.[4] There are no reliable estimates of how many were killed in the witch-hunts of the sixteenth and seventeenth centuries, but scholarly opinion suggests it was somewhere between 40,000 and 100,000 people, of whom about two thirds were women. The tract used to justify the witch-trials, the *Malleus Maleficarum* ('The Hammer of Witches'), was written by two Dominicans in 1486 and was banned by the Catholic Church in 1490. Nevertheless, it was reprinted many times and it continued to be used by the secular courts in the prosecution of witches over the next two centuries. Some modern scholars argue that the witch-hunts were motivated not only by religious fervour but perhaps more significantly by the drive to eliminate all traces of superstition from a society newly dedicated to asserting the power of reason over nature. Carolyn Merchant, in her book *The Death of Nature*, argues that the sexual torture of suspected witches provided many of the metaphors for Francis Bacon's writings.

Bacon is sometimes referred to as the 'father of modern science', and he was the inspiration behind the establishment of the Royal Society in 1660. In the following quotation, he likens the scientific investigation of nature to the gynaecological examination of witches, citing as an example the anti-witchcraft legislation of his mentor, King James I. Referring to 'superstitious narratives of sorceries, witchcrafts, charms, dreams, divinations, and the like', Bacon writes:

> howsoever the use and practice of such arts is to be condemned, yet from the speculation and consideration of them ... a useful light may be gained, not only for a true judgment of the offenses of the persons charged with such practices, but likewise for the further disclosing of the secrets of nature. Neither ought a man to make scruple of entering and penetrating into these holes and corners, when the inquisition of truth is his whole object – as your majesty has shown in your own example.[5]

Merchant argues that such language cannot be divorced from its social context. It suggests a link between the rise of science, the denigration of nature and the abuse of women associated with the witch-trials.

The early modern era saw the emergence of new and violent forms of misogyny, and it also saw the rise of the slave trade. Like the subordination of women, slavery is a phenomenon as old as humankind itself, and comparatively benign forms of slavery had been practised in the American colonies prior to the slave trade as we remember it today. However, the mid seventeenth century saw the emergence of more rigid rules of separation between slave and free. These were at first based on religious distinctions between Christians and heathens, so that initially they did not affect African Christians. In the 1660s and 1670s Virginia passed a series of laws which included the enslavement of Christian Africans, so that race became the central distinguishing mark which separated slaves from their masters. From then on, the contrast between the 'free' man of the Enlightenment and the slave to ignorance, passion and embodiment would be understood in racial as well as gendered terms.

James Walvin, who has written extensively on the slave trade, observes that 'between c. 1550 and 1860 slavery was integral to the way the Western world lived, functioned and prospered.'[6] He continues:

> To transport so many Africans, to force them to work, generally in the most difficult and oppressive of environments, Europeans and their American descendants devised systems of excruciating violence and cruelty ... There were, of course, great varieties of slavery, but in essence it remained a brutal system which was conceived in violence, maintained by draconian punishments, and all for the material betterment of the Western world.[7]

The rise of capitalism, the age of Enlightenment, the witch-hunts and the slave trade share an overlapping space on the spectrum of Western history. It was the Western man of reason who tortured and burned his fellow human beings and who reduced thousands of Africans to the status of shackled and abused beasts in his pursuit of the conquest of nature and the accumulation of wealth. Even as the enlightened men of Europe and America were celebrating the conquest of reason over the tyranny of God and religion, they were exercising innovative forms of tyranny over women and other races and cultures.

Rational men, hysterical women and inferior races

The phenomenon of the witch-trials had all but disappeared by the late seventeenth century, but the slave trade would not be finally eliminated until the nineteenth century. As we saw in the last two chapters, the belief that the white Western man stood at the pinnacle of the social and sexual hierarchy found scientific justification in Darwin's theory of evolution, and the nineteenth century saw new forms of racial and sexual prejudice flourishing under the cloak of science.

The witch-hunts had been fuelled in part by a fear of what was perceived as the dark, irrational power of female sexuality. By the nineteenth century, female sexuality had been tamed to such an extent that women were perceived as essentially passive and lacking in sexual desire – Freud did not believe that there was any such thing as the female libido. However, a different problem had emerged to challenge the skills of the newly established medical profession, for hysteria had reached near-pandemic proportions amongst the wives and daughters of the Victorian bourgeoisie.

The term 'female hysteria' (from the Greek *hystera*, meaning 'uterus') gained widespread usage to explain a range of women's 'ailments', from insomnia and fainting to causing trouble for other members of the family. Although the idea of hysteria can be traced back to ancient Greece, the nineteenth century has been described as its '*belle epoque*', for this was an era when 'scientific medicine flexed its muscles and spread its wings.'[8] Treatment for hysteria included genital massage to induce 'hysterical paroxysm', but physicians applying these 'treatments' did not acknowledge that they were bringing women to orgasm, owing to the commonly held belief that women did not have orgasms because of their sexual passivity. Doctors found the manual labour involved in this treatment tedious and time-consuming, as a result of which the electric vibrator was invented to deal with the problem.[9] Safely disguised as a medical device which would bring a sparkle to the eyes and a flush to the cheeks, the vibrator was widely advertised in women's magazines until the 1930s.

However, only middle-class white women were believed to be hysterical, weak, sexually passive and susceptible to a wide range of health problems. Poor women, and women of different races, were viewed quite differently. The ailments which afflicted the wives of the wealthy were a result of 'over-civilisation' and, as Freud argued along with others of his time, women were poorly adapted to meet the demands of civilisation. The British sexologist Havelock Ellis

(1859–1939) argued that women should wear corsets because in the evolutionary process they were less physically adapted than men to walking on two legs rather than four.[10] Poor white women, and even more significantly, African American women and the native women of the European colonies, were altogether more robust because they had not been over-exposed to the depleting effects of civilisation. Consider the opinion of the late-nineteenth-century American physician and corset manufacturer, Lucien Warner:

> It is not then hard work and privation which make the women of our country invalids, but circumstances and habits intimately connected with the so-called blessings of wealth and refinement. The African negress, who toils beside her husband in the fields of the south, and Bridget [the Irish immigrant woman] who washes, and scrubs and toils in our homes at the north, enjoy for the most part good health, with comparative immunity from uterine diseases.[11]

The so-called 'Hottentot Venus' is perhaps the most notorious example of the fascination of the nineteenth-century man of science and empire with his dark female 'other'.[12] Saartjie Baartman was a South African orphan who was shipped to England in 1810 and put on display naked, first in England and later in Paris, as an example of the extraordinary sexual character-istics of the Hottentot female. When abolitionists protested against her treatment, they were resisted by those who wanted to use her for scientific research, and Baartman herself assented to her treat-ment. When she died at the age of 25 her genitalia were preserved in the interests of science, and her skeleton was displayed in a Paris museum until 1974. Her remains were returned to South Africa in 2002.

It is easy to look back at examples such as these and to see where scientific thinking was clouded by unacknowledged preju-dices and driven by prevailing cultural norms. Those who believe in progress would argue that this in itself is evidence of the self-improving power of science and reason. Gradually, scientists learn from their mistakes so that scientific knowledge is slowly but surely advancing in its pursuit of truth. We no longer burn witches at the stake, slavery has been abolished, and we recognise that the theory of evolution does not prove that white men are superior to women and to other races. Women do have orgasms after all (even if these remain something of a mystery to scientists and sex therapists alike), and the vibrator has made a come-back without any need to disguise its real function. After two centuries, the Enlightenment vision of social equality and democracy has spread through all layers of Western society, the benefits of science and technology are clear for all to see, and we are pushing against the furthest frontiers of knowledge in our understanding of the universe. The only real enemy we face is religion, which threatens to undermine all that we Westerners have struggled to achieve because of its irrational beliefs, its superstitious practices, and its fanatical violence.

How plausible is this confidence in the power of science? Is it really true that scientific knowledge today is more objective and value-free than it used to be, or do we just discover a different set of prejudices – maybe even some of the same old prejudices – skulking beneath the apparently objective arguments of science?

'The Mother of All Burkas'

There is a fascinating chapter in *The God Delusion* in which Richard Dawkins explains the wonders of quantum physics to his readers. I shall come back to the scientific explanation in a later chapter, but for now I want to consider Dawkins' revealing choice of metaphor, which suggests an attitude every bit as blind to its sexual and racial prejudices as those of his Victorian predecessors.

Under the subtitle 'The Mother of All Burkas', Dawkins argues that our capacity to grasp the implications of modern physics is limited by our inability 'to cope with distances outside the narrow middle range of the ancestrally familiar.'[13] He uses the image of the *burka*-clad woman to illustrate his point:

not just a token of egregious male cruelty and tragically cowed female submission, I want to use the narrow slit in the veil as a symbol of something else … The one-inch window of visible light is derisorily tiny compared with the miles and miles of black cloth representing the invisible part of the spectrum, from radio waves at the hem of the skirt to gamma rays at the top of the head. What science does for us is to widen the window. It opens up so wide that the imprisoning black garment drops away almost completely, exposing our senses to airy and exhilarating freedom.[14]

In resorting to the cliché of the veiled Muslim woman as a metaphor for ignorance and oppression, Dawkins shows that culturally, his vision too is confined to the 'narrow middle range of the ancestrally familiar.' The sexual and racial 'other' is no longer the Hottentot Venus and her dark mysteries. Now, it is the veiled Muslim woman who must be exposed to the all-seeing, all-knowing gaze of the man of science.

Nowhere does Dawkins engage with the plurality of Muslim women's voices in discussing what the veil means to them, as everything from a symbol of oppression along the lines he suggests, to a positive assertion of their Muslim identity. In a similar vein, Polly Toynbee exhorts her readers to 'Forget cultural sensibilities' when she launches an attack on the burka as turning women into 'cowering creatures demanding and expecting violence and victimisation.'[15] She goes on to use the veil as an excuse for a sweeping attack on religion: 'Primitive Middle Eastern religions (and most others) are much the same – Islam, Christianity and Judaism all define themselves through disgust for women's bodies.'[16]

For Dawkins, scientific enlightenment involves the disrobing of that veiled female figure. Of course, it's only a metaphor, but is it really so far removed from those metaphors used by Francis Bacon, when he sought to probe the holes and secrets of the earth and/or the female body in the name of science? Is female nakedness in this context an apt metaphor for 'airy and exhilarating freedom', or might Muslim women themselves have something different to say if they were permitted to contribute to this debate? If removing the Muslim woman's veil is a modern metaphor for scientific knowledge, it too has its nineteenth-century antecedents. See, for example, the bronze statue by Louis-Ernest Barrias (1841–1905), entitled *Nature Unveiling Herself before Science*, in which a seductive woman parts her robe to reveal her breasts. The veiled female body stripped by the scientific male gaze is not a new phenomenon. It always masquerades under the guise of progress and enlightenment battling against the forces of religion, superstition and darkness. One of the most potent ways of defying the 'benefits' which modern, rationalising cultures such as ours have inflicted upon the world might be to deliberately take up the *persona* of the sexual and religious other, perfectly epitomised in the *burka*-clad woman.

I am not arguing with Toynbee's claim that religions often define themselves through disgust for women's bodies. However, I am appealing for a more nuanced evaluation of the extent to which women have benefited from Western notions of science and progress, not least by listening to what women themselves say in different cultural and economic contexts. Contrary to what Toynbee and others suggest, religion is not always the greatest obstacle in the path of women's flourishing. As long as science fails to deliver the benefits which it promises to the vast majority of the world's women, many will continue to seek meaning and support in religion, even at the expense of their personal freedom. Freedom is an abstract and meaningless concept for a mother whose children are starving.

Science and technology have transformed the lives of Western women. As a mother of four children, two of my pregnancies would probably have ended in the deaths of myself and my babies had it not been for emergency medical interventions. For the first time, women have access to reliable contraception which has ushered in a new era of sexual relationships and reproductive ethics. Across a vast range of factors, we in the Western world live longer, healthier and more comfortable lives than any of our forebears, and that is largely thanks to science. (Whether or not we are happier is another question.)

However, whatever benefits medical science has offered to women, the scientific obsession with women's bodies and reproductive capacities has hardly diminished. If contraception has given women some control over the processes of reproduction, the fertility industry has become a lucrative trade for scientists. Over all this hangs the shadow of eugenics, for recent developments in embryo research seem barely distinguishable from those early-twentieth-century beliefs about breeding programmes and their capacity to bring about a superior breed of human beings, based on the theory of natural selection. Whatever benefits embryology might offer in producing healthier or more intelligent children, these are likely to be for the exclusive benefit of a small minority of affluent white people in the Western democracies. Science today offers us the chance to genetically programme our rich white bodies to become stronger, more intelligent and healthier than poor black bodies − an exercise in social engineering that those early eugenicists could scarcely have dreamed of.

Meanwhile, the vast majority of the world's women still lack access to the most basic facilities in terms of reproductive health. These women gain nothing from expensive experiments in embryo research. Their needs are more fundamental than that, and could easily be met if there were the political and scientific will to do so. Yet public debate in the West is far more focused on the ethical dilemmas of researching on embryos and, in the United States, on the abortion controversy, than on the ethical outrage of the lack of basic health care for the majority of the world's women and children. In sub-Saharan Africa a woman has a 1 in 16 chance of dying in childbirth, whereas in the developed countries this is only 1 in 2,800. In 2005, the World Health Organization estimated that, during one year, 11 million children under 5 die from preventable causes, including 4 million babies during the first month of life. An estimated half a million women die every year in pregnancy and childbirth.[17]

Like their nineteenth-century predecessors, most scientists are still more interested in the elaborate pathologies and ailments of rich white women than in the age-old afflictions of the majority of the world's women who are poor, black and unable to pay for the increasingly expensive and elaborate treatments which science offers, often under the patented labels of the multinational drugs corporations. Meanwhile, many Christians expend considerably more energy fighting to defend unformed embryos and making unholy political alliances to block women's access to contraception, safe abortion and good maternity care, than they do fighting against war, hunger and poverty. In suggesting that science has not always served the interests of women, I am not promoting religion as a better alternative. Modern women have often found themselves caught between the devil of progress and the deep blue sea of religion.

Ethics and the ambiguity of science

Science, like religion, is an umbrella-term for a range of human ideas and practices. Neither of them can be judged in the abstract, for they are only as good or as bad as the people who practise them. They both include individuals who commit themselves wholeheartedly to working for the good of humanity, and they both include individuals who are driven by personal ambition, greed and the lust for power. This is why genuine humanists, religious or not, cannot afford the luxury of moral absolutes, particularly when these draw a line between science and progress on the one side (good), and religion on the other side (bad). These oversimplifications mask a host of ambiguities and complexities which do not lend themselves to such formulaic judgements. For an example of this, we might consider the vexed question of HIV/Aids and its prevention and treatment.

Many who loudly declare their concern for Aids victims are far more condemning of the Catholic Church than the drugs corporations. Yet the belief that the Catholic Church is largely responsible for the ongoing death toll of Aids because of its opposition to the use of condoms needs to be challenged. Polly Toynbee gave forceful expression to this idea in an article published on the day of Pope John Paul II's funeral, in which she savaged the Catholic Church for its moral corruption.[18] She wrote that 'In countries where 50% are infected, millions of very young Aids orphans are today's immediate victims of the curia.' She goes on to claim that the '"civilised" Catholics' who attended the Pope's funeral 'without rebelling on behalf of the helpless third world poor who die for their misplaced faith ... have as much blood on their hands as the Vatican they support'.

In fact, statistics show that there is very little correlation between the percentage of the population which is Catholic and the Aids mortality rate in third world countries. Some countries with a high Catholic population, such as Madagascar, have low rates of infection, while some with a low Catholic population, such as Botswana and South Africa, have high infection rates. Moreover, the Roman Catholic Church is a major provider of health care for third world victims of HIV/Aids, including the provision of anti-retroviral drugs and the care of Aids orphans. All the Catholic health workers I have met who are working in this field would advise the use of condoms for those infected with the virus who are in sexual relationships. This doesn't justify the Church's official position prohibiting the use of condoms, but it does invite a more careful evaluation of the impact of that teaching. It is simply wrong to claim that there is a direct link between the number of people dying of Aids, and the Roman Catholic Church's opposition to the use of condoms.

If we consider the role of scientists in the prevention and treatment of Aids, the picture is equally complex. For most HIV-positive people in the West, an expensive cocktail of patented drugs keeps the Aids virus at bay and enables them to lead more or less normal lives. When these drugs are unavailable, not only do people develop full-blown Aids, but the transmission of the disease from mother to child during birth or breast-feeding is much more likely. Scientists can play a crucial role in making patented drugs more widely available, when they have the collective will to do so. The fact that some of the drugs companies have reluctantly agreed to the distribution of generic drugs in poorer countries is partly due to pressure by concerned scientists, including doctors and researchers, as well as by politicians and public campaigners. But how much more might be achieved, if scientists were more united in their determination to work for the good of humankind, as Dawkins and others seem to suggest they are?

It is simply wrong to suggest that science and progress go hand in hand as forces for good, while religion is always and everywhere an obstacle in their path. Sometimes, religion provides a space of resistance and shelter for those who are forgotten or abandoned by science, or for those whose hopes and aspirations, communities and values, are sacrificed in the name of progress, which is usually closely allied to the West's political ambitions and economic interests. In clinging to the old-fashioned idea that science offers a value-free, objective view of the world, scientific rationalists remain blind to all the evidence which suggests that Western science is just one particular way of interpreting the world, and it never floats free of its cultural and historical moorings with all their vested interests and preconceived ideas.

Science and serendipity

Some radical postmodernists would argue that all science is socially constructed: that is, it is a way of relating to the material world which is entirely determined by its cultural and intellectual environment, and which lacks any grounding in objective reality and facts.[19] I think that's going too far, but it is a reminder that science and theology face similar challenges when they assert that there is an objective reality, not produced by the human mind, but which we are able to know and understand truthfully. As Thomas Kuhn argues, the scientific community operates with a set of 'received beliefs'[20] about the way the world is, which conditions its research. Scientists, like religious believers, need to be attentive to the ways in which their received prejudices and unchallenged assumptions can obscure their openness to new ideas. History is littered with the failures of science as well as being crowned with its many successes, and scientists do not operate in a privileged sphere of knowledge which makes them more objective or truthful than the rest of us.

Many scientific discoveries have come about through serendipity – scientists have stumbled upon life-changing discoveries when they have been researching something quite different – or as a result of miscalculations and mistakes in their research.[21] As I write this, newspaper reports are telling of how the disgraced Korean scientist, Hwang Woo-suk, who faked data on his research and claimed to have cloned the first human embryo, had in fact inadvertently made a scientific breakthrough in extracting stem cells from a single unfertilised egg. It is a fine example of the deceptions and failings of science, and of its serendipitous achievements.[22]

In the British newspaper, *The Guardian*, there is a weekly column written by Ben Goldacre called 'Bad Science'. Every week, Goldacre exposes some of the unsubstantiated claims, falsified research, inaccurate reporting and dangerous medical practices which masquerade under the umbrella of science, and result in a media diet of scare stories, health fads, wonder drugs and misinformation. Goldacre has revealed that scientific studies funded by drug companies are four times more likely to favour the drugs produced by the funding company; that a well-known television doctor and health guru had no medical qualifications; that a researcher working for a vitamin manufacturer had come out in support of claims that vitamin C was more effective than anti-retroviral drugs in preventing Aids; and that the medical journal *The Lancet* had published a highly favourable review of 'a slightly maverick book' on autism by a doctor working on the medical fringe with a track record of irresponsible research on children.[23]

All these examples indicate that science, like religion, has difficulty in policing its borders. For every good scientist, there is a multitude of cranks, charlatans and impostors claiming to be scientists, just as for every good religious believer there is a multitude of nutters and the occasional psychopath claiming to be religious. Josef Mengele was a scientist, and Osama bin Laden is a religious believer. Extremism can be just as terrifying in science as it is in religion, and indeed, it is only science which can give religious extremists the destructive capacity offered by a nuclear bomb or chemical weapons. Einstein is often quoted as saying that 'science without religion is lame, religion without science is blind.' This may be true, but in our own time one of the greatest threats to global security lies in the unholy alliance between religious extremists and unscrupulous scientists in the manufacture of weapons of mass destruction. Hand in hand, the two might help us to limp blindly towards our destruction.

Beyond the Enlightenment

With the benefit of hindsight, we can look back over the era of the Enlightenment and see that it cast long shadows in which new forms of abuse flourished, perpetrated by Western men of science against their sexual, racial and religious others. Claims to scientific objectivity mask the extent to which science, like all forms of knowledge, is shaped by its cultural contexts. Whatever the basis for our knowledge about the world – whether scientific, philosophical or religious – we are likely to regard as true that which our particular culture tells us is normal and natural, and to doubt anything which falls outside these parameters. Even apparently radical scientific discoveries are likely to be made to conform to existing social norms, as we saw with Darwin's theory of evolution and its implications in terms of gender, race and non-Western religions and cultures.

Science alone cannot lead us beyond our present crisis in knowledge. It has a significant role to play, but it is a means to an end, it is not an end in itself. We need to situate science in a wider context, making it the servant rather than the master of our dreams and aspirations. The era which began with the religious, scientific and political revolutions of the Enlightenment is drawing to a close. In an age of religious extremism and violent fundamentalisms, we should not be complacent about the destructive capacity of religion. However, in this twilight of reason, neither should we exaggerate the benefits of the Enlightenment in a way which blinds us to its negative aspects.

Democracy and liberalism are rooted in the values of the Enlightenment. They have become cherished ideals for many people in our world today, and they are under threat from the forces of political conservatism, religious extremism, and rampant globalisation with all its economic and social implications. But even as we seek to preserve these modern values, we also need to re-evaluate them and to tackle the injustices associated with them. We need to find new ways of understanding what we mean by freedom, equality and democracy, so that these do not simply open the floodgates to every kind of economic, environmental and political abuse.

We recognise now that the degradation and exploitation of nature in the name of science and progress may have brought us to the brink of an environmental catastrophe. We are also witnessing a new militancy among those who have been excluded and marginalised by modernity, having had access to few of the social or economic benefits which the more affluent nations have enjoyed. It is simplistic to portray this as a temporary setback in the project of scientific modernity, brought about primarily by religious extremism. The crisis is more profound than that, and it requires of us an honest evaluation of our historical legacy and an imaginative quest for a more creative way of being in the world.

The West has grown fat and corrupt on its myths of grandeur. From the time of the ancient Greeks through the conquests of Christendom, the adventures of imperialism and finally to the triumphant hubris of scientific rationalism, we Westerners have shaped the world according to our interests, our ambitions and our dreams. Sometimes these have been noble, sometimes they have been contemptible, most of the time they have been a complex mingling of the two. Today, we stand on the cusp of an era. Even as we fight the last bloody wars of our disintegrating empires, the shadow of a new and different empire looms on the horizon in the shape of China. But the battle for the future is not a battle between science and religion, Islam and the West, China and America. It is a battle between vast destructive systems which feed on sameness, uniformity and power, and the fragile diversity of the human species as we struggle to evolve, not according to some evolutionary myth of progress, but according to that innate desire within our species to make meaning, to imagine worlds, to create beauty, even in the midst of violence and destruction.

With this in mind, I turn now to the question of war and violence. If one single idea unites the new atheists – other than their shared rejection of the idea of God – it is the claim that religion and violence go hand in hand. In the next chapter, I want to consider this claim more closely, not only by examining the relationship between religion and war, but also by considering the role of modern science with regard to militarism and the arms trade. I suggested at the beginning of this chapter that knowledge and power have become inextricably linked in the Western imagination. Many of us have been appalled in recent years by the lengths to which our political leaders will go in their determination to shore up our global domination in the face of the growing threat from those who have been allowed no share in the benefits and privileges of scientific modernity. One of the more ingenious tactics of Western secularists has been to suggest that religion is the root cause of war and violence in the world, while justifying the violence of the Western nation state as a legitimate form of self-defence against the forces of terrorism and violence. Yet as we shall see in the next chapter, the new atheists are far less united in their attitudes to war than their united condemnation of religion suggests, and it is worth exploring their arguments and differences in more detail.

Chapter 4

SCIENCE, RELIGION AND WAR

As I write these words, and as you read them, people of faith are in their different ways planning your and my destruction, and the destruction of all the hard-won human attainments that I have touched upon. *Religion poisons everything.*

Christopher Hitchens[1]

Imagine, with John Lennon, a world with no religion. Imagine no suicide bombers, no 9/11, no 7/7, no Crusades, no witch-hunts, no Gunpowder Plot, no Indian partition, no Israeli/Palestinian wars, no Serb/Croat/Muslim massacres, no persecution of Jews as 'Christ-killers', no Northern Ireland 'troubles', no 'honour killings', no shiny-suited bouffant-haired televangelists fleecing gullible people of their money ('God wants you to give till it hurts'). Imagine no Taliban to blow up ancient statues, no public beheadings of blasphemers, no flogging of female skin for the crime of showing an inch of it.

Richard Dawkins[2]

Ideas which divide one group of human beings from another, only to unite them in slaughter, generally have their roots in religion. It seems that if our species ever eradicates itself through war, it will not be because it was written in the stars but because it was written in our books; it is what we do with words like 'God' and 'paradise' and 'sin' in the present that will determine our future.

Sam Harris[3]

The claim that religion is a major cause of violence is perhaps one of the most frequently repeated shibboleths of modern secular discourse. Get rid of religion, the argument goes, and you will significantly reduce the amount of war and violence in the world. However, this idea involves a highly selective historical memory and considerable distortion of the motives and ideologies of some of the most genocidal regimes in history – namely, the atheist and post-Christian regimes of the twentieth century's various forms of totalitarianism, communism and fascism.

Richard Dawkins wriggles and squirms around the question of twentieth-century atheism and violence. In the end, he comes to the ingenious conclusion that 'Individual atheists may do evil things but they don't do evil things in the name of atheism ... Religious wars really are fought in the name of religion, and they have been horribly frequent in history.'[4] A little later on, it becomes clear that Dawkins does not *really* think that even an individual atheist would do evil things, when he declares that 'I do not believe there is an atheist in the world who would bulldoze Mecca – or Chartres, York Minster or Notre Dame, the Shwe Dagon, the temples of Kyoto or, of course, the Buddhas of Bamiyan.'[5] Setting aside the awkward fact that, if it were not for religion, none of these buildings would have existed at all, it should be noted that the learned professor has a touching faith in the goodwill of his fellow atheists. Perhaps he should take a look at Robert Bevan's book, *The Destruction of Memory: Architecture at War*,[6] which uses the term 'cultural cleansing' to describe the destruction of people's architectural heritage as a deliberate strategy of war. In the twentieth century, Maoists destroyed temples and monasteries in China and Tibet, Stalinists destroyed many of Russia's Orthodox churches, Ceausescu destroyed churches and cathedrals in Romania, and Pol Pot ordered the destruction of Cambodia's Buddhist temples. The elimination of all traces of religious culture by atheists or anti-religionists was the driving force behind all these destructive acts. If we add to these the desecration and burning of synagogues by the Nazis, we have an awesome catalogue of acts of cultural cleansing committed against religious artefacts by anti-religious forces during the last century.

Religion and the causes of war

In 2004, the BBC commissioned the Department of Peace Studies at the University of Bradford to conduct a 'War Audit' for its programme entitled *What the World Thinks of God*.[7] The authors refer to 'the over-simplifications that have crept into media reporting about the prominence that war occupies in one religion or another.'[8] In seeking to offer a more informed perspective, they compiled two tables – one showing major wars in the 3500 years up to the end of the nineteenth century, and the second showing major wars of the twentieth century. In each case, they evaluated the significance of religious ideas and justifications in relation to the wars being fought, based on five criteria:

- religion as a mobiliser
- religious motivation and discourse by political leaders
- attacks on symbolic religious targets
- conversion goals
- strong support from religious leaders[9]

Wars which had a clear religious motivation included the Arab conquests (632–732), the Crusades (1097–1291), and the Reformation wars of the sixteenth and seventeenth centuries. However, they found that religion was not a motivating factor in any of the major wars of the twentieth century. With regard to the conflicts of the early twenty-first century, the audit sees the same trend – namely, that 'what many represent as religious wars have more convincing explanations as manifestations of policies, not religion, and that religion is more likely to be a cause of war when religion and the state authorities become closely allied or intertwined.'[10]

This report invites a more balanced and historically contextualised approach than that offered by militant atheists in their blanket condemnation of religion, particularly in the aftermath of a century which was the least religious and bloodiest century in world history. The death tolls of the twentieth century constitute an unimaginably dark legacy of an era in which, for the first time in history, large numbers of political regimes shrugged off their religious traditions and values, in order to experiment with a range of post-religious ideologies and political utopias.[11] Stalinism claimed somewhere between 9 and 60 million victims, Hitler's regime murdered as many as 15.5 million people, including 6 million Jews, and Maoism killed an estimated 30–40 million. To quote the authors of the War Audit, 'Atheistic totalitarian states … have perpetrated more mass murder than any state dominated by a religious faith.'[12] If we add to these the total death tolls of the First World War (15 million) and the Second World War (50–55 million), and we bear in mind that many of these deaths occurred in the heart of Europe in the aftermath of the nineteenth-century triumph of science and reason over religion and superstition, we should surely be sceptical of those scientific rationalists who continue to blame religion for most of the violence in the world.

Violence is a complex phenomenon whose origins lie deep within the human psyche, whatever names it borrows and whatever justifications it seeks. Our capacity for violence moves restlessly from cause to cause, justification to justification, attaching itself to whatever happens to be the dominant ideology or value system. If this is religious, then violence takes on a religious character. If it is racist or tribal, then violence takes on racist and tribal dimensions. If it is ideological atheism, then violence turns against religion. If we are to understand why violence happens, we also have to understand where and how it happens, and the conditions under which it flourishes. Contrary to the claims of the new atheists with their short historical memories, rationalism too has its murdered victims. Have they never heard of the Terror which followed the French Revolution? In 1793, the Goddess of Reason was enthroned in Notre Dame Cathedral in Paris, while her 'devotees' slaughtered tens of thousands during their year-long Reign of Terror, in an outpouring of anti-Christian fervour which particularly victimised Catholic priests.

Perhaps, though, the focus of this debate about religion and war needs to shift from asking if religion causes war, to asking why religion has done so little to prevent it. If we concentrate only on Christianity, at the very least we might ask why Christians have been so willing to commit themselves to war. After all, they claim to be followers of a man whose resistance to all forms of religious and political tyranny, violence and oppression led to him being crucified by a coalition of religious and political power-brokers, and whose earliest followers were dedicated pacifists. As John Ferguson writes:

> The historic association of the Christian faith with nations of commercial enterprise, imperialistic expansion and technological advancement has meant that Christian peoples, although their faith is one of the most pacifistic in its origins, have a record of military activity second to none.[13]

How did this religion, modelled on the self-sacrificing example of Jesus Christ, become the inspiration behind so many of history's conflicts and atrocities?

The Bible, war and violence

The controversial decision to include the Old Testament in the Christian scriptures meant that Christianity acquired a scriptural perspective on war which is almost lacking from the New Testament.[14] The early Christian thinker Marcion (c. 85–c. 160) argued that the God of the Old Testament was a violent and flawed deity who had no place in the story of love, grace and peace associated with Jesus Christ. However, the early Church accused Marcion of heresy, and decided that the Old Testament story of the Hebrew people was inseparable from the revelation of God in Christ. When the new atheists fulminate against the violence of the biblical God, it is usually this Old Testament view of the deity to which they are referring. There is a thread of violence running through many of the Old Testament writings, and this sometimes erupts with quite spectacular and shocking force.

The vast majority of biblical scholars – Jewish and Christian –

readily acknowledge the difficult nature of many of these texts, and this is not the place to offer an extended survey of their arguments. The problem is that militant atheists are fundamentalists when it comes to interpreting scripture. Sweeping aside the careful scholarship which should go into any reading of ancient texts, they throw out quotations from the Bible with a literalistic zeal worthy of any Christian fundamentalist. For example, Dawkins asks, 'Do those people who hold up the Bible as an inspiration to moral rectitude have the slightest notion of what is actually written in it?'[15] He goes on to cite a list of sins from Leviticus which would incur the death penalty, then refers to an account of a man being stoned to death in the Book of Numbers, before declaring:

> What makes my jaw drop is that people today should base their lives on such an appalling role model as Yahweh – and, even worse, that they should bossily try to force the same evil monster (whether fact or fiction) on the rest of us.[16]

I would hazard a guess that most Jews and Christians are far less literalistic than Dawkins in their understanding of how these scriptures are to be read and interpreted. Yes, there are people who take them literally, and yes, there are aspects of the biblical deity which are abhorrent to modern sensibilities. But we have to read these texts in the context in which they were written, if we are to discern in what ways they might be relevant for us today.

The Hebrew scriptures – a collection of books including different literary genres – offer us a glimpse into a world that is as remote from ours as it is possible to be. Here we have preserved some of the most ancient myths, histories, poems, prophecies, love songs and legal codes that human beings have produced. These are documents of inestimable historical and literary worth, but their value has been all but destroyed for a modern generation of readers, because they carry the burden of divine revelation which demands that they be read as more than literature. Even Hitchens and Dawkins acknowledge their literary worth, in terms of their influence on Western culture. For that reason alone, we should lament the widespread levels of scriptural and religious illiteracy which prevail in Western society. It is quite possible to read the Bible as a collection of historical and literary texts without having to adopt any faith perspective, and for those who refuse even to read it in that context, it is hard to see how they can acquire the interpretative resources needed to appreciate the West's artistic heritage and literary canon. One of my sons jokes that the Bible is a very good book, but it ought to have one of those disclaimers at the front: 'The characters featured in this book are completely fictional. Any resemblance to any person living or dead is purely coincidental. No similarity to any person either living or dead is intended or should be inferred.' For people repelled by the Bible's claim to 'truth', perhaps this would be a good starting place for revisiting the Bible as fiction, but fiction worth reading.

However, if one does approach the Bible as a source of potential revelation and inspiration, there are intelligent ways of negotiating a relationship with the text which avoid the literalisms of either religious or atheist fundamentalists. The shocking stories of destruction and violence and the repugnantly misogynistic tone of some of the Old Testament writings can be read against the grain, as warnings of what happens when divine justification becomes too closely associated with human institutions and relationships. Many of these texts invite such readings, since their account of divine action often calls into question human behaviour rather than simply endorsing all that is done in God's name.[17] There are also many Old Testament passages which offer enduring insights into the human condition. In the Psalms, the Book of Job, the Prophets and the Wisdom literature, there are many, many riches to be found as inspiration and wisdom for life. For those who seek the shimmer of transcendence and the whisper of revelation in the Old Testament, it is not hard to find, even if this calls for discernment and understanding in the task of interpretation.

Moreover, there is something a little arrogant about modern critics claiming to view the violence of ancient cultures from a more enlightened and informed perspective. Even if we set aside the recent violence that has been done in our name in Iraq and Afghanistan, and in the prison camps of Abu Ghraib and

Guantanamo Bay, our modern secular cultures have given rise to an entertainment industry which is glutted with gratuitous violence, to an extent that would have appalled many of our less 'civilised' forebears. The British censors have recently taken the almost unprecedented step of banning a video game called *Manhunt 2*. The director of the British Board of Film Censors described the game as involving 'sustained and cumulative casual sadism' which 'encourages visceral killing with exceptionally little alleviation or distancing'.[18] The human fascination with violence has survived the end of public religion in the Western democracies, and the line between fantasy and reality remains as blurred as it always has been. Human beings indulge in violent fantasies and sometimes we act them out. We may have banished religion in the name of democracy and freedom, but this has done very little to banish violence.

Turning to the New Testament, we encounter neither the militarism nor the poetry of the Old Testament – with the exception of the vivid apocalyptic rhetoric of the Book of Revelation. Again, most educated Christians are well aware of the contradictions, difficulties and cultural anachronisms found in the New Testament.[19] If one reads it as Dawkins and Hitchens do – with cavalier disregard for any questions of scholarship, interpretation and contextualisation – then of course there is ample ammunition for ridiculing Christians. But there is also a coherent social vision running through the Old and New Testaments, focused on a God who demands justice, who takes the side of the poor and the marginalised, and who calls for an understanding of love, commitment and responsibility that is radically different from that which informed other societies in the ancient world.

Any collection of texts must be read with a view to its overall coherence and vision. New atheists and Christian fundamentalists both distort the biblical story when they quote verses at random, without trying to situate them in a wider context. The ambiguity of the Bible is such that there will always be those who see its overall message as one orientated towards violence, social division and sexual oppression, while others will read its overarching narrative in terms of reconciliation, love and justice. But whichever side we incline towards, we should at least acknowledge its complexity and its potential plurality of interpretations, just as we would with any other great work of literature.

Christianity, war and pacifism

In claiming that the God of the Old Testament was most perfectly revealed in the suffering humanity of Christ, the earliest Christians rejected all forms of violence, and for the first three centuries, Christianity was largely pacifist in its teachings and practices.[20] The surviving literature suggests that soldiers who were baptised were expected to give up serving in the Roman army. Although Christians may not have been fed to the lions in quite the numbers that Christian folklore recalls, they were a persecuted minority who were victims rather than perpetrators of violence. While many decided to worship the Roman gods rather than face death in the arena, the early saints and martyrs defied the Roman empire by their willingness to face slow and savage death rather than bow down before the tyranny of the pagan deities. The great leitmotiv of these early Christian martyrs was freedom: Christ offered dignity and freedom to his followers, and one did not give up eternal freedom for the brief respite which came from willing obeisance to the gods of the cults, with their degrading and abusive practices.[21]

In later chapters I shall discuss in more detail the significance of Christianity in shaping our modern Western values, but perhaps most significant of all is this early privileging of the fundamental equality and freedom of all human beings, made in the image of God and redeemed in Christ. In reading the New Testament and the stories of the early Church, we are reading about the pioneers of many of our modern Western values in which the freedom, dignity and rights of the individual take precedence over the power and tyranny of the state. In the words of St Paul in the Letter to the Galatians, 'It is for freedom that Christ has set us free. Stand firm, then, and do not let yourselves be burdened again by a yoke of slavery' (Gal. 5:1). This spirit of freedom is the radical core at the heart of the Christian message, and it is a message which institutionalised Christianity has failed to eradicate, despite all its strenuous attempts to control and subjugate the human spirit. Wherever Christianity has travelled under the protection of empire and conquest, it has carried this hidden seed of freedom within it. That is why, from American slaves to African post-colonialists, Christianity has often proved to be a more robust and enduring faith in the lives of the oppressed and liberated than in the lives of their former oppressors.

The early Christians were willing to die rather than surrender their freedom of religion and speech. Under threat of torture, they refused to keep quiet. They had no power at all except the power of language and the power of their lives to witness to the truth of their beliefs. They adopted the language of war in a way which was intended to subvert violence through a war-like rhetoric of peace. They were part of a radical and courageous social experiment in pacifism which lasted for several centuries – and which continues to inspire Christian pacifists such as the Quakers and a growing number of individuals in all churches as modern warfare becomes ever more destructive and potentially annihilating.[22]

The shift from early pacifism to an acceptance of the occasional necessity of engaging in war was a gradual process, but it was Augustine (354–430) who, faced with the collapse of the Roman empire and the conflicts which followed, introduced the concept of the just war into the Christian tradition.[23] In setting out the criteria which might justify war, Augustine argued that, subject to rigorous terms of engagement designed to minimise the impact and lasting effects of violence, war was necessary in order to defend the innocent and preserve peace. However, for Augustine all war was evidence of the inherent sinfulness of the human condition, and those who engaged in it could not avoid its contaminating influences.

Writing under different historical and social conditions in which Christianity occupied a more secure position, Thomas Aquinas (c. 1225–74) lacked the more pessimistic aspects of

Augustine's thought. In his synthesis of Augustinian theology and Aristotelian philosophy, he introduced self-defence as a justification for war (Augustine had believed that Christians should not fight in self-defence but only in defence of an innocent third party). Aquinas's just war theory has had a continuing influence on Western philosophy and politics, and still today the rules which govern the justification for going to war (*just ad bellum*) and the legitimate conduct of war (*jus in bello*) are shaped by these Christian influences. The idea of the holy war which prevailed during the Crusades transformed the fighting of war from an undesirable but sometimes necessary duty, to a virtuous activity for Christians. However, outside the George W. Bush camp, few modern Christians would support the possibility of a holy war. While many Christians support the idea of a just war in certain extreme situations, many others see pacifism as the only conscientious Christian response to a world of proliferating violence and economic investment in the arms trade and weapons research. Although the Roman Catholic Church retains the just war theory, it has in practice shifted to a position of virtual pacifism since the 1960s, particularly under the papacy of John Paul II. For the first time since the conversion of Rome, Western nations now go to war without the sanction of their churches' leaders.

The new atheists and the Iraq war

Once again, then, the picture becomes significantly more complex when we move away from polemics and rhetoric, to consider the evidence more closely. If we concentrate only on the 2003 war in Iraq, then we are confronted with a situation in which many secular liberals in Britain and America supported the war while most Christian leaders and most of the international community opposed it. Far from encouraging religious believers to take a stand for peace, some secular commentators such as Hitchens poured derision on those who were opposed to the war. On 10 March 2003, Hitchens wrote mockingly that 'An awful realization has been dawning upon the Bush White House. Christianity is a religion of peace. From every pulpit, an appalling ecumenicism is preached, which calls for "more time" at best and for a "hands-off Saddam" line at worst.'[24]

Hitchens remains unrepentant over his support for American and British intervention in Iraq. At an event at the Garrick Theatre in London in June 2007 to publicise his book, *God Is Not Great* (rarely have I heard anyone so capable of combining erudition and ignorance, moral passion and misanthropy, with such confident aplomb), he repeatedly used the word 'evil' to describe religion, then finished the evening by telling his audience that we should be very thankful for America's 1/34th Brigade Combat Team fighting in Iraq. They might, he said, be 'snake-charming Pentecostalists', but they are patrolling the boundary between barbarism and civilisation in order that we can sleep securely in our beds at night.

In his continuing support for the war in Iraq, Hitchens is a member of a dwindling minority. Former neo-cons such as Francis Fukuyama who initially supported the war have broken ranks to heap condemnation on the Bush administration. British journalist Johann Hari, also a new atheist, remains convinced that it was right to go to war, although he is rather less gung-ho than Hitchens. In published correspondence between Hari and Dawkins, Dawkins spells out his own position.[25] Hari had written a column expressing his support for the invasion of Iraq, and had defied 'one person to dare to write to this newspaper and say with a straight face and a clear conscience that the Iraqi people would be better off now if we had left Saddam Hussein in power. Just one.' Never one to miss a challenge, Dawkins responded in typically understated style:

> Oh, do please tell Johann Hari to grow up … Of course nobody thinks Iraq would be better off with Saddam. That is not the point. The point is that the world thought it had left behind the bad old days when a strong country could unilaterally impose regime change on a weak country by invading it. We had painstakingly built up international law, and Bush (with contempt) and Blair (in agony) broke it.

> By Mr Hari's logic, we should all go and blow up McDonalds, and then challenge objectors to deny the resulting improvement in children's diet.

Clearly flattered that such an eminent reader had taken up his challenge, Hari offered an ingratiating response in which he declared himself 'extremely grateful for your role in the fight against superstition and the absurdities of religion.'

Polly Toynbee shares Dawkins' repugnance for what has been done in Iraq. Toynbee is a passionate campaigner for social justice, as well as being a militant atheist. At a time when the politics of the left have become something of a fringe movement, she has dedicated her career in journalism to speaking out on behalf of the most vulnerable and victimised members of society, providing a sustained critique of economic policies which create conditions of social exclusion.

In April 2007, two days after Seung-Hui Cho gunned down 27 of his fellow students and five faculty members at Virginia Tech, nearly 200 Iraqis died in a series of car bombs in Baghdad. Toynbee compared the excessive media coverage given to the shootings in America with these Iraqi deaths. She wrote:

> The pictures and the thoughts tell the same dismal story day after day, raising the same terrible questions: what have we done, what have we unleashed, how can it end? This is our war, our fault, our bloodshed for aiding America's reckless and incompetent invasion and for failing to stop civil war.[26]

Toynbee concludes her article with the suggestion that

> An age of over-individualism is demanding individual recognition for every painful death, me-me mourning regardless of its collective significance. Near-pornographic fascination with the gory details of a meaningless madman's murders in Virginia was just grisly. This week's deaths in Iraq are the ones we should all be contemplating with due solemnity, because they belong to us.[27]

What Toynbee fails to recognise is that the relentless assault by atheists like herself on religion in all its forms may contribute to this climate of indifference towards the deaths of Muslims. In another article, Toynbee describes the war against terrorism as 'a rationalist jihad'.[28] Just as in Islam, *jihad* can be a metaphor for a spiritual struggle or a call to arms, so we must be aware that Toynbee's 'rationalist jihad' may be intended metaphorically, but it is a dangerous metaphor when we are spilling so much Muslim blood in a very real war.

So far then, the new atheists represent a spectrum of attitudes towards war and violence which is similar to the kind of spectrum one might find among religious believers. American Christians may not include large numbers of 'snake-charming Pentecostalists', but they certainly include a large number of conservatives from all churches who have views very similar to those of Hitchens. Indeed, two American Catholic theologians, George Weigel and Michael Novak, have unsuccessfully lobbied the Vatican to change the just war rules to include pre-emptive strikes, so as to justify America's attack on Iraq. Other Christians – perhaps the majority – support the idea of a just war in theory, but do not accept that the war in Iraq meets the just war criteria. A significant minority – including some Catholic bishops – take a principled stand against any modern resort to war, arguing instead that there must in the modern world be an effective system of justice to allow for conflict resolution by way of international law rather than armed force. In responding to Weigel and Novak, Cardinal Ratzinger (now Pope Benedict XVI), argued that

> There were not sufficient reasons to unleash a war against Iraq. To say nothing of the fact that, given the new weapons that make possible destructions that go beyond the combatant groups, today we should be asking ourselves if it is still licit to admit the very existence of a 'just war'.[29]

Sam Harris, Islam and torture

Where are we then, in making any sense of the relationship

between war and religion? Just as the Bradford study pointed to the complexity of analysing reasons for war, so in looking at the Iraq war, there is simply no consistency among either religious believers or secularists as to whether it was right or wrong. On this issue, Dawkins is closer to the Catholic hierarchy than to some of his fellow atheists such as Hitchens and Harris, although there is not a whisper of this in his book. A sustained rant against religious violence includes not a squeak of protest against the no less significant threat of military violence perpetrated in the name of the modern democratic nation state and supported by some of his co-atheists. This is odd, since Hitchens and Harris really do represent an attitude as extreme as any to be found among the most militant Islamic or Christian religionists.

Harris stands out as someone who makes no attempt at all to mask his contempt, not only for radical Islamism but for Muslims in general, and who is willing to justify any violence, however extreme, to fight the threat which he thinks they represent. For Harris, Muslims represent a world-view which is opposed to modern ideas of progress and reason, and which leads them to unite against America. According to Harris,

> many Muslims [are] standing eye deep in the red barbarity of the fourteenth century … Any honest witness to current events will realize that there is no moral equivalence between the kind of force civilized democracies project in the world, warts and all, and the internecine violence that is perpetrated by Muslim militants, or indeed by Muslim governments.[30]

This negative evaluation of Islam leads Harris to conclude that the killing must continue, even if it means 'an even greater cost to ourselves and to innocents abroad, elsewhere in the Muslim world. We will continue to spill blood in what is, at bottom, a war of ideas.'[31] This blood-letting includes torture and the bombing of women and children, for 'Given what many of us believe about the exigencies of our war on terrorism, the practice of torture, in certain circumstances, would seem to be not only permissible but necessary.'[32] A little later in his book, he writes:

We cannot let our qualms over collateral damage paralyze us because our enemies know no such qualms. There is a kill-the-children-first approach to war, and we ignore the fundamental difference between their violence and our own at our peril. Given the proliferation of weaponry in our world, we no longer have the option of waging this war with swords. It seems certain that collateral damage, of various sorts, will be a part of our future for many years to come.[33]

Harris has great faith in the benign intentions of Western leaders, including George W. Bush: 'Whether or not you admire the man's politics – or the man – there is no reason to think that he would have sanctioned the injury or death of even a single innocent person.'[34] Like Dawkins' atheists, Harris's Americans are essentially benign individuals who are sadly sometimes compelled into violence by the religion of their enemies. Referring back to the My Lai massacre of 1968, he claims that Americans have now 'clearly outgrown our tolerance for the deliberate torture and murder of innocents. We would do well to realize that much of the world has not.'[35] This is interesting from a man who still condemns religion because of the violence of the Old Testament. While Americans can apparently outgrow violence in the space of a few decades, religious believers are held accountable for violence dating back some three millennia.

But let me recommend that anybody who supports Harris's defence of the fundamental trustworthiness of Americans over and against Islamist extremists should spend some time surfing the web. Google 'Guantanamo Bay' or 'Abu Ghraib'. If you have a strong stomach, Google 'Fallujah' and watch the online videos of that shattered city which was attacked by American forces in 2004 using napalm and white phosphorus. Google 'Abeer Qasim Hamza' and read about how this 14-year-old girl was raped and shot in the head by American soldiers, before her parents and her 6-year-old sister were also murdered. True, the soldiers in question were charged and the United States issued an apology, but we have no idea how many similar atrocities may have escaped public scrutiny. After the murder, a blogger drew attention to a video on the internet which showed a song written by an American soldier, being 'performed before thousands of U.S. troops in Iraq who could be heard wildly cheering and laughing in the background'. The song tells of how an Iraqi woman seduces an American Marine into her home where her insurgent family tries to murder him:

> They pulled out their AKs so I could see
>
> And they said ...
> *Durka Durka Mohammed Jihad*
> *Sherpa Sherpa Bak Allah*
> (with humorous emphasis:)
> So I grabbed her little sister, and pulled her in front of me.
>
> As the bullets began to fly
> The blood sprayed from between her eyes
> And then I laughed maniacally.
>
> Then I hid behind the TV
> And I locked and loaded my M-16
> And I blew those little f*ckers to eternity.[36]

One does not have to be anti-American nor does one have to be an Islamist extremist to regard America as a society unhealthily obsessed with war and violence, from its entertainment industry to its gun laws and its foreign policy. Many liberal Americans share that perception. Whatever restraint America has exercised in its fight against terrorism, this is more likely to be because of the vigilance of the international media than because of any self-restraint on the part of its present political leaders or the many confused and brutalised young people serving in the country's military. So, Mr Hitchens, you can be grateful if you choose, but do not preach gratitude to me when I come to hear you promote your book.

Given Dawkins' anti-imperialist stance on Iraq, one would

think that he would be at least mildly perturbed by the belligerence of his co-atheists, Hitchens and Harris. One might even expect from Hitchens an attempt to distance himself from some of Harris's more extreme positions. But no. In this back-patting world of militant atheism, what are a few small differences over war and torture between buddies? Dawkins repeatedly praises Harris for his insights: 'Sam Harris is magnificently scathing ...';[37] 'as so often, [he] hits the bullseye';[38] 'I cannot improve on Sam Harris's chilling comment ...';[39] 'Once again, Sam Harris put the point with percipient bluntness ...'[40] A similar lack of discernment can be found in Dawkins' review of Hitchens' book, *God is Not Great*. Addressing 'those critics who can't resist the ad hominem blow: "Don't you know Christopher Hitchens supported the invasion of Iraq?"', Dawkins retorts, 'I'm not reviewing his politics, I'm reviewing his book.'[40] Readers of *The God Delusion* might be surprised to discover that its author has acquired a sudden aversion to ad hominem arguments (that is, arguments which seek to score points by criticising the personalities involved in a debate rather than tackling the arguments themselves), since his book is riddled with them. It would be interesting to know what the learned professor actually thinks about the role which carpet-bombing and torture play in the struggle of militant atheism against Islam, with particular reference to Harris and Hitchens.

Violence and the human condition

This brief sketch of differing attitudes to war among the new atheists is intended to illustrate my argument that the projection of war and violence onto religion masks a more complex and dangerous scenario. To draw the fault-lines between religion and secularism is profoundly misleading and distorts the political, economic and military realities of the contemporary world. There is a review of Hitchens' book, *God is Not Great*, by Chris Hedges in *The New Statesman*, which is worth quoting from at some length:

The danger, which Hitchens fails to see, is not Islam or

Christianity or any other religion. It is the human heart – the capacity we all have for evil. All human institutions with a lust for power give to their utopian visions divine sanction, whether this comes through the worship of God, destiny, historical inevitability, the master race, a worker's paradise, *liberté-fraternité-égalité,* or the second coming of Jesus Christ. Religion is often a convenient vehicle for this blood lust. Religious institutions often sanctify genocide, but this says more about us, about the nature of human institutions and the darkest human yearnings, than it does about religion.

This is the greatest failing of Hitchens's book. He, like Harris, externalises evil. And when such writers externalise evil, all tools, including violence and torture, become legitimate in order to eradicate an evil outside of them. This world-view – one also adopted by the Christian right – is dangerous. It fails to acknowledge the impulses within us, both dark and seductive, that permit us to carry out evil, often in the name of good. [42]

The division today is not between believers and non-believers. Rather, it is between those who see violence as the solution to the world's problems, and those who recognise the urgent need for a more just and peaceful international order. While the new atheists preach division at their book launches and public debates, there is a growing coalition who recognise the need for us to overcome our religious and ideological differences in order to struggle together for justice for all the world's people. This will come about not through uncritical support for Western policies but through the transformation of global politics and the defence of human rights. The challenge to protect the vulnerable and limit the power of all who would use violence to achieve their ends applies equally to the legally sanctioned violence of the nation state and to the anarchic violence of the revolutionary and the militant. There is a saying that war is the terrorism of the rich and terrorism is the war of the poor. If we seek a world free of both forms of terrorism, then we must achieve it not through ever increasing expenditure on ever more deadly weapons, but through a robust and effective system of international law and through the elimination of the highly lucrative international arms trade. Along with the drugs multinationals, this is a major source of corporate investment in the world economy, and they both fuel a thriving illegal trade as well.

Scientific research and the profits of war

This brings me to another issue which is highly relevant to the campaign against religion waged by scientists such as Dawkins, and that is the relationship between science and war. There always have been and always will be madmen and fanatics willing to kill in the name of ideas, beliefs and tribal loyalties which override the demands of compassion, justice and reason. Situations such as the Rwandan genocide are savage reminders that human beings can slaughter one another in unthinkable numbers with the most primitive of weapons. Nevertheless, for the international escalation of war and violence we need military technology capable of extending the threat and effects of war beyond regional boundaries. Chemical, nuclear and biological warfare have been made possible by the dark genius of modern science, when it becomes focused not on the service of but on the destruction of humankind.

In 2005, an organisation known as Scientists for Global Responsibility published a report entitled *Soldiers in the Laboratory*, the purpose of which was 'to document the power and influence of the military in the governance and direction of science, engineering and technology in the UK.'[43] The report points to the sharp increase in global military expenditure since the start of the 'war on terror', so that in 2003 it amounted to US$956 billion. Over 40 per cent of this is attributable to the USA, while Britain is the world's third largest spender, and the world's second largest investor in military science, engineering and technology research (SET). Thirty per cent of Britain's total public research and development budget goes on military research – in 2003/4 this amounted to £2.6 billion of public money. The report also refers to the increasingly close collaboration between the military sector and British universities, in a number of new research initiatives which all, according to the report, 'reflect a narrow technological approach to security issues.'[44] In summarising its findings, the report argues that

> Our investigations show that SET programmes in conflict prevention, poverty alleviation, and environmental protection often yield clear benefits for relatively little cost, yet these areas get a fraction of the budget allocated to military technology. Disarmament and peacebuilding initiatives also tend to be smaller scale. Equally, R & D budgets for renewable energy technologies, essential to tackle the threat of climate change, are dwarfed by budgets for the development of weapons technology.[45]

It goes on to suggest that 'The military sector, especially in the UK and USA, has a very large and disproportionate effect on science, engineering and technology.'[46] Among their recommendations, the researchers urge the UK government to

> Devote more resources to implementing a far more inclusive concept of security within policy. Such a broadened concept would place social justice, peace and environmental sustainability at the centre of considerations of security. Such an approach would lead to the Ministry of Defence relying to a much lesser extent on the development and implementation of military technology and the use of force, and a much greater support where SET and other activities can contribute to peacebuilding and non-violent conflict resolution.[47]

In Dawkins' role as an Oxford Professor for the Public Understanding of Science, one would think that he would be at least as engaged with this kind of issue as he is with the conflict between scientific atheism and religious fundamentalism. But in becoming so obsessively and exclusively focused on religion, he has missed an opportunity to play a leading role in the vital debate about the role of science in modern life. This has not only created a monumental distraction from urgent ethical issues to do with the uses and abuses of science, it has also contributed to the sense of panic about religious violence which lends justification to the West's ever-increasing expenditure on weapons research, even though the kind of military hardware being developed is hardly likely to prevent murderous fanatics from flying aeroplanes into buildings. Many scientists today have committed themselves to working in the public interest and to making themselves ethically accountable for their research and the uses for which it is produced,[48] but Dawkins has created a smokescreen around these ethical issues with his anti-religious polemics. It is hardly surprising that a growing number of his fellow scientists seek to distance themselves from his ideas.

In these first four chapters, I have attempted to go beyond the black-and-white picture presented by the new atheists, in order to suggest a much more ethically complex relationship between science and religion with regard to questions of power, politics, gender and violence. In the next two chapters, I look at the role played by religion in the development of Western concepts of science, reason and progress. Again, I want to demonstrate that attempts to wrest modern Western values away from their religious moorings constitute a superficial and ahistorical understanding of the ways in which ideas and social institutions evolve organically. It is as foolish to suggest that Enlightenment values dropped into Western thought free from all their ancestral Christian influences, as it is to suggest that Adam and Eve showed up in the Garden of Eden free from all their ancestral stages of evolution.

Chapter 5

SCIENCE,THEOLOGY AND POLITICS

It is as true today as it was in the nineteenth century that the violent war of words between religious and scientific dogmatists masks a plurality of mutually respectful encounters between theologians and scientists. Since long before Dawkins fired the opening salvoes in the present conflict, theologians and scientists have been conversing with considerable intellectual rigour about the limits of science and the possibilities of God in the light of evolutionary theory and quantum physics. In this chapter I focus on Christianity rather than religion in general. If the political confrontation between the new atheism and religion is primarily concentrated on Islamist extremism, the intellectual confrontation is between Christian theology and science.[1]

The creative exchange between theology and science is as old as science itself, even if religious authorities and scientists have sometimes treated one another with mutual contempt. John Polkinghorne, a Christian theoretical physicist, argues that

> Religious thought and scientific thought have been interacting seriously with each other ever since the rise of modern physics provided the mature second partner to participate in the dialogue.[2]

Polkinghorne dates the most recent phase in the dialogue between science and theology to the publication of Ian Barbour's *Issues in Science and Religion* in 1966. Among the key issues he identifies in this dialogue, Polkinghorne refers to the historical relationship between science and religion, a rejection of scientific reductionism in favour of a more complex appreciation of our human make-up, and an acceptance of evolutionary biology and an evaluation of its significance for the doctrine of creation.

In the last few years, the nature of the dialogue between science and religion has been affected – or perhaps 'distorted' is a better word – by religious and scientific combatants in the form of creationists on one side and militant atheists on the other. Meanwhile, academic theologians have also entered the battle, seeking to develop a reasoned response to the challenge of scientific atheism. Oxford theologian Keith Ward has repeatedly locked horns with Dawkins, in *God, Chance & Necessity*,[3] and more recently in *Is Religion Dangerous?*[4] and *Pascal's Fire: Scientific Faith and Religious Understanding*.[5] Alister McGrath – as much a one-man publishing industry in theology as Dawkins is in popular science – has written *Dawkins' God: Genes, Memes and the Meaning of Life*,[6] and he also published *The Dawkins Delusion*[7] within a few weeks of *The God Delusion* appearing on the shelves. Catholic theologian Nicholas Lash has published a paper entitled 'The Dawkins Delusion',[8] and John Cornwell's book, *Darwin's Angel: A Seraphic Response to 'The God Delusion'*[9] is about to be published as I write this. My intention here is not to evaluate these various theological arguments, but to position them in a wider context.

Theology, quantum physics and evolution

There is widespread awareness among scientists as well as theologians that a quantum universe dissolves the boundaries by which modern science has sought to insulate itself from theological and philosophical questions, even if the challenge which quantum physics poses to the traditional Christian understanding of God is as significant as the challenge it poses to Newtonian physics. The cosmologist Paul Davies has been more radical than most theologians in exploring the implications of the new physics for belief in God. Davies points out that

The success of the scientific method at unlocking the secrets of nature is so dazzling it can blind us to the greatest scientific miracle of all: *science works*. Scientists themselves normally take it for granted that we live in a rational, ordered cosmos subject to precise laws that can be uncovered by human reasoning. Yet why this should be so remains a tantalizing mystery. Why should human beings have the ability to discover and understand the principles on which the universe runs?[10]

Davies argues that modern science increasingly points towards 'the ultimate superlaw'.[11] This suggests an intelligence not itself constrained by the laws of physics but necessary to explain how these vastly complex laws interact to sustain the physical universe. Davies writes, 'Physics can perhaps explain the content, origin and organization of the physical universe, but not the laws (or superlaw) of physics itself.'[12] Although Davies recognises the challenge that such ideas pose to traditional religious beliefs, he also argues that 'The existence of mind … as an abstract, holistic, organizational pattern, capable even of disembodiment, refutes the reductionist philosophy that we are all nothing but moving mounds of atoms.'[13]

With regard to the biological sciences, there is probably far greater acceptance among theologians than there is opposition to the theory of evolution.[14] In theology as in science, we should not let the polemics of a noisy minority deafen us to the quieter voices of reason and dialogue which represent the more widespread reality. In his 1996 address to the Pontifical Academy of Sciences, Pope John Paul II invoked the traditional Catholic belief that 'truth cannot contradict truth' to insist upon the importance of scientific research for theology.[15] The Pope referred to the support given by his predecessors to further research into the theory of evolution, and he pointed to the need to recognise a plurality of theories of evolution. His main concern was to reject any suggestion that the human mind was itself a product of evolution, and to assert the Christian belief in 'an ontological difference' between the human and the rest of creation. Defending the compatibility of this suggestion with the theory of evolution, he appealed for a recognition of the different tasks of science, philosophy and theology:

> The sciences of observation describe and measure the multiple manifestations of life with increasing precision and correlate them with the time line. The moment of transition into the spiritual cannot be the object of this kind of observation, which nevertheless can discover at the experimental level a series of very valuable signs indicating what is specific to the human being. But the experience of metaphysical knowledge, of self-awareness and self-reflection, of moral conscience, freedom, or again, of aesthetic and religious experience, falls within the competence of philosophical analysis and reflection while theology brings out its ultimate meaning according to the Creator's plans.

If scientists want to dismiss this argument as yet more evidence of religious dogma, they also have to dismiss Davies's argument which is based not on theological claims but on cosmology and the laws of physics. Both John Paul II and Davies suggest that it is at the level of consciousness or mind that questions of God become relevant in the light of modern theories of physics and evolution.

Polkinghorne, who has written widely on the relationship between science and religion, appeals for a balanced approach to questions of mind and matter against the reductive materialism of some scientific arguments. Along with many other scientists, he sees the existence of order in a quantum universe as evidence of a purposeful and meaningful cosmos. He writes:

> That unconscious atoms have combined to give rise to conscious beings is the most striking example known to us of the hierarchical fruitfulness of our being, in which there is a nesting and ascending order of being, corresponding to the transitions from physics to biology to psychology to anthropology and sociology.[16]

These observations reflect a shift in theological thinking from reflection on the actions of God in creation, to reflection on God as creating the possibilities in which evolution can happen, particularly the evolution of human consciousness, in a quantum universe which appears radically unpredictable and random in its behaviour at the sub-atomic level. The term 'the anthropic principle' is sometimes used to describe speculations such as these, which seek to understand how the universe can be so finely tuned as to allow intelligent life to emerge. However, the term is confusing because it is applied to a wide range of conflicting theories, from cosmological theories of multiple universes, to intelligent design theory.[17]

The point about these encounters between theology and science is not whether or not they succeed in converting people from atheism to belief. In the end, they may only succeed in demonstrating the impossibility of proving or disproving the existence of God according to the criteria of science. For atheist rationalists, the absence of empirical evidence and the theory of evolution are sufficient proof that God does not exist, accepting that one cannot ultimately prove a negative. For scientists with a religious faith, the evidence points in a different direction. Of course they may be wrong – just as atheists may be wrong – but at this point in our scientific understanding it is not irrational to believe in God. Even if it were, that does not necessarily disprove the existence of God. As Davies argues, 'It is a fact of life that people hold beliefs, especially in the field of religion, which might be regarded as irrational. That they are held irrationally doesn't mean they are wrong.'[18]

The Dawkins delusion

Dawkins mocks all attempts to reconcile science with theology. Referring to scientists of faith such as Francis Collins, Peacocke, Polkinghorne and others, he claims that 'The efforts of apologists to find genuinely distinguished modern scientists who are religious have an air of desperation, generating the unmistakably hollow sound of bottoms of barrels being scraped.'[19] He is particularly contemptuous of scientists (including Davies) who participate in research sponsored by the Templeton Foundation, which offers generous grants to academics who contribute towards an improved understanding of the relationship between scientific and spiritual values. Referring to prestigious scientists who have received Templeton funding, Dawkins accuses them of making a Faustian deal, before admitting that he too has participated in a Templeton-sponsored event at which the theologians he was debating with were apparently uniformly evasive, overly subjective, and self-deceiving.[20]

Yet Dawkins does not seem to recognise that, in his own attempts to explain quantum physics, he undermines many of the arguments elsewhere in *The God Delusion*. After a book which is committed to arguments about empirical evidence, proof, facts and the certainty of scientific knowledge, Dawkins ends with a chapter which offers a tantalising insight into how little we actually know or understand about the physical universe and the laws which govern it.

In an attempt to communicate to his readers the wonders of a quantum world, Dawkins uses the metaphor of the *burka* (to which I've already referred in Chapter 2) to explain how limited our understanding of the universe is, and how inadequate our consciousness is with regard to being able to experience the real nature of the cosmos. He doesn't seem to appreciate that this means that science itself has undermined the faith of scientific rationalists that the material world constitutes a 'given' to which our knowledge must conform. On the contrary, Dawkins suggests that our perceptions of the material world are a product of human consciousness – not vice versa – in a way which challenges not only scientific empiricism, but perhaps the whole idea of evolution as we currently understand it. If the human brain produces our perceptions of the world to make it possible for us to inhabit a universe which at least appears to be predictable and orderly, then the idea that we are nothing more than a highly evolved species which has adapted to its environment becomes difficult to justify. By Dawkins' own account, we are a species which adapts its environment to conform to its senses and to enable our survival, rather than having adapted ourselves to suit our environment. Dawkins writes that

> Science has taught us, against all evolved intuition, that apparently solid things like crystals and rocks are really composed almost entirely of empty space. The familiar illustration represents the nucleus of an atom as a fly in the middle of a sports stadium. The next atom is right outside the stadium. The hardest, solidest, densest rock, then, is 'really' almost entirely empty space, broken only by tiny particles so far apart that they shouldn't count. So why do rocks look and feel solid and hard and impenetrable?[21]

Now, pause for thought here. In a materialist world, science must be a product of 'evolved intuition'. So where does science discover a truth that is somehow beyond human consciousness, and that is indeed profoundly counter-intuitive? Dawkins responds to this question by appealing to the theory of evolution: 'Our brains have evolved to help our bodies find their way around the world on the scale at which those bodies operate.'[22] But our brains are part of our bodies. How then have they acquired an evolved capacity different from the capacity of the rest of our bodies, to such an extent that they are able to deceive our bodies about the nature of the world, in order to enable those bodies to survive? Dawkins goes on to argue that 'What we see of the real world is not the unvarnished real world but a *model* of the real world, regulated and adjusted by sense data – a model that is constructed so that it is useful for dealing with the real world.'[23] I admit I'm confused, because I thought the whole point of his argument was that our secure knowledge of the real world makes belief in God unreal and therefore irrational.

Immanuel Kant would have agreed with Dawkins that all we know of the world is that which our senses perceive and our minds interpret. However, even though Kant rejected the idea of an interventionist or personal God, he still believed that a divine creator was a necessary hypothesis to lend coherence to this idea. In eliminating the idea of God, I am not convinced that Dawkins can offer a coherent explanation as to why we should have evolved as rational entities with an illusory sense of being solid objects in a world of solid objects, when in fact we are part of a much more ephemeral and insubstantial universe.

Referring to Steve Grand's book, *Creation: Life and How to Make It*, Dawkins writes, 'Steve Grand points out that you and I are more like waves than permanent "things".' He goes on to quote a passage where Grand invites his reader to recall an experience from childhood, before declaring that

> here is the bombshell: you *weren't* there. Not a single atom that is in your body today was there when that event took place ... Matter flows from place to place and momentarily comes together to be you. Whatever you are, therefore, you are not the stuff of which you are made. If that doesn't make the hair stand up on the back of your neck, read it again until it does, because it is important.[24]

Far from challenging a theological understanding of human existence, this vision of a continuity of memory and experience which transcends the body's flux and impermanence might legitimately look to theology for an explanation. Similarly, if Christians turn to natural law for a deeper understanding of the claims of faith, then quantum physics brings an awesome new perspective to their theological vision. The universe described by Dawkins – a universe in which '"Really" isn't a word we should use with simple confidence'[25] – is a universe more like than unlike that envisaged by a certain theological vision of the world. At the very least, the quantum world described by Dawkins cannot rationally be divided into natural and supernatural, body and spirit, experience and imagination, faith and science, for these are far less separate than Newtonian physics has led us to believe.

Intelligent design theory

Despite the protests of scientists such as Dawkins, most academic debates about the relationship between theology and science respect the autonomy of science, just as scientists such as Davies take seriously the questions raised by theology, even if they are not themselves religious. However, a different kind of engagement is happening in America. There, the encounter between science and Christianity is driven not by theology but by intelligent design theory, and here there is indeed a hidden agenda operating. Intelligent design theory (sometimes referred to as ID) is a recent attempt by American Christians to combat the teaching of evolution in schools by introducing a different, ostensibly non-religious, theory of life.[26] In order to understand its arguments, we have to situate it in the context of the various forms of natural law theory which have influenced the Christian understanding of creation.

The idea that the universe points to a creator God or a divine intelligence can be traced back to Greek philosophy, and its best-known advocate in the Christian tradition is Thomas Aquinas. As I mentioned in an earlier chapter, Catholic theology still adheres to a natural law tradition, which teaches that the human mind is created with the gift of reason so that we are able to interpret something of the will of God from our study of nature. Christians have sometimes interpreted this in terms of the two books of revelation – the book of nature and the book of scripture.

In its early modern versions, the idea of intelligent design is associated with the watchmaker analogy which was used by several philosophers in the eighteenth and nineteenth centuries, although its best-known proponent is William Paley (1743–1805). Paley argued that, just as the mechanism of a watch points to a purposeful design rather than a random or arbitrary occurrence, so the universe points to a designer and could not have come about by accident. He used the eye as a particular example of a complex organism which he believed was evidence of design rather than a random process of evolution. In keeping with other natural theologians, Paley believed that it was possible to know something about 'the mind of God' by studying natural organisms and the laws of nature. Darwin was impressed by Paley's *Natural Theology* when he read it at university, but he later believed that his own theory of natural selection provided a conclusive account of how complex life forms evolve without any need for an original creator or designer. Nevertheless, James Moore suggests that Darwin's theory of evolution still owes much to Paley's theology.[27]

The idea of intelligent design is therefore not new, although in its present form some would argue that it is a propaganda exercise aimed at getting the teaching of Christian beliefs about creation into the education system in America and, to a lesser extent, Britain. The theory became popular after an American Supreme Court ruling in 1987 declared the teaching of creationism in public schools unconstitutional because it promoted one particular religion.[28] However, the Supreme Court also allowed for the teaching of a variety of scientific theories, and this provided the impetus for the development of intelligent design theory. It was after this that a range of books began to appear on the theme of intelligent design, beginning in 1989 with *Of Pandas and People: The Central Question of Biological Origins* by Percival Davis and Dean H. Kenyon.[29] Most intelligent design theorists are associated with the Center for Science and Culture at the Discovery Institute in Seattle, a politically conservative think-tank dedicated to projects in technology, science and culture, national defence, foreign affairs, and religion in public life.[30] The best-known proponents of the theory are the biochemist Michael Behe and the mathematician William Dembski.

Although intelligent design theorists are Christians, they are not creationists in the sense of believing in a literal interpretation of Genesis, and they acknowledge that evolution may play a role in the development of species. Supporters of intelligent design argue that, because it is a scientific theory rather than a religious belief, it ought to be taught in schools alongside evolution. Dembski appeals to Aquinas to justify the claim that belief in a creative intelligence does not imply belief in the God of Christianity:

Intelligent design may for the time being be operated mainly by Christians. But it is not owned by Christians. It is not even owned by theists. Thomas Aquinas, writing in the *Summa Contra Gentiles*, remarked, 'For seeing that natural things run their course according to a fixed order, and since there cannot be order without a cause of order, men, for the most part, perceive that there is one who orders the things that we see. But who or of what kind this cause of order may be, or whether there be but one, cannot be gathered from this general consideration.' … [F]or Thomas the 'cause of order' that we infer strictly from reflection on the natural order does not even issue in a generic monotheism.[31]

Intelligent design theorists argue that the existence of complex organisms such as bacterial flagella and biochemical phenomena such as blood clotting and the immune system offer evidence of a design in creation which cannot be explained by evolution. The mechanism of some living organisms is so complex and finely tuned that it suggests a teleological intention – that is, the organism exists for a purpose that could not be internal to the evolutionary process itself, which is neither purposeful nor intelligent. The bacterial flagellum has been described by Harvard biologist Howard Berg as 'the most efficient machine in the universe',[32] a quotation which has been seized upon by anti-evolutionists. With a finely tuned tail rotating at phenomenally high speeds and capable of subtle changes of direction, the purpose of this microscopic organism is to act as a cellular motor. In the opinion of intelligent design theorists, organisms such as these challenge the atheistic materialism of the theory of evolution by natural selection.

One argument put forward by Behe in his book *Darwin's Black Box* is that of irreducible complexity with regard to such organisms.[33] These are complex mechanisms in which form and function are so perfectly united that the one is entirely dependent upon the other. He likens this to the mechanism of a mousetrap, in which every component is essential to its function. Dembski develops Behe's argument with his idea of 'specified complexity', in which something has both a complex structure and a specified meaning. A complex structure, such as a string of letters, might be meaningless, and a specific item might have meaning but lack complexity, but when a structure's complexity coincides with its significance or meaning, then there is a strong mathematical improbability of this being a random occurrence. Dembski uses the example of poetry, arguing that 'A single letter of the alphabet is specified without being complex. A long sentence of random letters is complex without being specified. A Shakespearean sonnet is both complex and specified.'[34] He argues that the improbability of specified complex patterns emerging by chance indicates an intelligent designer.

Dawkins offers a range of arguments against intelligent design and the appeal to irreducible complexity. In *The Blind Watchmaker* – a title which invokes Paley's watchmaker analogy – he argues that evolution can account for the development of complex organisms through a process of natural selection. He points to apparent flaws and mistakes in the evolutionary process, which suggest a random and purposeless series of adaptations rather than an intelligent designer. Over vast periods of time and through subtle genetic adaptations, the theory of natural selection can account for the development of even the most complex and finely tuned organisms. Moreover, Dawkins argues that the appeal to complexity as evidence of design is self-defeating, because a designer would have to be even more complex, which raises the question of who designed God.

Some would claim that this is a nonsensical question from a theological perspective – Lash describes it as seeming to talk 'about the Wizard of Oz, not the creator of this world and all the worlds there are.'[35] As Lash points out, Dawkins

> has failed to notice that simplicity, like most interesting words, has a wide variety of uses and that when we say that God is simple, we are speaking, as it were, of a simplicity on the *other* side, not on *this* side, of complexity; a simplicity more like wisdom than like simple-mindedness.[36]

One might by analogy think of comparing Bach's music with Bach the man. It would be absurd to say that Bach must have been even more complex than his most complex symphony, for we are not comparing like with like. The relationship between the creative process in the mind of the creator and the creation which results from that process is not susceptible to the kind of comparison which Dawkins seeks to make. This is not to lend support to intelligent design theory, but to point out that some of Dawkins's arguments work better than others.

His refutation of what he calls 'the Ultimate Boeing 747 gambit' is more persuasive. This is a reference to an argument attributed to the British astronomer Fred Hoyle (1915–2001), which claims that 'the probability of life originating on Earth is no greater than the chance that a hurricane, sweeping through a scrapyard, would have the luck to assemble a Boeing 747.'[37] Dawkins points to the inadequacy of this comparison because the theory of evolution by natural selection envisages the emergence of complexity through a very long process of trial and error and of incremental changes. Dawkins refers to Daniel Dennett's metaphor of the 'skyhook' which he uses to criticise creationism and intelligent design theory. Dennett contrasts the skyhook with the crane – the one suggests a concept of complex designs delivered from above, the other suggests a concept of equal complexity built up gradually from below.[38] From this perspective, one can accept that even an apparently perfectly 'designed' organism, such as the bacterial flagellum, only acquired its function at a particular point in its development, which in turn could have a knock-on effect on the evolution of other genetic adaptations and cellular functions.

Intelligent design theory has been widely criticised by other scientists and by theologians.[39] However, the dogmatic certainty of evolutionists such as Dawkins and Dennett also raises questions, particularly when evolution is offered not only as a biological explanation for the development of life forms, but as a totalising theory of the meaning of life which allows for no dissent and no alternative. Although the evidence is persuasive, the theory of evolution remains a hypothesis which cannot be definitively proven or demonstrated in all its aspects. When it extends beyond biology to include theories such as Dawkins' idea of memes as the replicators by which cultural trends and values are spread, it becomes every bit as speculative and unscientific as creationism.

Competing ideologies

The main objection to intelligent design theory may be not so much its lack of scientific evidence as its political influence. Critics draw attention to a manifesto issued by the Discovery Institute's Center for the Renewal of Science and Culture under the title *The Wedge Strategy*.[40] As I mentioned above, most intelligent design theorists work under the auspices of the Discovery Institute. In the 'wedge document', as it is often referred to, the Institute makes clear that its overall aim is to defeat materialism in all its forms by a sustained assault across a range of intellectual, political and social frontiers. The document begins by affirming that 'The proposition that human beings are created in the image of God is one of the bedrock principles on which Western civilization was built.' It goes on to attack the legacy of modern science, particularly of Darwin, Marx and Freud, for introducing a 'materialistic conception of reality [which] eventually infected virtually every area of our culture' and 'spawned a virulent strain of utopianism'. It sets out its manifesto as follows:

> Discovery Institute's Center for the Renewal of Science and Culture seeks nothing less than the overthrow of materialism and its cultural legacies. Bringing together leading scholars from the natural sciences and those from the humanities and social sciences, the Center explores how new developments in biology, physics and cognitive science raise serious doubts about scientific materialism and have re-opened the case for a broadly theistic understanding of nature.

This is a manifesto which might disconcert any liberal-thinking person, religious or not. It is the work not of a small enclave of religious extremists but of a highly influential think-tank which has the sympathies of the most powerful government on earth. It is hardly surprising that American atheists such as Dennett and Harris have been driven into the opposite corner by such an attack on intellectual freedom, and it is also right that we in Britain should be aware of the threat posed by this closing down of intellectual frontiers.

But cultures caught up in this war of ideas must also recognise that this debate is becoming polarised between two equally dangerous ideologies. On the sides of both intelligent design theory and militant atheism, science has been co-opted in a battle for hearts and minds which impinges on every aspect of our culture and extends far beyond the frontiers of scientific enquiry.

Like all ideologies, militant atheism has a tendency to stifle reasoned debate in its proselytising zeal. With Dawkins as its commander-in-chief, this movement is no less committed to the total transformation of educational, social and political structures than intelligent design theorists are, and its treatment of religion is overly simplistic and often unreasonable. Just as Christians are often the last to manifest the core Christian value of love in their dealings with others, so rationalists are often the last to manifest their core value of rationality in their treatment of religions and theology.

Dennett claims that 'It is commonly supposed that it is entirely exemplary to adopt the moral teachings of one's own religion *without question*, because – to put it simply – it is the word of God (as interpreted, always by the specialists to whom one has delegated authority)'.[41] In a similar vein, Dawkins repeatedly claims that faith is a form of ignorance which is promoted by religions, because 'Faith (belief without evidence) is a virtue. The more your beliefs defy the evidence, the more virtuous you are'.[42]

But these claims deny the fact that the relationship between faith and reason has been the motor which has driven much of the intellectual development of Western society. The kind of irrationality condemned by Dawkins and Dennett is a relatively modern phenomenon associated with religious fundamentalisms, and it flies in the face of the mainstream theological and philosophical traditions which have shaped Western society and politics for some two millennia and more. The Roman Catholic authorities might repeatedly disgrace themselves in their handling of dissent, and we do not here need to repeat the story of Galileo as evidence of their failure to rise to the challenge of science. Nevertheless, at the core of the Catholic tradition is the belief that truth cannot contradict science, because the truth of God is revealed through the intelligibility of the laws of nature to human understanding. Ultimately, from the belief that the earth revolves around the sun to the belief that the theory of evolution explains the emergence of complex life forms, Catholicism has accepted the judgements of science. While some forms of Protestant evangelicalism are resistant to the claims of science and reason, there is also a widespread conversation in liberal Protestantism between philosophical and theological arguments, with an ongoing negotiation between the traditional claims of theology and the new challenges posed by the physical and social sciences.

Hitchens quotes Sigmund Freud on the last page of his book: 'The voice of Reason is soft. But it is very persistent.'[43] This is an unintentionally ironic note on which to end such a bombastic and ill-informed rant against religion, but it is vitally important that we attend to the soft voice of reason amidst this din of conflicting ideologies. If we attune our ears to the arguments and beliefs of Christian theology, we shall find that the voice of reason is as persistent there as it is elsewhere in the philosophical discourses of Western thought, for the Christian understanding of God and humankind bears the imprint of the Greek philosophical tradition. For better or worse, Christianity and scientific modernity form an inseparable world-view. If we try to sever the two in the interests of either religious or scientific fundamentalism, we risk unleashing a greater violence than any we have witnessed so far. Reason alone does not express the fullness of our humanity, but it is the condition upon which all our other social and artistic endeavours rest. I turn now to consider more closely the ways in which reason has shaped the Western religious tradition and its secular inheritance.

Chapter 6

HISTORY, FAITH AND REASON

There is a widespread belief that the Enlightenment represented the triumph of reason over faith and set Western societies on the road to progress by liberating scientific rationalism from religious ignorance. The new atheists represent the culmination of this point of view, in their battle against religion in the name of reason. For example, AC Grayling, a British professor of philosophy and an ardent new atheist, writes that 'Most of what was achieved in the history of the West from the 16th century onwards ... was wrested from the bitter reactionary grip of religion inch by painful and frequently bloody inch.'[1]

This creates the impression that we Westerners owe our cherished freedoms and values to a fragile secular ethos which must be constantly defended against the dangerous power of religion. Such ideas need to be challenged, for they represent a superficial and distorted understanding of the history of ideas in the West. In this chapter, I reflect on the suggestion made by some scholars that our modern democratic societies cannot be understood without some awareness of their Christian roots.

The role of reason in Western religion

Christianity, like many religions, has syncretistic elements insofar as it emerged through the encounter of two quite different worlds of thought – namely, the scriptures of the Hebrew people, and the ideas of Greek philosophy.[2] From the beginning, the Christian understanding of God was informed both by the God of revelation and history discovered in the Hebrew scriptures and the life of Christ, and by the God of rationality and order found in the writings of the Greek philosophers. Within the different denominations and groupings of the Christian tradition, these two influences have often wrestled with one another. The Catholic tradition has always affirmed the importance of reason in its theological and doctrinal debates, so that some might argue that it has too often favoured the God of the philosophers over the God revealed in the Bible and in the person of Jesus Christ. On the other hand, the Protestant tradition has tended to privilege biblical revelation over philosophical reasoning, which can lead to fundamentalisms and to a failure to challenge irrational beliefs.

The patristic era (that is, the first six centuries or so of the Christian faith) represented the first great flowering of philosophical reflection in Western religious thought. The Dark Ages probably never were as dark as popular history records, but in the social and political turmoil which followed the fall of Rome and the subsequent disintegration of Western order, Christian thinkers no longer engaged with the texts of ancient philosophers. It was Muslim scholars who preserved these texts, translating them into Arabic and keeping them in the libraries of their universities in Baghdad, Cairo, Toledo and Cordoba, at a time when Arab civilisation spread a swathe of learning and prosperity across North Africa, Persia and the southern reaches of Europe. Western Europeans regained access to the philosophical and scientific knowledge of ancient Greece through these Arabic sources. They translated Greek philosophical texts from Arabic into Latin with the help of Muslim scholars, so that a rich philosophical dialogue flourished among the three faiths, associated with thinkers such as the Muslims Avicenna (980–1037) and Averroes (1126–98), the Jewish Maimonides (1138–1204), and the Christian Thomas Aquinas (1225–74). It was Aquinas who most fully integrated Aristotelian philosophy into Christian thought, and his influence has shaped Catholic theology ever since.

Richard E. Rubenstein, in his book *Aristotle's Children*, argues that today we might learn from these medieval philosophical encounters. He suggests that the Aristotelian perspective which they shared offers a more integrated and humane approach to questions of truth than the modern division between 'the provable, apparently objective truths of science and the intuitive, subjective truths of religion and personal philosophy'.[3] Referring to the medieval West's rediscovery of Aristotle, Rubenstein writes that 'the reappearance of Aristotelian ideas in Europe had a transformative effect totally unlike that of any later discovery.'[4] He continues:

> more than four centuries before Francis Bacon and René Descartes proclaimed the Scientific Revolution, a recognizably modern perspective – rationalist, this-worldly, humanistic, and empirical – ignited cultural warfare throughout Western Europe, challenging traditional religious and social beliefs at their core. The struggle between faith and reason did not begin, as is so often supposed, with Copernicus's challenge to earth-centered cosmology or Galileo's trial by the Inquisition but with the controversy over Aristotle's ideas during the twelfth and thirteenth centuries.[5]

Rubenstein asks why the significance of this intellectual revolution is not more widely acknowledged. He suggests that it is because it challenges deeply held convictions about the inherent superiority of Western culture and Christian civilisation over all others. When Europeans were feuding lords and illiterate peasants, the Islamic world was a flourishing empire of culture, prosperity and scholarship on the fringes of Western life.

As Rubenstein argues, revisiting these ancient and medieval philosophies might enable us today to recover a more holistic approach to questions of wisdom and reason. They invite us to go beyond the idea that there is an irreconcilable conflict between faith and reason, and between Islam and the West, pointing the way towards a new maturing of faith through reason, and a new appreciation of the role played by reason in the formation of faith. Without this maturing process, Rubenstein suggests that powerful elites on both sides will fuel the idea of a conflict between faith and reason in order to extend their power.

In a different vein, Rodney Stark has also written on the long association between Christianity and Western ideas in the formation of modern values of equality, democracy and freedom. Stark argues that Christianity was the catalyst for the West's unique story of progress, capitalism and democracy, and that for many centuries it provided a sustaining intellectual and ethical framework within which these could develop.[6]

Thinkers such as these are witness to a long tradition of philosophical debate and scientific enquiry in Western religion. They demonstrate that Christianity and, to a lesser extent, Judaism and Islam, constitute an integral aspect of the historical development of modern Western life and values. While Jewish and Christian thinkers have continued to play a significant role in the philosophical, scientific and political debates of modernity, Islam has experienced a decline in its traditions of learning and philosophy. However, the rise of Islamic fundamentalism since the 1970s has prompted a renewal of intellectual activity among Muslim thinkers in their engagement with Western ideas. Some Muslim scholars such as Tariq Ramadan have called for a reformation in Islam similar to that which transformed Christianity in the sixteenth century.[7] Far from stifling religious thought, the combined challenges of secularism and fundamentalism may well be the catalyst for a new flourishing of philosophical and theological debate among the world's religions.

Celestial teapots and other nonsense

None of this is likely to convince those whose atheism is entrenched in contempt for these historical and philosophical arguments about the positive influence of religion. The rubbishing of all religion as uniformly ignorant, irrational and violent closes off any opportunity for a more intelligent conversation based on the strengths as well as the weaknesses of religious intellectual traditions. Both Richard Dawkins and Sam Harris dismiss such attempts at engagement as doing more harm than good. Dawkins asserts that 'even mild and moderate religion helps to provide the climate of faith in which extremism naturally flourishes.'[8] Harris claims that

> religious moderates are themselves the bearers of a terrible dogma: they imagine that the path to peace will be paved once each of us has learned to respect the unjustified beliefs of others … [T]he very ideal of religious tolerance – born of the notion that every human being should be free to believe whatever he wants about God – is one of the principal forces driving us toward the abyss.[9]

The history of Western theology and philosophy shows a quite different trend to Harris's highly individualistic description of tolerance. The validity of beliefs about God and the need to evaluate these rationally in terms of their doctrinal and/or philosophical coherence have been central to the Western intellectual enterprise from the time of the ancient Greeks, and they have been the cause of rich theological and philosophical debates as well as bitter and bloody conflicts. However, the unwillingness of militant atheists to explore these ideas results in an impoverished slanging match, in which witticism, insult and anecdote take the place of reasoned and informed debate.

Take, for example, Christopher Hitchens' description of St Augustine as 'a self-centered fantasist and an earth-centered ignoramus'.[10] I am tempted to say it takes one to know one, but I would not flatter Hitchens by comparing him to Augustine. Having read some of the less than enthusiastic reviews of his book, I only wonder what might be said of him if by some remote chance he is still being read and talked about 1600 years from now.

St Augustine (354–430) is arguably one of the most complex and interesting characters of the early Church, and his legacy to Western culture has been profound. His *Confessions* remains one of the greatest autobiographical works in the Western canon, and his *City of God* is a reflection on politics, religion and ethics which still informs political theory as well as theology today. His collections of sermons and other writings constitute an invaluable resource for those who are interested in the understanding of Christian doctrine and identity at a time when the established order of the Roman empire was disintegrating.

It is also true that Augustine's libidinal struggles cast a long shadow over the Christian understanding of sex. Like many religious converts, he was somewhat over-enthusiastic in embracing the moral precepts of his new religion, turning his back on the promiscuity of his youth and the beloved mistress of his more mature years, in favour of a life of sexual renunciation. When I notice my students flagging in lectures on sexual ethics, I sometimes tell them that Augustine's linking of original sin with sex was primarily because he was worried that his penis had a life of its own which refused to be controlled by his rational mind. That certainly gets their attention, although the strategy can backfire. One year I had to send a batch of essays to an external examiner who was a rather genteel and elderly academic at Oxford University. The only significant fact which some of the students had remembered was that 'the doctrine of original sin came about because Augustine could not control his erections.' The essays came back with the comment that there was rather a lot of sex and not much about other aspects of marriage in this course.

A common resource for atheists wanting to deride religious faith is Bertrand Russell's comparison between belief in God and belief in orbiting teapots. Dawkins quotes Russell to pour scorn on those who argue that the lack of evidence against God's existence makes it reasonable to continue to believe in God. According to Russell,

> If I were to suggest that between the Earth and Mars there is a china teapot revolving about the sun in an elliptical orbit, nobody would be able to disprove my assertion provided I were careful to add that the teapot is too small to be revealed even by our most powerful telescopes. But if I were to go on to say that, since my assertion cannot be disproved, it is intolerable presumption on the part of human reason to doubt it, I should rightly be thought to be talking nonsense. If, however, the existence of such a teapot were affirmed in ancient

books, taught as the sacred truth every Sunday, and instilled into the minds of children at school, hesitation to believe in its existence would become a mark of eccentricity and entitle the doubter to the attentions of the psychiatrist in an enlightened age or of the Inquisitor in an earlier time.[11]

Dawkins devotes rather more space to rubbishing theology by appealing to this kind of analogy than he does to entering into any serious philosophical engagement with theological ideas. For example, in a chapter titled 'Arguments for God's Existence' which begins with a quotation from Thomas Jefferson – 'A professorship of theology should have no place in our institution' – he dismisses Aquinas's five proofs for the existence of God in a mere three pages. Yet his book is riddled with page after page of anecdotal evidence about teapots, tooth fairies, Mother Goose, 'two enormous green lobsters called Esmerelda and Keith',[12] and 'the Flying Spaghetti Monster', in order to inform his readers that

> I have found it an amusing strategy, when asked whether I am an atheist, to point out that the questioner is also an atheist when considering Zeus, Apollo, Amon Ra, Mithras, Baal, Thor, Wotan, the Golden Calf and the Flying Spaghetti Monster. I just go one god further.[13]

One of the blessings of a liberal society is that we are all free to believe more or less what we want to believe (so long as we remain religiously 'moderate'). People may indeed opt to worship a Flying Spaghetti Monster or Baal or a Golden Calf or a two-dimensional cardboard cut-out Jesus drawn from a literal interpretation of the Bible, or a megalomaniac and warring God who incites his followers to butcher their opponents without mercy, whether by way of ancient rape and pillage or by way of modern military technology. Others may decide to throw their lot in with the new atheists – although that will not preclude them being willing to wage war on Muslims, to bomb innocent civilians and to torture suspected terrorists, if they are followers of Hitchens' or Harris's brand of atheism. Either way, to opt for either god-fearing fanaticism or atheist fundamentalism is to opt for philosophical and historical illiteracy, moral bigotry and blind dogmatism. This is quite different from entering into the challenging intellectual struggle for truth in the open-ended tradition of scholarship and debate which constitutes the philosophical and theological heritage of the world's religious traditions, including those three which have most profoundly made us what we are today in the West – Judaism, Christianity and Islam.

As I have argued earlier, the existence of God cannot be proven or disproven, but this does not mean that belief in God is akin to belief in celestial teapots or tooth fairies. There are indeed some odd religions out there – Dawkins cites the Polynesian cargo cults, and there are many others. But there are also some odd scientific theories, and science too has its lunatic fringe, its blind zealots and its ignorant devotees. I cannot see what there is to be gained by citing endless examples of these as an argument against either religion or science, and that is partly what makes it so difficult to respond to Dawkins' and Hitchens' books. They show no serious interest in engaging with the arguments of their opponents, and they have very little aptitude for philosophical or theological argument and analysis. Terry Eagleton suggests that Dawkins writing on theology is akin to 'someone holding forth on biology whose only knowledge of the subject is the *Book of British Birds*.'[14]

Heavenly hopes and utopian nightmares

Christianity is a diverse tradition woven out of many different strands, not all of which are compatible with one another. Whatever my disagreements with the new atheists, I probably have considerably more in common with Dawkins and Polly Toynbee than with George W. Bush and his Christian supporters, and many of my Christian friends would say the same. That is why the task of thinking through the relationship between Christianity and modern Western values is so complex.

If one reads authors such as Rubenstein and Stark, then the rational strand of Christianity has something vital to offer to modern society in its resistance to both religious and scientific fundamentalisms. The furious attempt by the new atheists to deny any positive significance to the role of religion in modern culture is an act of intellectual denial which is also socially dangerous. It pushes us towards a rationalism stripped of humanity, intuition and hope on the one hand, and towards a religiosity stripped of rationality, common sense and pragmatism on the other. Nothing fuels religious fanaticism more effectively than persecution. In their militant campaign against religion, the new atheists are playing into the hands of those extremists who say that Western society is a godless and destructive force in the world. But I sometimes wonder if a global explosion of religious fury would not in some sense be deeply satisfying to the new atheists, for then they could say, 'We told you so', and many more moderate secularists might be converted to their cause. At that point, I suspect we would begin to see the elimination not only of religious beliefs but of the people who hold them, because, as John Gray argues, the Enlightenment faith in progress always trails in its wake the justification of extreme violence as a legitimate means in the struggle for social transformation.

Scholars such as Rubenstein and Stark take a benign view of the relationship between Western values and the religious traditions which shaped them. However, Gray is more pessimistic about the human condition in general and the Western tradition in particular. I want to turn to his recent book, *Black Mass*,[15] before I negotiate a way through these complicated and sometimes conflicting ideas.

Gray is Professor of European Thought at the London School of Economics, and he is far more critical of post-Enlightenment ideas, including scientific rationalism, than he is of their religious antecedents. In *Black Mass*, Gray argues that there is a dangerous strand of utopianism running through all modern political ideologies with their faith in progress and in the potential perfectibility of human society. This utopianism includes the latest atheist ideologies represented by figures such as Dawkins and Daniel Dennett, and American neo-conservatism represented by Tony

Blair and George W. Bush (Gray regards Blair as an American neo-con).

Gray argues that this utopian streak with its violent totalitarian and fascist tendencies is a phenomenon which is unique to societies shaped by Christianity. Its origins derive from the innovative belief, communicated by Christ to his followers, that the world was on the brink of a dramatic and redemptive transformation. However, this Christian eschatological hope was always expressed in the context of an awareness of the effects of original sin and the impossibility of human perfection in this life. Although millenarian Christians have believed that Christ would return and rule the earth in peace for a thousand years, this perfect society would be brought about by divine intervention, not by human endeavour. This awareness of human limitations and a trust in the providence of God restricted any tendencies towards the kind of revolutionary violence which has been the result of all post-Enlightenment utopian movements since the French Revolution. Secular Western societies have inherited Christianity's millenarian hope but not its moderating theological influence. Modern secular fundamentalisms share with their religious counterparts a misplaced certainty about the world and the human condition. In their confident faith in the power of knowledge and reason, they have lost sight of the 'civilizing perception' which traditional religion offers in its 'attempt to deal with mystery rather than hope that mystery will be unveiled.'[16] As a result, they have repeatedly descended into bloody revolutions and tyrannical regimes, fuelled by the conviction that the utopian transformation of human society is a realisable political goal. Gray writes:

> If anything defines 'the West' it is the pursuit of salvation in history. It is historical teleology – the belief that history has a built-in purpose or goal – rather than traditions of democracy or tolerance, that sets western civilization apart from all others … What is unique to the modern West is the formative role of the faith that violence can save the world. Totalitarian terror in the last century was part of a western

project of taking history by storm. The twenty-first century began with another attempt at this project, with the Right taking over from the Left as the vehicle of revolutionary change.[17]

AC Grayling has written a scathing review of Gray's book,[18] pouring scorn on the idea that Christianity has ever offered anything of value to Western Enlightenment values, and repeating all the old shibboleths about religion which I have discussed earlier. Grayling describes religion as 'a view which essentially premises commitment to belief in the existence of supernatural agencies in the universe' and declares that 'the history of the modern European and Europe-derived world is precisely the history of liberation from the hegemony of Christianity.' Ignoring the work of recent historians, Grayling refers to 'the Christianity of the Inquisition, which burned to death' those who asserted the values of individual freedom associated with the Enlightenment. I have already referred to studies which show that the witch-hunts were at least as closely associated with the rise of reason in Western society as they were with any religious impulses (see Chapter 2). Toby Green's recent study of the Spanish Inquisition suggests that it was primarily motivated by the secular, political ambitions of Spanish and Portuguese rulers, and that the Vatican actually had a restraining influence on the excesses of the Inquisition when it had the power to do so.[19]

These are inconvenient truths for those still dogmatically committed to the myth that there is an irreconcilable conflict between Christianity and Enlightenment ideals. However, if we are to find a way through these messy entanglements of fact and fiction, myth and reason, conflicting theories and multiple interpretations of history, politics and our place within them, we all need to face up to the inconvenient truths which challenge our particular views of the world. We have to set aside the certainties of faith – whether it is faith in progress or faith in God – in order to inhabit these dangerous times in a spirit of doubt, uncertainty and openness to the possibility of new ways of thinking and living. Only if we can lose our arrogant belief that we Westerners stand at the pinnacle of human truth and endeavour, whether in the name of religion or in the name of science, might we recognise that we share the human condition of vulnerability, ignorance and dependence which is common to our species. Recognising our limitations, we must struggle in darkness and confusion to find our way towards the pinpricks of light which constitute our hope. This is not a utopian striving for a perfect world, but a patient attentiveness towards creating the conditions in which we might live as beings whose capacities for benevolence and kindness must always struggle against the temptation to violence and hatred which lurks within us and among us, and which is nurtured in the crucible of fear, alienation and despair.

Contextualising rationality

I have suggested that reason has an indispensable role to play in moderating religious excess and in sustaining a climate of tolerant pluralism in which those of different beliefs might co-habit in relative acceptance of one another, if not in perfect peace. I think Gray underestimates the role that reason has played in the development of the more positive aspects of Western secular culture with its Christian influences. However, I also stop short of the kind of optimism expressed by Stark with regard to the unambiguously beneficial effects of democracy, capitalism and Western individualism. If, as Stark argues, Christianity's emphasis on reason, progress and freedom has indeed played a significant role in the development of these values, then perhaps we might begin a critique of the more negative aspects of late modernity by reconsidering the Christian understanding of reason.

Implicit in the discussion so far has been a suggestion that reason is universal. Both philosophical theology and scientific rationalism have tended to agree that reason provides a means by which human beings can transcend their particular cultural and religious contexts, in order to arrive at universal ideals and aspirations which are – or should be – shared by all rational subjects.

Thus the Enlightenment project, epitomised today in the thinking of philosophers such as Grayling, holds to the confident belief that universal reason alone is the means by which all humans might share in the benefits of science and progress which so far have been enjoyed only by a few 'enlightened' Westerners.

However, other philosophers argue that reason is culturally conditioned. We may have a common human capacity to think rationally, but the content of rationality – that is, what counts as rational behaviour and ideas – is a product of historical and cultural contexts.[20] If we want to understand whether or not a person is rational, we must not look for some universal yardstick against which to judge their actions, but must rather understand why they believe and behave as they do in the context of the worlds they inhabit. Rationality does not float free of all the particularities of our lives but is embedded within them and flows from them. It is a way of organising our ideas and informing our actions to conform to the goals we aspire to, the hopes we nurture, the visions we seek, but it does not produce those goals, hopes and visions. So in the Christian tradition, reason has been employed in the service of a certain vision of the world. According to Stark, that has been a positive and progressive vision. In Gray's interpretation, it is a vision which has introduced a dark strain of violent utopianism into the Western narrative.

Feminist critiques of Western reason

Many would say that what has passed for reason in the Western tradition has been too closely allied to power, privilege and male domination.[21] Feminists and postcolonial Christians argue that the Christian narrative has been distorted by an over-emphasis on a particular form of rationality associated with the values and projections of a Western male elite, which has left women and non-Western cultures in positions of silence and marginality in relation to the dominant trends of history.[22] To take seriously such challenges means expanding what we mean by reason. From the perspective of Christian theology, this means going beyond its patriarchal and androcentric moorings, in order to enter into a creative engagement with radical new perspectives which are emerging from those who have traditionally been excluded from the study of theology and the formulation of doctrine.[23]

I have argued that Christianity arises out of the encounter between the Bible and Greek philosophy. There is an extensive body of feminist biblical criticism which analyses the ways in which the patriarchal views of the biblical world have continued to shape the Christian tradition.[24] However, feminist theologians also argue that a gendered understanding of God entered Christianity through the doorway of Greek thought, so that biblical patriarchy was shored up by a range of sexual stereotypes associated not with the Bible but with Greek philosophy. In particular, some would argue that the identification of philosophical concepts of masculine reason with the human capacity to image God referred to in the story of Genesis 1:27 has had a disastrous impact on the understanding of sexuality and gender in the Christian tradition. It is man, not woman, who has been understood to be made in the image of God. As a result, masculinity has come to signify transcendence, divinity, reason and order, while femininity signifies bodiliness, nature, passion and chaos. In their aspirations towards godliness, men must struggle to transcend the desire, sexuality, embodiment and mortality which they associate with the female flesh. This creates a culture of contempt for sexuality and the female body, and also for nature and the earth, which are construed as maternal and feminine in relation to the masculinity of the Father God. The struggle for order over chaos, transcendence over immanence, spirituality over the flesh, reason over passion, thus becomes a struggle of man against woman and culture against nature. I discussed some of the implications of this for modern science and philosophy in the first three chapters.

The associations between masculinity and divinity mean that Christian beliefs about God are influenced by masculine fantasies and projections. The nineteenth-century philosopher Ludwig Feuerbach (1804–72) argued that God is a projection of the highest inner aspirations and ideals of man.[25] Feminists would say that, in this case, the word 'man' is exclusive, not inclusive. God is a projection modelled on the ideals of the Western man of reason. In a critique of Richard Swinburne's philosophical conceptualisation of God, the feminist philosopher of religion Grace Jantzen writes that 'anyone who can imagine "himself" as an infinitely extended (and disembodied) version of an Oxford professor is an analogue of the divine.'[26] The problem is, if one abandons Swinburne's theological world-view to follow Dawkins, one simply gets more of the same. In the case of Dawkins' angry atheism, God becomes a mirror image – not an ideal so much as a projection of the very worst excesses of masculine power and violence. Dawkins describes the God of the Old Testament as

> arguably the most unpleasant character in all fiction: jealous and proud of it; a petty, unjust, unforgiving control-freak; a vindictive, bloodthirsty ethnic cleanser; a misogynistic, homophobic, racist, infanticidal, genocidal, filicidal, pestilential, megalomaniacal, sadomasochistic, capriciously malevolent bully.[27]

With perhaps just a little embellishment, this sounds remarkably like the sorry fusion of religion and torture that one might get in old-fashioned English public schools, where every sadistic master makes God in his own image. The God that Richard Dawkins does not believe in may be the God of his own childhood experience, as the son of affluent colonial middle-class parents who gave him 'a normal Anglican upbringing'[28] and sent him to an English public school from an early age. Dawkins' God is as much a thoroughly modern English bully as an ancient supernatural tyrant. In a similar vein, Hitchens describes the God of the Old Testament as 'an ill-tempered and implacable and bloody and provincial god, who was probably more frightening when he was in a good mood (the classic attribute of the dictator).'[29] Those who have witnessed Hitchens growling and grumping his way through an interview or pubic lecture may detect just a distant echo of a man made in the image of the God he rejects.

Assessing the Christian legacy

The God of the philosophers shaped early Christian theology, but this philosophical concept sat uneasily alongside the God of the Christian scriptures who was incarnate in the human vulnerability and mortality of Christ. This duality persisted in medieval theology, devotion, art and culture, in which we see a tension between intuitive, expressive, mystical and artistic forms of faith and the emergent theologies of the new universities with their more rationalised approaches to questions of faith. The Reformation cast a stern eye over the more expressive forms of faith associated with Catholic devotion, and it put in their place a more rigorous biblical austerity. However, it was the theism of the Enlightenment which finally stripped God of his humanity and gave us a more abstract and remote deity akin to the God of the ancient philosophers – a god who was more of a master architect or a celestial engineer than the incarnate God of the Christian faith.

This brings me back to the tension I referred to at the beginning of this chapter. Christian theology is informed by both the Bible and Greek philosophy, so that some of the more radical challenges of the biblical narrative have been made to fit comfortably within existing social hierarchies. Aquinas's theology, for example, was developed in the stratified societies of medieval Europe which, like the societies of ancient Greece in which Aristotle lived, had clearly defined ranks of social and sexual responsibilities and duties, sustained by an appeal to natural law. God intended men to have authority over women, children, slaves and animals, even though this was to be regulated by principles of justice according to each kind of relationship and its place in the social hierarchy.

This belief in the natural superiority and leadership of the Western male has persisted through centuries of Western domination, and I suggested in the first few chapters that it has infected modern science as thoroughly as it infected Christianity. But the historical legacy of Christianity is complex, because alongside its imperial and warring tendencies there has always been another tradition of social justice and solidarity with the poor and the marginalised. This was the prevailing ethos of the earliest Christian communities, and it has survived in one form or another through-out Christian history. After 600 years of Christianity being impli-cated in the growing power of Western global domination, it still retains this radical edge. While Western military and economic powers collude to sustain a world order of burgeoning inequality and exploitation, Christians are often in the forefront of the struggle against poverty, disease, violence and oppression.

The World Social Forum is a loose-knit collective of activists and anti-globalisation campaigners who seek to promote alterna-tive economic and political models to those represented by the G8. Every January the Forum gathers in a different international venue at the same time as the Davos Economic Summit in Switzerland, bringing together tens of thousands of campaigners on a wide range of issues. Reporting on the Forum in Nairobi in January 2007, the *Economist* magazine commented on 'the strong Christian contingent', and went on to note that 'The biggest single group of anti-poverty campaigners in Nairobi were Roman Catholics, who accounted for 20,000 or so of the dele-gates.'[30] Any attempt to evaluate the impact of religious traditions in ethical and humanitarian terms must take into account this quite different aspect of religious activism. It does nothing to jus-tify or excuse the more aggressive and ignorant forms of religion, but it is motivated by religious convictions about the meaning of life and the intrinsic value and dignity of the human made in the image of God which shape the Christian understanding of human nature, and which still implicitly inform all our Western concepts of what it means to be human.

The privileging of reason by Catholic Christianity laid the foundations for Western science and created the conditions in which the values of secular modernity gradually germinated and outgrew their religious habitat. Today, that flowering of secular reason is itself turning to seed. As we survey the withering remains of Europe's great intellectual flourishing, we face three equally terrifying possibilities if we ask what might take root and grow in its place. First, there is the prospect of an advanced form of scientific rationalism which would strip away the last vestiges of our humanity and transform us into the kind of intelligent robots which have inspired so many dystopian science-fiction novels and films. Second, we face the emergence of new forms of religious totalitarianism – particularly Islamism and Christian fundamentalism – with the potential to destroy a host of fragile modern freedoms, not least in the area of women's rights. Third, we face various forms of postmodern anarchy, in which every quest for truth and coherence is sacrificed on the altar of a violent and chaotic struggle for survival, such as that which is already emerging in Iraq. This has the potential to become a widespread reality through the combined forces of weapons of mass destruction used in proliferating wars, and a series of environmental catastrophes, all unleashed by the power of a species which has forgotten what it means to be a rational animal and has become instead a species in the grip of its own violent and terrifying animal desires.

In this twilight of reason, postmodernists, postcolonialists and feminists embrace the present as a moment of opportunity and potential liberation. Free from the overarching stories – the metanarratives – which both Christianity and the Enlightenment told about the world, those who have been silenced and excluded from active participation in these great Western dreams of re-demption and transformation are beginning to tell their stories. As we shall see in the next chapter, this may indeed be the dawning of a new era of plurality, diversity and freedom, but it may also be the beginning of a long night of violence and conflict.

Chapter 7

KITSCH, TERROR AND THE POSTMODERN CONDITION

The term 'postmodernism' refers to a loose-knit movement of ideas which extends from popular culture, art and architecture across the academic spectrum of the arts and humanities, including theology and philosophy. It is a world-view which asserts that there is no world-view, paradoxically laying claim to the universal truth that there is no universal truth. The concept was first made popular by Jean-François Lyotard in 1979 in his book, *The Postmodern Condition*,[1] although in its earliest usage in the late 1940s it referred to a trend in architecture. Postmodernity as an era rather than a concept emerged in the aftermath of European imperialism and in the crisis of confidence in Enlightenment values which followed the Second World War.

While European thinkers contemplated the disintegration of reason, civilisation and modernity in the trenches of the First World War and the gas chambers of the Holocaust, new voices emerged to challenge the dominance of the Western man of reason. Questions of race, gender, sexuality, ethnicity, cultural particularity, identity and difference, embodiment and desire, the environment and animal rights, have surged in to occupy the vacuum left by the collapse of the project of modernity with its ruling elite of white Western heterosexual men. The rise in communications technology and what Lyotard saw as the commodification of knowledge have given these different perspectives and discourses wide circulation, so that knowledge is no longer controlled by an educated minority. The language of universal human rights has attempted to spread some kind of ethical canopy over this babel or Pentecost (which?) of competing discourses and narratives. Postmodernism's celebration of particularity, relativism and contextuality over universality, rationality and truth, can provide a window of opportunity for the emergence of new ethical visions, but it can also serve the purposes of radical individualism and extreme forms of nationalism and religious fundamentalism.

Postmodernism and identity politics

Under the banner of postmodernism, with its dissolution of universal truths, identity politics comes to the fore. Postmodernism creates a forum in which individuals and minority groups can claim rights to self-expression and self-determination rooted in particular identities and cultural narratives which are not accountable to the judgement of outsiders. In the case of Western individualism, postmodernism privileges the here and now over the bonds of tradition, history and community. It allows for an experimental lifestyle through the expression of multiple identities – a sort of metropolitan fancy-dress parade where we act out fictional identities because there is no such thing as the 'I' based on the idea of a gendered, communal, historical self with a fixed identity.

In its most extreme manifestations, the postmodern self is a voracious consumer, who requires a cultural *habitus* capable of constantly feeding his or her desire for novelty, innovation and change, and who demands a proliferating range of individual rights to satisfy his or her infinitely varied appetites. Switch on the television and you will see such individuals filling the spaces of low and high culture, from *Big Brother* to the late-night arts shows.

But the tolerance which makes us tolerate every kind of narcissistic excess is not really tolerance at all. The ostensible diversity which proliferates under the banner of postmodernism is a banal and barren sameness, masked by a surface gloss of corporate images, brand names, fashions and lifestyles. Postmodernism cannot accommodate genuine, meaningful difference. When post-modern culture encounters the truly different, it must either force it to conform to its own valueless values, or label it as extremist, violent and dangerous. While the intellectual community is distracted from any real political engagement by its apparently insatiable appetite for postmodern discourses of alterity and difference (or *différance*, to use a Derridean term), democracy withers and freedoms are slowly corroded by a political system which has acquired excessive power through its cynical exploitation of the general public's insecurity and susceptibility to fear. This social melt-down is happening in an era when only a minority of people has any interest in or commitment to religious values. It cannot therefore be blamed on religious influences. It is the consequence of a secularism which has cast aside its Christian heritage but has found nothing to put in its place except a proliferation of vacuous choices which masquerade as freedom.

Religious extremism and nationalism flourish in the long shadows cast by our Western charades of freedom, multiculturalism and diversity, for outsiders see better than we do ourselves what it costs to maintain our illusory postmodern freedoms. The assault on religion by a clique of Western polemicists risks becoming a self-fulfilling prophecy in its labelling of religion as violent and extremist, for it is stoking the fires of resentment at a time of global volatility when, for many of the world's people, religious faith holds out the only possibility of living a meaningful and dignified life. Only a small minority of the world's people has access to the wealth needed to live out the postmodern consumerist lifestyle. Poverty provides a potent breeding ground for anti-Western hostility, while within Western cultures themselves, there are many who are appalled by what they see as a loss of traditional values and increasing social chaos. Where can such people turn to for different values, for more enduring visions, for a transcendent sense of truth which will allow them to rise above the postmodern abyss? The answer – to God, and to all the fervent causes associated with 'him', including nationalism, homophobia, fundamentalism and patriarchy.

Religious extremism in a postmodern context

In recent decades we have seen the widespread resurgence of religion in some of its most extreme forms – from the Christian fundamentalists of the American Bible belt and their Zionist counterparts, to the jihadists of Islamist uprisings and the Hindu nationalists of India's BJP (Bharatiya Janata Party). Even Buddhists – stereotypically portrayed by Westerners as peace-loving pluralists – have embraced militant nationalism in Sri Lanka, and a Japanese Buddhist sect known as Aum Shinrikyo was responsible for the nerve-gas attack on the Tokyo subway in 1995. Wherever we look, it seems that religiously inspired extremists are rising up against the West's hard-won values of tolerance, democracy and freedom. Far from religion disappearing, it has become in its various manifestations a significant threat to modernity. Hence, the belief that it would eventually vanish under the weight of its own deceptions has given way to a more militant crusade against religion – a 'rationalist jihad', to quote Polly Toynbee (see Chapter 4) – waged by the new atheists and their supporters.

But ignorance is no response to ignorance, and atheist intolerance sets itself on a collision course with religious intolerance. If we are to maintain a more open and constructive debate, we have to begin by trying to understand why so many of our species – 'mammals' like us, to use a word favoured by Hitchens – are resorting to such desperate forms of self-expression and violent assertions of anti-modernist values.

Malise Ruthven, a scholar of Islam, argues that postmodernity poses a particular challenge to those who seek religious certainty, because of its relativising of all truth claims. While modernity and progress were meant to spell the end of religion by ushering in a new era of secularisation, postmodernism has once again opened up public spaces for religious expression, but only by refusing to privilege any one truthful story about the world:

> By saying, in effect, 'Your story is as good as mine, or his, or

hers', post-modernism allows religious voices to have their say while denying their right to silence others, as religions have tended to do throughout history.[2]

In traditional societies, dominant concepts of truth are rarely challenged, and social and religious conformity avoids the need for complex negotiations with others of different beliefs and practices. However, in the pluralist cultures of postmodernity, religious believers have to negotiate boundaries and make compromises, and this can produce feelings of alienation and a loss of identity. For this reason, Ruthven sees fundamentalisms as 'distinctly modern phenomena':

> like the New Religious Movements that have sprouted in some of the most industrialized parts of the world (notably South-East Asia and North America) they feed on contemporary alienation or anomie by offering solutions to contemporary dilemmas, buttressing the loss of identities sustained by many people (especially young people) at times of rapid social change, high social and geographic mobility, and other stress-inducing factors.[3]

Some of these themes of identity, alienation and postmodernism also feature in Mark Juergensmeyer's study of religious violence, *Terror in the Mind of God*.[4] In an extensive series of interviews with perpetrators of religious violence, and by studying contexts in which religion has been a significant factor in political and nationalist conflicts, Juergensmeyer analyses the justifications offered for different acts of religiously inspired violence. He argues that these are not the work of lonely fanatics or mad psychopaths. Rather, they are a radical form of protest against the present order which usually enjoys at least the tacit support of wider groups. He refers to 'postmodern religious rebels' and 'guerrilla nationalists' who 'have dreamed of revolutionary changes that would establish a godly social order in the rubble of what the citizens of most secular societies have regarded as modern, egalitarian democracies.'[5]

Juergensmeyer argues that the late-twentieth-century eruption of religious violence can be seen as a reaction to the anti-religious sentiment which has been a feature of Western societies since the Enlightenment. The manifest failures of the Enlightenment project have created an environment in which religious extremism flourishes by proclaiming 'the death of secularism'. Religious extremists

> have dismissed the efforts of secular culture and its forms of nationalism to replace religion. They have challenged the notion that secular society and the modern nation-state can provide the moral fiber that unites national communities or the ideological strength to sustain states buffeted by ethical, economic, and military failures. Their message has been easy to believe and has been widely received because the failures of the secular state have been so apparent.[6]

Yet none of this offers a satisfactory explanation as to why religion provides a focal point for the gathering together of explosive forces of nationalism, resistance and violent revolution. Juergensmeyer argues that, when religion becomes a justification for violence, it is because religious extremists are motivated by a sense of cosmic war between good and evil. He suggests that religious visions of 'personal wholeness and social redemption',[7] although often expressed in non-violent forms, can also legitimate confrontational violence against systems and structures perceived to be unjust, decadent or immoral, so that religious activists become motivated by 'a spiritual conviction so strong that they are willing to kill and to be killed for moral reasons.'[8]

Secular kitsch, religious wrath and postmodern ambiguity

The upsurge of religious violence is in part an explosive confrontation between the postmodern West and its religious 'others', fermented in a climate of political instability, economic inequality, and social disintegration. There is a widespread loss of confidence in political structures and ethical values among postmodern secularists and religious extremists, and in both cases questions of identity and self-expression acquire exaggerated significance. Religious violence and anarchy are rooted in identity politics as surely as the ironic parodies and performances of the postmodern Western subject in his or her rejection of all traditional values and concepts of an essential or given self. The clashing perspectives of Western secular individualism and religious extremism collided in the 9/11 attack on America, and the dust has yet to clear in order for us to see the full historical significance of that event. On that day, postmodern kitsch was blasted into reality by fundamentalist wrath. With brilliant cunning and ruthless rationality, bin Laden and his suicidal supporters targeted the ultimate symbols of Western global domination – the Twin Towers and the Pentagon. If it is true that their third, failed target was the White House, then it is hard to imagine a more symbolically eloquent act of violent protest against Western values. We can rest assured that, if Islamist militants win the so-called war on terror and rewrite the history books, Osama bin Laden will become the greatest hero of the twenty-first century and possibly of the coming millennium. That is unlikely, however, and it remains to be seen what history will make of the two self-appointed commanders-in-chief of the war against terror – George W. Bush and Tony Blair.

None of this is to deny the positive aspects of postmodernity, and its potential to nurture flourishing societies capable of accommodating diversity and difference. Nobody who lives in a great multi-cultural city such as London should deny our human capacity to live side by side with those whose values may be very different from our own, and rare eruptions of violence should not blind us to the small daily acts of kindness, acceptance and good will which are the far more pervasive and unremarkable reality. Most of us do not fear terrorist attacks every time we board an aeroplane or travel on the underground. Many of us experience our lives as richly enhanced by the challenge of living and learning alongside those of different cultures, races and faiths to our own. The equality which we enjoy today across boundaries of race, religion, sexuality and gender owes more to postmodernity than to the Enlightenment for, as I suggested in the first few chapters, the Enlightenment did little to challenge Western hierarchies of power and domination.

The enemies of these fragile postmodern freedoms are not confined to religious fundamentalists, for they also include secular and scientific fundamentalists who lay claim to a truth which tolerates no dissent and no diversity. Like religious fundamentalists, militant atheists are threatened by the ideological free-for-all of the postmodern marketplace, which opens up public spaces for a competing plurality of cultures, traditions and truth claims. In their vehement defence of secular rational modernity, they too manifest all the insecurities of a universal ideology under threat from cultural relativism and intellectual and ethical diversity. Like the liberal religious apologists they so despise, they put a rationalising gloss on some of the more sinister aspects of their own tradition and its followers. The fact that the theory of evolution might itself validate the use of violence in the struggle for survival of different groups and cultures, the fact that it has been used to justify the extermination of racial and economic groups and the elimination of disabled and mentally ill human beings, the fact that it is a random and amoral biological process which offers no basis for a social vision based on humanitarian values – these are all dismissed in favour of a mythology of the improving power of evolutionary science which gripped the late Victorian imagination and remains alive and well in the new atheism.

What role for religion?

In the face of all these contradictions and debates, a question remains as to what role religion might occupy in this postmodern era, given that the alternatives of scientific atheism, religious fundamentalism or a return to traditional Christian values are probably all equally unattractive to the majority of the West's citizens. The need to live and let live presents two particular challenges: the first is to find a way for the followers of different traditions, religious and secular, to cohabit in peace. This means negotiating a delicate balancing act between allowing space for a diversity of beliefs and cultures, while upholding the vision of human rights which is enshrined in the 1948 Universal Declaration of Human Rights. Although this document is riddled with inconsistencies and contradictions, it is the only ethical vision which has broad consensus among the world's cultures and nations. No universal ethos will ever iron out all the contradictions and incompatibilities in what counts as the good life for different cultures and individuals, but the modern idea of human rights is the only shared language we have that is capable of resisting the torture and tyranny which go hand in hand with the darker aspects of modernity and its political structures. To abandon the struggle for human rights because it is too demanding – intellectually as well as ethically – is to clear the way for the abuses which proliferate under the guise of the war on terror no less than under those regimes which it claims to oppose. But none of this *per se* will tackle the question of religion and spirituality. So the second challenge is, how can we find a more positive role for religious traditions within liberal democratic societies?

In secular societies, the religious impulse often finds expression in the New Age spiritualities which proliferate in the climate of postmodernity, offering a psychic brew of ancient and Eastern religions (particularly of the Celtic and mystical varieties), homeopathic remedies, nature cults and neo-pagan devotions. If there is one common theme uniting all of these, beyond the spiritual hunger they represent, it is hostility to any form of institutionalised religion. Even Sam Harris, doyen of American militant atheism, makes the surely heretical claim, in the light of the movement's non-credo, that there is 'a sacred dimension to our existence'[9] so that 'The roiling mystery of the world can be analyzed with concepts (this is science), or it can be experienced free of concepts (this is mysticism).'[10]

It is an illusion to believe that there can be a mysticism which is free of concepts. Scholars of mysticism argue persuasively that, even if there is some dimension of human consciousness which transcends conceptualised thinking, as soon as we attempt to communicate anything of this experience, we must do so in the language and concepts which religions make available to us.[11] More importantly, however, if we accept that there was a quasi-religious or spiritual dimension to twentieth-century ideologies such as Nazism, then we should be wary of seeking spiritual forms of expression which are free of the restraints of reason and conceptualisation. Harris himself says of Stalin and Mao:

> although these tyrants paid lip service to rationality, commu-nism was little more than a political religion. At the heart of its apparatus of repression and terror lurked a rigid ideology, to which generations of men and women were sacrificed. Even though their beliefs did not reach beyond this world, they were both cultic and irrational.[12]

If one asks what transforms a political tyranny into a religion, then perhaps one has to look for signs of a transcendent vision, a mys-tical or utopian dimension, which breaks free of the restraints of a strictly materialist rationality and of the restraining influences of any historical religious tradition.

Psychoanalysis reveals the dark and violent desires which shape the human psyche, and the new atheists are right when they remind us how often religion taps into these desires to produce extremes of sado-masochistic behaviour and malevolent fantasies of hell and punishment.[13] When Freud referred to the 'soft voice of reason', he meant the constant struggle of the human subject to rise above these unconscious desires and instincts to function as a responsible moral agent in society. Postmodernism has the poten-tial to unleash new forms of religious irrationality which are always likely to be accompanied by expressions of violence or psychosis. As John Gray suggests, 'Along with evangelical revivals, there is likely to be a profusion of designer religions, mixing science and science fiction, racketeering and psychobabble, which will spread like internet viruses.'[14]

If we take such threats seriously, then we may need to re-evaluate the role of traditional religions as an endeavour to control our psychological impulses towards violence and fear more than as an attempt to exploit them. Indeed, if religion were as uniformly ignorant and wicked as militant atheists suggest, it is hard to see how humanity has survived at all, let alone progressed, for it would imply that for most of our history we have been prey to the darkest possible forces of violence, corruption and fear, cunningly manipulated by religious authorities to keep us servile and ignorant.

The teachings and practices of the world's enduring religious traditions have often been abused, but overall they have enabled human beings to refine and develop their primal religious impulses by channelling their energies and controlling their more irrational tendencies. They all contain guidance for ways of disciplining and nurturing our inner worlds in order to orientate these towards the glimmers of goodness, compassion and hope that flicker within us all, despite the sometimes overwhelming psychological tyranny of violence and fear. Every religious tradition is home to millennia of wisdom and reflection on the human condition and its contradictory and competing desires, torn as we are between life and death or, to use Freud's language, *eros* and *thanatos*.

Let's consider, for example, the most notorious area of religious control, namely, that of sex. Hitchens declares that 'the divorce between the sexual life and fear, and the sexual life and disease, and the sexual life and tyranny, can now at last be attempted, on the sole condition that we banish all religions from the discourse.'[15] I am not interested in defending the sorry track record of Christianity in particular, in its ongoing attempt to police the sex lives of its followers according to particularly narrow criteria of monogamous heterosexuality. But it is more than 40 years since the sexual revolution of the 1960s, and during that time Britain has become an increasingly secularised society in which relatively few people allow religious considerations to regulate their sex lives. Even those of us who remain within religious traditions such as the Roman Catholic Church usually exercise a fairly high degree of autonomy when deciding how to live in terms of sexual and reproductive matters. I always tell my students, it is a mistake to think that the pronouncements of religious authority figures are reflective of the practices of religious followers, because sometimes the opposite is the case. Vigorous papal attempts to control contraception and abortion since the 1960s have to be understood in the context of women's liberation and a new generation of Catholic adults who simply do not invite priestly scrutiny of our sex lives and child-bearing capacities.

But it is also true that the increasing secularisation of British culture has not resulted in a healthier sexual environment. Britain has one of the highest teenage pregnancy rates in Europe, abortion rates continue to rise in spite of the ready availability of contraception, and there is evidence of widespread depression and social alienation among our ostensibly sexually liberated and thoroughly secularised youth. Casting the net wider, more vulnerable human beings, including children, are being trafficked, enslaved and exploited for sexual purposes than ever before, owing to the combined forces of poverty, communications technology and unbridled sexual appetites which have created a global culture of sexual predation. The liberal myth that sex would all be good clean fun if only religion would get off our backs has been exploded both by the Aids pandemic and by the proliferation of sex-related crimes and abuses in our modern secular society. That some of these are perpetrated by priests and other religious authority figures is scandalous, but this does not change the fact that the relationship between sex, oppression and violence continues to flourish long after the decline of religion.

The undercurrents that tug at human consciousness are made up of powerful eddies which we do not fully understand, and sex is often caught up in the whirlpools of violence. The world's religions may not have produced great expertise in their understanding of human sexuality but, if we restrict our focus to Christianity, we can argue that it has attempted to negotiate a difficult path between acknowledging the dangerous potential of sex, while also affirming the capacity of sex to express love and creativity as well as violence and destructiveness. This must be understood in the context of a larger social vision which aspires to transform human society from relationships of exploitation, domination and oppression, to relationships of mutual respect, equality and freedom in which the dignity of the human made in the image of God can find expression. However often this Christian vision has failed, we should take seriously the arguments of those who suggest that we owe our present Western values to the maturing of this religious tradition, beyond its institutions and structures perhaps, but not beyond its visions and hopes.

Faith in a postmodern world

As I suggested in the last chapter, far from encouraging violence and injustice, the long Christian project of combining revelation and reason in the service of human redemption may have been indispensable to the development of Western liberal values. Christianity's doctrines and theological insights have moderated the dangerous extremes of our religious instincts in the service of a vision which seeks to balance the freedoms of the individual with the common good. In the twentieth century, the casting off of this moderating influence by previously Christian societies in the Soviet Union and Nazi Germany did not produce greater levels of freedom but barbaric cruelties on a scale which would have been unthinkable to our Christian forebears. Whatever atrocities may have been perpetrated by the followers of Christ, none can rival the systematic extermination of millions of human beings in the service of these post-Christian ideologies. Nazism was fuelled by a strong quasi-mystical cult rooted in fantasies of blood, race and soil and free from the restraints of reason and ethical reflection. Spirituality without religion and mysticism without concepts to order its insights are not necessarily avenues to peace. They may simply draw us more deeply into the darkness.

Few cultures have developed such profound antagonism towards their own historical traditions as Western secular societies have towards Christianity. This has been a movement which has gained momentum during the last 200 years, but it may well have peaked with the rise of postmodernism. Some Christian post-modernists such as Alasdair MacIntyre, John Milbank and Stanley

Hauerwas argue that the only way in which Western society can rediscover its values is to reclaim its Christian heritage.[16] In a postmodern world, they argue that the universalising project of modernity has to yield before an acceptance of tradition, community and history as the narratives wherein our values and visions acquire truthfulness and meaning. This appeal to community-based traditions and values is sometimes referred to as 'communitarianism', and its influence extends considerably beyond that of Christian postmodernism to describe a range of political and ethical ideas.

Whether or not these postmodern Christians will succeed in articulating a radically new form of Christianity relevant to the questions of the post-Christian West remains to be seen. They are mainly eurocentric male thinkers who gloss over the manifest failures of Christianity through history, and who tend to overlook the many conflicting traditions which make up Christianity. They offer little by way of engagement with other postmodern Christian voices, particularly those of feminists and post-colonialists, who pose a more radical and far-reaching challenge to traditional forms of Christianity. Christian communitarians also underestimate the power of conservatism to dominate the religious landscape. In the present political climate, if the Western nations do rediscover their Christian heritage, it is likely to be through a combination of American evangelicalism and ultra-conservative Catholicism. As a practising Roman Catholic, I thank God for the gift of modernity and the insights of secularism. I would not want to live in a theocracy governed from Rome or Canterbury – far less from Washington – nor would I want the homophobes and misogynists who form a noisy and growing constituency in the Christian Church to triumph over secular liberal values. Those of us who care for the integrity of religious faith have a corresponding duty to resist religion's power. One way of doing that might be to value and nurture the positive aspects of secular postmodernity, even as we recognise and resist its nihilistic and relativistic excesses.

This means speaking out against the ongoing injustices perpetrated by Christian churches, and it means cultivating a spirit of resistance to the ethical abuses which proliferate when Christians value unity more highly than integrity. In a fractured world such as ours, the idea that gun-toting fundamentalist housewives who hate Muslims and gays with equal fervour belong within the same world-view as Christians working tirelessly for peace and reconciliation among the world's religions and peoples is not viable. Militant atheists make much of the fact that the Roman Catholic Church has never excommunicated a single person for membership of the Nazi party, and the Catholic Church is still sheltering some of its priests and nuns who took part in the Rwandan genocide. These are scandals which people within the Church ought to speak out against, forming alliances with secularists and atheists who share our concerns rather than with co-religionists, when fundamental issues of justice, freedom and human dignity are at stake. The great threats facing our world today are not homosexuality and abortion but war and other forms of violence, economic injustice and environmental degradation.

But no matter how much we struggle against injustice and oppression, we will never eliminate the causes and effects of suffering in our world, for they are woven into the human condition. In the last chapter, I considered Gray's warning that visions of utopian transformation tend to mutate into dystopian nightmares, multiplying the injustices which they set out to eradicate. With that in mind, I want to end this chapter by briefly considering the challenge which suffering poses to faith, and the different responses which this has evoked amidst the fading hopes of a postmodern world.

Suffering, mystery and God

Postmodernism flourishes in the shadows of a nihilism which it often denies. The hidden face of postmodern culture is a form of despair, for our multi-cultural jamboree conceals an abyss of meanings and values. In the twentieth century, faith in God became an impossibility for many people, not because science and reason had provided answers to the mystery of life, but because the scale of humanity's suffering and capacity for violence had outstripped any possibility of believing in a just and loving God. If postmodernism challenges the thoroughly modern scientific faith of the new atheists, it also provides a nurturing habitat for other more profound forms of atheism.

The challenge of reconciling faith with the reality of suffering has preoccupied religious thinkers since the time of the Buddha and the author of the Book of Job. The Buddha taught that the material world, including the self, is an illusion, and suffering is caused by our attachment to this illusory world. To be free of suffering, we must be free of attachment. The author of Job called attention to the mystery of God revealed in creation, and to the impossibility of the human mind being able to understand that mystery. These represent two quite different ways of responding to the challenge and mystery of suffering, which reflect something of the differences which run through Eastern and Western cosmologies and religions.

Theological attempts to reconcile faith in a good and all-powerful God with the reality of suffering and evil are known as theodicy. Christian theodicy has tended to be informed by two main arguments. The first argues that suffering is the price we pay for freedom. A God who intervened to prevent us from doing evil and causing suffering to ourselves and others would be a God who violated human free will. Second, it is argued that suffering teaches us the meaning of altruism and patience. When faced with the sufferings of others, we are moved to compassion, and when called to cope with our own suffering, we learn endurance and courage. These are the forms of theodicy associated with the philosopher of religion Richard Swinburne, and I tend to agree with Dawkins that there is something 'grotesque' about them.[17]

For a start, they seem to ask us to believe in a God whose respect for freedom works in favour of the powerful and against the vulnerable. Why should Hitler's freedom be more worthy of God's respect than the lives of millions of men, women and children whose freedom was utterly violated by Hitler's abuse of power? Why should a woman's freedom to walk safely down a street at night be less important to God than the freedom of the man who rapes her? Why should a drunk driver's freedom be more important to God than the child he mows down and kills? As for suffering as an opportunity for personal growth and compassion, most of us experience compassion and kindness in many situations where there is no visible suffering, and there are other situations where people experience extremes of suffering which evoke very little by way of human kindness. Torture chambers and prison cells are not noted for their ability to inspire compassion among witnesses to suffering. Those who kill themselves in suicidal despair are evidence that suffering is not always ennobling – it can and often does overwhelm the human spirit. In the end, most attempts to resolve the question of suffering flounder on the shores of insensitivity or ignorance. The darkness is sometimes too great, the suffering and futility too intense.

Atheisms forged in the crucible of human suffering are quite different both from standard Christian theodicies and from the new atheism with its hubristic confidence in the power of science. From the perspective of the new atheists, suffering is not a mystery, it is only a problem waiting to be solved. But science will never banish the ashes of Auschwitz by the light of understanding, for these will continue to cast a pall over the earth for as long as there are humans more aware than scientists like Dawkins of their significance. Science will never provide an answer to the question 'why?' which Job asks, and which every human being must surely ask when we contemplate the sometimes unbearable reality of belonging to a species afflicted with the capacity, not only to experience pain, but to imagine suffering as well, so that our memories and imaginations are haunted with the spectres of past and future agonies. The new atheism is a puritanical brand of godless Protestantism, full of moral bombast and preachy rhetoric, but intellectually limited and culturally parochial in its lack of engagement with the kind of existentialist questions which haunt the texts of modern European literature and philosophy, rooted as they often are in the dark loam of a century of unthinkable evil and misery.

Nietzsche and the death of God

Perhaps the greatest and darkest genius among modern atheists is Friedrich Nietzsche (1844–1900) who, on the cusp of the twentieth century, proclaimed the death of God, and whose nihilistic madness looms over us still today as the ultimate gesture of defiance of the divine.[18] Like the new atheists, Nietzsche saw Christianity as a vast corrupting influence on human history and aspirations. If 'man' could shake off the mantle of meekness which Christianity had spread over him, he would unleash within himself the *übermensch*, the Superman, in whom the full greatness of the human spirit would at last be manifest, as it had been in the ancient Greek gods. But Nietzsche also recognised that there was madness in letting go of the idea of God, for it constitutes an experiment in meaninglessness beyond anything that has been tried before. Humans would become the murderers of God, and in so doing they would cut themselves off from all compass-points and plunge themselves into an unimaginable and terrifying darkness. These are the two faces of Nietzschean atheism – the hubristic triumph of the Superman, and the futile fantasies of the nihilist.

Nietzsche became the favoured philosopher of Hitler and Nazism, and some would argue that the spirit of his philosophy, with its emphasis on unbounded human power, trails this possibility in its wake. But more recently, Nietzsche has been rehabilitated by postmodernists, who believe that his ideas invite a more nuanced and thoughtful engagement. His insistence that we must interrogate all truths, all apparent realities about the world which find their affirmation in the language we use, constitutes an extreme form of scepticism which, paradoxically, has the ring of truth about it for many who study him. Theologians as well as philosophers and cultural theorists recognise in his critique of religion and in his challenging of established truths, values and meanings a profound unmasking of the deceptions which allow power and ideology to masquerade as truth, often in the name of God. That is why Nietzsche, along with Marx and Freud, has been called one of the 'masters of suspicion'. These three thinkers invite us to question what society presents to us as normal, natural and true. They ask us to explore the hidden dynamics of power, exploitation and deception which posture under the guises of morality, religion and language, and to probe the hidden under-belly of our ways of speaking and relating in order to discover the oppressions that lurk there, but also the moments of insight by which we might rupture the established order so as to recognise different ways of being and relating.

Recognition of the role played by language in the construction of meaning brings with it the realisation that all our talk of divine revelation and inspiration can only be shown to be true in terms of its coherence and relevance in the context of human lives. Whether or not God exists above and beyond human experience, as humans it only makes sense to say that God 'exists' insofar as we embody that existence within the fabric of our own lives and within the language by which we give meaning to the world.

Stories of God

The second form of atheism I want to consider is not really atheism at all, for it constitutes a form of tortured defiance against every attempt to justify, explain or defend God, which paradox-ically must position itself before the utter darkness of God's apparent betrayal of the world. It is motivated by the spirit of Job, but without the resolution of the biblical ending. It is perhaps most famously expressed by the character Ivan in Dostoyevsky's great novel *The Brothers Karamazov*. After a harrowing description of the many ways in which human beings inflict torture and cruelty on one another, Ivan concludes that there is no possible harmony in this world or the next which would allow a mother to forgive the torturer of her child:

harmony has been overestimated in value, we really don't

have the money to pay so much to get in. And so I hasten to return my entry ticket. And if I am at all an honest man, I am obliged to return it as soon as possible. That is what I am doing. It isn't God I don't accept, Alyosha, it's just his ticket that I most respectfully return to him.[19]

Christopher Hitchens claims that he and his fellow atheists 'find that the serious ethical dilemmas are better handled by Shakespeare and Tolstoy and Schiller and Dostoyevsky and George Eliot than in the mythical morality tales of the holy books.'[20] He conveniently overlooks the fact that Tolstoy and Dostoyevsky devoted many of their literary endeavours to addressing the profound human dilemmas and divine mysteries expressed in those same holy books. Perhaps not surprisingly, Hitchens' reading of *The Brothers Karamazov* focuses exclusively on Ivan, so that he fails to acknowledge that Dostoyevsky's story is slanted not towards the convincing power of Ivan's atheism, but towards the redemptive compassion of Alyosha's faith. According to Hitchens, 'Dostoyevsky in his *Brothers Karamozov* was extremely critical of religion'.[21] He was, but he was an infinitely wiser critic than the new atheists.[22]

While the Book of Job calls attention away from the human to God as a response to suffering, existentialists such as Dostoyevsky and Albert Camus shift our gaze from God to the human. They confront us with the absurdity and pathos of the human condition in a world in which our freedom brings only torment and misery, a world in which God seems impotent in the face of our human capacity for evil.

But never have divine impotence and human evil encountered one another so profoundly as in the Holocaust, and it is Jewish survivors who have produced some of the greatest writings on suffering and the absence of God. In Eli Wiesel's short memoir, *Night*, he describes his experience when, at the age of 16, he was taken from his small Hasidic community and transported to Auschwitz:

Never shall I forget that night, the first night in camp, which has turned my life into one long night, seven times cursed and seven times sealed. Never shall I forget that smoke. Never shall I forget the little faces of the children, whose bodies I saw turned into wreaths of smoke beneath a silent blue sky.

Never shall I forget those flames which consumed my faith forever.

Never shall I forget that nocturnal silence which deprived me, for all eternity, of the desire to live. Never shall I forget those moments which murdered my God and my soul and turned my dreams to dust. Never shall I forget these things, even if I am condemned to live as long as God Himself. Never.[23]

In the memories of Wiesel's tortured youth, we have moved far beyond the vulgar atheism of scientific rationalism, and we have also moved beyond the theodicies of theologians and philosophers like Swinburne. That is because we have moved beyond God as a scientific conundrum or a philosophical concept or a theological proposition, to God as a character in literature and story-telling.

Great literature does not seek to persuade us or to convert us. Rather, it draws us into the heart of the inescapable mystery of the human condition, and it lays before us the losses and opportunities inherent in that condition in the face of joy and suffering, love and violence, desire and denial. When it invokes the name of God, it does so because there is something deep within us which asks a fundamental question of God when we contemplate our own humanity. What we make of that question lends itself to perhaps an infinite variety of responses, for there are many different ways of inhabiting the shadowy worlds of unknowing, in this era in which dogmatism, certainty and absolutism are the trademark of every kind of fundamentalism and extremism, whether atheist or religious.

Wiesel's writing is inspired by a Hasidic legend which goes as follows:

When the great Rabbi Israel Baal Shem-Tov saw misfortune threatening the Jews it was his custom to go into a certain part of the forest to meditate. There he would light a fire, say a special prayer, and the miracle would be accomplished and the misfortune averted.

Later, when his disciple, the celebrated Magid of Mezritch, had occasion, for the same reason, to intercede with heaven, he would go to the same place in the forest and say 'Master of the Universe, listen! I do not know how to light the fire, but I am still able to say the prayer,' and again the miracle would be accomplished.

Still later, Rabbi Moshe-Leib of Sasov, in order to save his people once more, would go into the forest and say, 'I do not know how to light a fire, I do not know the prayer, but I know the place and this must be sufficient.' It was sufficient and the miracle was accomplished.

Then it fell to Rabbi Israel of Rizhyn to overcome misfortune. Sitting in his armchair, his head in his hands, he spoke to God: 'I am unable to light the fire and I do not know the prayer; I cannot even find the place in the forest. All I can do is to tell the story, and this must be sufficient.' And it was sufficient.

God made man because he loves stories.[24]

Theology may well be dead in the water for everyone but theologians, but God's story is alive and well. In cinema, popular culture, art, music and literature – even in the popularity of the new atheism – the story of God is an implicit theme running through the imaginative life of Western culture as pervasively today as it ever has.

This idea of a God who loves stories, the idea that we are living characters in God's story, brings me to the last chapter of this book. I want to shift our focus now to questions of creation and creativity, imagination and story-telling, as perhaps a more fruitful way of reflecting on what it means to speak of God, than debates about rationality, science and religion. So, let me conclude by turning to stories which may not begin with 'once upon a time' and which may not end 'happily ever after'.

Chapter 8

CREATIVITY AND THE STORY OF GOD

In a postmodern age, the power of narrative and story-telling to shape our lives has replaced appeals to universal reason and truth. Each of us is part of a living story about the world, for we are born into communities and traditions whose histories, values and meanings tell us who we are. Together, these many different narratives make up the human story. Religious traditions are the most enduring of these narratives, each with its own claims to truth and its own understanding of the ultimate purpose of the cosmos and our place within it. The Enlightenment is a narrative which can be interpreted in continuity or conflict with the Christian narrative which it has gradually replaced in Western society. The new atheism is a particular version of the Enlightenment narrative which, as John Gray and Mary Midgley argue, has the same myth-making function as religious stories, in seeking to offer an over-arching vision of the meaning and purpose of life. To be human is to be a story-telling creature. 'God made man because he loves stories.'

This is not to suggest that our stories about the world are fictions with no basis in truth. For example, to say that Christianity is a story about God is not necessarily to say that God does not exist except as a character in a human story. It is, however, to say that the truthfulness of Christian beliefs about the nature and revelation of God can only be evaluated by considering their coherence in the context of the Christian faith and its traditions, and the same is true of any religion.[1] As Dawkins and others rightly point out, we can never 'prove' the existence of God through appealing to external facts and objective evidence. We can only evaluate the credibility of any narrative of meaning by considering its arguments and beliefs in the context of the people who inhabit that narrative and the ways in which they have shaped their world through philosophy, doctrine and ethics, but also through art and literature, music and poetry, devotion and prayer.

Midgley argues that scientific rationalism has severed the connection between science and poetry, so that it offers too reductive an understanding of what it means to be human.[2] She argues that the atomistic philosophy which emerged with a scientific worldview in the seventeenth century has led to an over-emphasis on individualistic, competitive and exploitative models of life, over and against more organic and co-operative models. Faced with the urgency of the environmental crisis as well as the many other challenges confronting us at the beginning of the new millennium, we need to move beyond what she calls the 'omnicompetence' of science in its attempts to explain the world, and to rediscover the power of the imagination to generate meaning and shape our visions of who we are.

The new atheism and the arts

In a televised debate, Richard Dawkins declares that he would miss nothing about religion if it were to be eradicated altogether. Referring to the role of religion in inspiring great art, he suggests that

> the B Minor Mass, the Matthew Passion, these happen to be on a religious theme, but they might as well not be. They're beautiful music on a great poetic theme, but we could still go on enjoying them without believing in any of that supernatural rubbish.[3]

He tells of how, when he was on the British radio programme, Desert Island Discs, the presenter Sue Lawley expressed surprise that he chose a piece of music from St Matthew's Passion. He explains how an atheist can enjoy religious music, by using an analogy from literature: 'You might as well say how can you enjoy Wuthering

Heights, when you know that Cathy and Heathcliffe never really existed. It's fiction. It's good fiction. It's moving fiction. But it's still fiction.'[4]

Is it really as simple as that? Our capacity to enjoy *Wuthering Heights*, as with any other great work of literature, is not dependent upon our belief that Cathy and Heathcliffe actually existed, but it is dependent upon the capacity of their characters to communicate something truthful about the human condition. The obsessive passions which Emily Brontë explores in her novel speak to us because we recognise their truth in ourselves. Cathy and Heathcliffe are fictional characters but they are also truthful, and that is why *Wuthering Heights* is good and moving fiction. The same can be said of all literature, poetry and music which transcend their time and place to communicate across cultural and historical boundaries. If religious music, art and literature have this transcendent capacity, they are not simply referring to 'supernatural rubbish'. We might not share Bach's Christian faith, but can we really appreciate his music without having at least some sense of what it means to praise the glory of God or to evoke the passion of Christ? If we regard the beliefs which inspired him as just so much 'supernatural rubbish', and if we remain mired in an adamant materialism which refuses any glimpse of transcendence, how can we allow ourselves to be transported by music, art or literature?

After citing the example of *Wuthering Heights* in *The God Delusion*, Dawkins goes on to suggest that religion had little to do with the great achievements of Christian art such as the Sistine Chapel or Raphael's *Annunciation*. He claims that, even if Raphael and Michelangelo were Christians,

> the fact is almost incidental. Its enormous wealth had made the Church the dominant patron of the arts. If history had worked out differently, and Michelangelo had been commissioned to paint a ceiling for a giant Museum of Science, mightn't he have produced something at least as inspirational as the Sistine Chapel? How sad that we shall never hear

Beethoven's *Mesozoic Symphony*, or Mozart's opera, *The Expanding Universe*. And what a shame that we are deprived of Haydn's *Evolution Oratorio* – but that does not stop us from enjoying his *Creation*.[5]

Setting aside Dawkins' misguided understanding of how artistic patronage works and his rubbishing of the motives of Christian artists (throughout *The God Delusion*, Dawkins privileges insult over argument when seeking to express disagreement), why should there not in the fullness of time be a work of scientifically inspired genius to match the genius of Beethoven or Mozart? Given that science has enjoyed increasing economic and intellectual power for the past century and a half, shouldn't we be experiencing something of this flowering of art in the name of science? Where is it?

We may struggle to find artistic or musical examples of scientific atheists at work, but literature is a more fertile source. I have already referred to the novelist Martin Amis who has apparently joined the new atheists in their anti-religious polemics, but I want to consider Ian McEwan as offering perhaps the best example of what we might call new atheist literature. McEwan appeared on Dawkins' television series, *The Root of All Evil?*, and Hitchens' book, *God Is Not Great*, is dedicated to him. Hitchens says of McEwan that his 'body of fiction shows an extraordinary ability to elucidate the numinous without conceding anything to the supernatural.'[6] McEwan's novel *Saturday* is about the dilemmas facing a liberal scientific rationalist in the months leading up to the Iraq war, and it offers a literary exploration of many of the ideas which preoccupy the new atheists.

Saturday focuses on a day in the life of surgeon Henry Perowne and his family. The blurb on the dust-jacket gives a good sense of Perowne's life: 'Henry Perowne is a contented man – a successful neurosurgeon, the devoted husband of Rosalind, a newspaper lawyer, and proud father of two grown-up children, one a promising poet, the other a talented blues musician.' Not quite an Aga saga then, but a homely story of English domesticity in Blairite

Britain, which risks being smashed apart by the combined forces of religiously inspired violence and individual insanity.

The Saturday of the book's title is not just any Saturday – it is Saturday, 15 February 2003, the day of massive anti-war demonstrations in London. McEwan puts Perowne through his paces in an increasingly frenetic day, as every possible issue has to be confronted and dealt with in 24 hours. The hapless Henry wakes up to what he initially thinks is a terrorist hijacking in the skies over London, gets caught up in the war demonstrations, crashes his car, reflects on the intricacies of brain surgery, contemplates middle age in a breathless game of squash, visits his mother who has senile dementia and therefore offers a pause for reflection on old age and madness, frets about his teenage son, discovers that his unmarried daughter is pregnant, saves his family from a murderous attack, and performs brain surgery on their attacker before snuggling up in bed with his wife at the end of the day:

> He fits himself around her, her silk pyjamas, her scent, her warmth, her beloved form, and draws closer to her. Blindly, he kisses her nape. There's always this, is one of his remaining thoughts. And then: there's only this. And at last, faintly, falling: this day's over.[7]

It is a moving ending. Bourgeois England is secure, at least for the time being, behind its solid front door. Perowne is shown to be a moderate man, a man capable of a quiet act of altruism without any religious justification. His reward is not resurrection and eternal life, but the warm body of a beautiful and clever woman. What man could want for more? Early in the book, the author quotes Darwin: 'There is grandeur in this view of life'.[8] Perhaps this fragrant nesting down is all we can aspire to, at the end of the day – for those of us who can afford silk pyjamas and scent.

Saturday is a much more intelligent book than either *The God Delusion* or *God Is Not Great*, but it covers all the same ideas and arguments. Perowne is reading *The Origin of Species*. His garden is his 'own corner'[9] of London, and it is a shrine to the Enlightenment and its achievements:

an eighteenth-century dream bathed and embraced by modernity, by street light from above, and from below by fibre-optic cables, and cool fresh water coursing down pipes, and sewage borne away in an instant of forgetting.[10]

The tediously long passages on neurosurgery are not just McEwan showing off. They are making the point that we are highly complex animals whose behaviour and emotions are dominated by chemicals in our brains. The book suggests that we should look no further than this to explain the range of human emotions from love and altruism to violence and fury.

Perowne is a fictional character, but he brings to mind Terry Eagleton's description of Dawkins, if we substitute London's Fitzrovia for North Oxford. Eagleton says of Dawkins that his opinions are those of

> a readily identifiable kind of English middle-class liberal rationalist. Reading Dawkins, who occasionally writes as though 'Thou still unravish'd bride of quietness' is a mighty funny way to describe a Grecian urn, one can be reasonably certain that he would not be Europe's greatest enthusiast for Foucault, psychoanalysis, agitprop, Dadaism, anarchism or separatist feminism. All of these phenomena, one imagines, would be as distasteful to his brisk, bloodless rationality as the virgin birth … His God-hating, then, is by no means simply the view of a scientist admirably cleansed of prejudice. It belongs to a specific cultural context. One would not expect to muster many votes for either anarchism or the virgin birth in North Oxford.[11]

Dawkins himself refers to theorists such as Foucault, Roland Barthes and Julia Kristeva as 'icons of haute francophonyism.'[12]

Saturday has the potential to be a deeply ironic novel, which might have invited reflection on the idea that, after the death of all religious visions, we are left with 'the British gods'[13] watching over the middle-class family slumbering beneath threatening skies emptied of angels but not of aeroplanes. It could also have been a profoundly unsettling existentialist novel about the challenge of living in a world without gods or promises of salvation, in the shadow of our own mortality. But its author fails to communicate that sense of paradox which is the hallmark of the best existentialist writers. His central character is too complacent in his knowledge, too secure in his environment. Perowne is a man of certainty and, like McEwan himself, he resists the ambiguity of religious doubt. Unlike the great anti-heroes of existentialist literature, he is not a man in the grip of absurdity and pathos. Although we are told that he is 'Baffled and fearful'[14] about the times he lives in, he comes across as a rather dull and unadventurous Englishman who experiences no existential dread about his place in the universe and no real thirst for knowledge beyond the closed horizons of his own scientific world. He is, in other words, quite a good character study of the new atheist temperament, at least in some of its more famous incarnations.

Saturday is threaded through with biblical motifs and images, with references to angels and gods, but these never leave the printed page and take flight because of the book's unyieldingly materialistic perspective. It is an intelligently designed novel which provides a vehicle for the author's pet beliefs, and that is why it lacks the spark of creative genius. As with most of McEwan's novels, one senses that he plots his stories and designs his characters with meticulous care, so that it is hard to believe that he is ever taken by surprise or caught off guard by the worlds he has brought into being. There is something a little robotic about the way his characters think and behave, because at no time do they quite break free of the author's intentions. (I would exempt *Atonement* from this criticism, but this is not the place for an extended discussion of McEwan's writing.)

Shortly after reading *Saturday*, I read Zadie Smith's romping novel *On Beauty*, which is loosely based on E. M. Forster's *Howard's End*. Smith's characters surge into life, and one has the sense that they are not compliant enough to serve the demands of a tidy and coherent plot. Her book is a bitter-sweet comedy about love and loss, about knowledge and values and meaning. Unlike McEwan's representation of orderly family life, Smith celebrates the love that is to be found in the midst of chaos and disorder. She offers no tidy ending of domestic bliss, however uneasy. Instead, she leaves us where much great fiction leaves us – with the ending unknown, but with an intimation of the subtle hope of beauty and love in the face of the inevitability of death and decay.

I am edging towards the suggestion that divine creativity might be more like Zadie Smith's kind of creativity than Ian McEwan's. Something risky, experimental, not quite in control of its material, capable of giving rise to characters who leap off the page and subvert the author's intentions. God as a creative genius rather than an intelligent designer. The author of life as a black postcolonial woman, perhaps, rather than as a white establishment Englishman. But we'll come back to these suggestions later.

'The long day's journey of the Saturday'

I don't know if McEwan is familiar with George Steiner's book on literature and transcendence, *Real Presences*, but I suspect that the novel's title is taken from Steiner's exploration of the significance of Saturday for the times we live in. I want to quote Steiner at length, as he ushers in the closing reflections of this book. Here is what he writes:

> There is one particular day in Western history about which neither historical record nor myth nor Scripture make report. It is a Saturday. And it has become the longest of days. We know of that Good Friday which Christianity holds to have been that of the Cross. But the non-Christian, the atheist, knows of it as well … We know, ineluctably, of the pain, of the failure of love, of the solitude which are our history and private fate. We know too about Sunday. To the Christian, that day signifies an intimation, both assured and precarious, both evident and beyond comprehension, of resurrection, of a justice and a love that have conquered death. If we are non-Christians or non-believers, we know of

that Sunday in precisely analogous terms … The lineaments
of that Sunday carry the name of hope (there is no word less
deconstructible).

But ours is the long day's journey of the Saturday. Between
suffering, aloneness, unutterable waste on the one hand and
the dream of liberation, of rebirth on the other … The appre-
hensions and figurations in the play of metaphysical imagining, in the poem and the music, which tell of pain and of
hope, of the flesh which is said to taste of ash and of the spirit which is said to have the savour of fire, are always
Sabbatarian. They have risen out of an immensity of waiting
which is that of man. Without them, how could we be
patient?[15]

There are profound resonances between Steiner's reflections and
McEwan's novel. However, if McEwan has read *Real Presences*, his
allegiance to the new atheism shows that he has ignored Steiner's
argument, for Steiner insists that 'a wager on transcendence'[16] is the
necessary condition for all forms of artistic expression. This means
that 'It is a theology, explicit or suppressed, masked or avowed,
substantive or imaged, which underwrites the presumption of
creativity, of signification in our encounters with text, with music,
with art.'[17] Art in its broadest form is, according to Steiner, an
encounter with the freedom of the other, and the possibility of that
encounter is a willingness to position ourselves before God. After
the twentieth century, 'one of the cruellest, most wasteful of hope
in human record', the artistic endeavour is a form of 'shadow-
boxing' in the absence of God, a 'negative theism, a peculiarly vivid
sense of God's absence or, to be precise, of His recession.'[18]

The dramatic climax of McEwan's book focuses on Daisy's
recitation of one of the most famous of all poems about the loss
of faith: Matthew Arnold's 'On Dover Beach'. Here, we read of the
'melancholy, long, withdrawing roar' of the Sea of Faith, which
leaves us

> as on a darkling plain
> Swept with confused alarms of struggle and flight,

Where ignorant armies clash by night.

In a world torn apart by ignorant armies, what glimmers of salvation are to be found in the arts?

Art, freedom and humanity

Art has no power to change the world, for great art exerts a different kind of power – not the power of violence and revolution, but the potent vulnerability of imagination and memory, of mourning and of hope. Art is powerless in itself, and yet it stands as an obstacle in the path of every destructive and oppressive force. That is why every tyrant and ideologue has sought to silence or to control the artistic imagination. This battle against art witnesses to the nature of the relationship between art and freedom, for it suggests that there is an inseparable link between the spirit of freedom and the creative impulse. Those who would destroy human freedom must first destroy the art which expresses that freedom in its most perfect form.

Art is a form of expression in which the quest for truth breaks free of the struggle for domination. It opens up spaces for the exploration of truth in a different idiom, in which many visions and voices can co-exist. The Czech writer Milan Kundera makes the point that the word 'history' changes its meaning in different contexts, so that the history of art is not the same as the history of science. 'The history of science has the nature of progress', but art is different: 'Applied to art, the notion of history has nothing to do with progress; it does not imply improvement, amelioration, an ascent; it resembles a journey undertaken to explore unknown lands and chart them.'[19]

In these imaginary journeys to unknown lands, we exist not in competition but in creative co-operation with one another. We can all be seekers after truth along the pathways of art. Of course, art alone will not feed the hungry nor visit those in prison nor clothe the naked, but it may answer to a much deeper need than our basic physical needs. It may be of the very essence of our humanity that we hunger for beauty as much as we hunger for food, and those who seek to do good in the world must be providers of beauty as well as of food to those in need.

There is an extract from a diary in London's Imperial War museum, written by Lieutenant Colonel Mervin Willett Gonin DSO, one of the first British soldiers to enter Bergen-Belsen, the Nazi death camp:

> It was shortly after the British Red Cross arrived – though it may have no connection – that a very large quantity of lipstick arrived. This was not at all what we men wanted, we were screaming for hundreds and thousands of other things and I don't know who asked for lipstick.
>
> I wish so much that I could discover who did it. It was the action of genius, sheer unadulterated brilliance. I believe nothing did more for these internees than the lipstick. Women lay in bed with no sheets and no nightie but with scarlet red lips, you saw them wandering about with nothing but a blanket over their shoulders, but with scarlet red lips. I saw a woman dead on the post mortem table and clutched in her hand was a piece of lipstick.
>
> At last someone had done something to make them individuals again; they were someone, no longer merely the number tattooed on the arm. At last they could take an interest in their appearance.
>
> That lipstick started to give them back their humanity.

From Bergen-Belsen to Beijing to Bosnia to Beirut to Baghdad, creativity has marked out the space of our humanity in the midst of the worst forms of destruction, violence and oppression. As long as we can still create beauty, we are free, and as long as we are still free, we are human.

This suggests that the Christian privileging of reason as the essential characteristic which separates out the human from all other creatures is too narrow, for creativity is a more fundamental human attribute than rationality. A child rejoices in splashing paint on paper and moulding clay into shapes, long before he or she learns to reason. Even when Christian theologians talk about the creativity of God, they tend to talk in terms of rationality rather than art.[20] I am suggesting that we might shift the whole idea of creation and of the human made in the image of God away from the tyranny of reason, and locate it instead in the freedom of art.

The dreaming ape

Studies of cave paintings in sites such as Altamira and Lascaux suggest that it was the capacity for art which first marked us out as a unique species, and that this creative spark was kindled into being through the awakening of a religious imagination.[21] It was when we began to ask questions about life beyond the material horizons of our own existence, when we acquired the capacity to dream of other possibilities and to think symbolically, that we became *homo sapiens*. This lends added weight to the argument by some neuroscientists that we are 'hard-wired' for religion.[22] The human brain may be such that it has a genetic capacity for transcendence.

We are *homo creativus*, and the primal expression of our humanity takes place at the level of creativity. It is creativity which constitutes the difference between a human and an animal, between a prison and a zoo. What are the implications of this for the Christian understanding of what it means to be human made in the image of God?

Nowhere in this book have I attempted to offer arguments for the existence of God in terms familiar to systematic theologians or philosophical rationalists. I do not find those arguments particularly interesting or persuasive. Christian theology has been hamstrung by its preoccupation with rationality, at the expense of other ways of speaking intelligently about God. A great work of art or music is not rational in the way that a philosophical argument or a scientific experiment is rational, but it is charged with meaning and capable of communicating a potent sense of transcendence and truth. Steiner argues that this cannot help but open our minds to eternity and to God, even if that is an absent, unknowable God more like the character in Samuel Beckett's

Waiting for Godot than the all too knowable and assured God of religious fundamentalisms.

Christian authorities have always had an ambivalent attitude towards the power of the arts to communicate the truth of the Christian story, from the iconoclastic controversies of the early Church through the Reformation and beyond. The artistic imagination has eluded the control of theology and doctrine with their rationalising and authoritarian tendencies, and it still lays before us a more visceral and compelling account of the story of Christ than those theological tomes gathering dust in libraries which cater to a bygone era.

While the men of God have glowered disapprovingly on human sexuality, Christian art and music have given expression to a potent eroticism in their celebration of human and divine love. While the men of God have written the maternal feminine face of God out of the texts of theology, she smiles and weeps and sings and laughs with us in the face of a million Madonnas. While the men of God have refused the imaginative capacity of wisdom to romp playfully amidst the creative endeavours of the human species, we have always discovered in the caves of our minds the whispers and seductions of a different God, luring us into forbidden fantasies of desire and dread, enticing our spirits into sublime manifestations of hope and transformation.

David Lewis-Williams, in his study of cave art, speaks of a 'creative explosion' in the Upper Palaeolithic period some 40,000 to 10,000 years ago, which connects the caves of France, South Africa and Australia, and which suggests a species-wide transformation in the evolutionary process.[23] This is a short time-scale in evolutionary terms, but it is still difficult for us to imagine in terms of human experience. Maybe though, the religious awakening which flashed through a whole species also happens in each individual consciousness when we experience an awakening to transcendence. Here is how St Augustine describes that experience, addressing God as 'beauty so old and so new':

And see, you were within and I was in the external world and sought you there, and in my unlovely state I plunged into those lovely created things which you made. You were with me, and I was not with you. The lovely things kept me far from you, though if they did not have their existence in you, they had no existence at all. You called and cried out loud and shattered my deafness. You were radiant and resplendent, you put to flight my blindness. You were fragrant, and I drew in my breath and now pant after you. I tasted you, and I feel but hunger and thirst for you. You touched me, and I am set on fire to attain the peace which is yours.[24]

To be human is to be a species which has been set on fire with longing for peace. It is to be a creature endowed with consciousness, capable of turning from an exterior world of lovely things to an interior world wherein we discover God in the form of a hunger and thirst that nothing can satisfy. It is this longing, this 'peculiarly vivid sense of God's absence', to use Steiner's words, which is the source of our own creative capacity. Faced with a world of 'lovely created things' which cannot satisfy that inner desire, we too have become creators of beauty, co-creators with God invited to participate in the ongoing creativity of making the world anew.

Intelligent designer or creative genius?

While cosmology invites reflection on human consciousness and therefore on God, intelligent design theorists argue that evidence of God can be found in the order of creation which defies some aspects of the theory of evolution. Evolutionary theorists such as Dawkins argue that the randomness of the evolutionary process, the fact that it is a process of trial and error which is often wasteful and futile, is evidence against an intelligent designer. Yet I want to come back to my earlier suggestion that we might think of God not as an intelligent designer but as a creative genius, in which case there may be considerably more freedom and more trial and error woven into the universe than we normally recognise.

Creativity is not the same as design. Design implies a process of planning which is functional and controlled. It is not an end in itself but a means to an end. The plot and characters of *Saturday* are driven by the author's desire to make a point, subtle and incisive no doubt, but it is as much a book about McEwan as it is about Henry Perowne. Zadie Smith's *On Beauty* has something of creative genius in its energy and vitality, in its failure to control the plot, and in the sense that the characters have acquired a life beyond the author's intentions. The book is too long, and there are many superfluous passages where one senses that the young author has been carried away by the joy of writing. It leaves us up in the air at the end, wondering about possible outcomes, and yet with a vivid sense that we 'know' Kiki and Howard and their unruly family. We care about them. We want it all to end well for them.

When we talk about God's creation, we need to understand ourselves as characters in a work of creative genius rather than as a unique kind of godlike being in an intelligently designed universe. Design seeks to eliminate risk, because it is concerned with efficiency, function and purpose. Creativity is measured by the risk it is willing to take, for the greater the creative endeavour, the greater the risk of failure. That is why there is ultimately no great creative work which does not involve suffering. All art expresses sorrow and beauty, loss and desire, tragedy and hope. All art stands under threat of its own destruction, of imploding under the weight of meaning it is asked to bear. In Christian art, the weaving together of nativity and crucifixion, the cross which casts its shadow over the crib, the mother of sorrows who hovers over the virgin's joy, all speak to us of the inseparability of suffering and hope in the story of God's creative love for humankind.

But Christianity invites us to go further still, for it tells us that we are endowed with a freedom beyond any created freedom, for we have within us the infinite freedom of God. I suggested that characters in a great work of fiction acquire a freedom beyond the author's intention. The writing process involves a mysterious moment when the characters begin to tell their own story, and there is a sense in which the story takes over, and the author follows where it leads.

But however vivid the characters in a story might become, they are still the product of the author's mind and, if the author died before the story was finished, the story would not write its own ending.

Yet Christianity suggests a creative process in which God does what no human author can do, for God steps inside the story and becomes one of the characters. When the plot gets out of hand and violence threatens to unravel the whole creative endeavour, the creator takes the most radical possible risk in becoming wholly identified with the work of creation. Christian theologians have continued to project images of virile masculinity onto God in the language of omnipotence and omniscience, but at the heart of the Christian faith is a different story about God – a God of vulnerability, love and compassion, who surrenders all claims to divine power by becoming the child in Mary's womb and the tortured man on the cross. This is a story in which the characters are given a freedom which no fictional character ever had, for they have the freedom to kill the author of the story in which they find themselves. That is why the incarnation and death of Christ ushers in a whole new way of understanding the relationship between human freedom and divine creativity, but Christianity may have been premature in thinking it knows how the story will end.

In the earliest versions of Mark's Gospel, believed to be the earliest of all the Gospel accounts of Christ's life, there is no account of the resurrection. Even the Bible, then, is indeterminate as to the ending of its own story. The Christian story is not yet finished, and it offers many possible endings. It might, as Paul Davies suggests, find its story dissolved into a sense of mysticism associated with quantum physics and the mystery of consciousness. It might find itself radically transformed through its encounters with other religions, and through the questions and challenges that feminists and non-Westerners pose to its traditional values and beliefs. Nietzsche offers another possible ending. We can murder God and become the authors of our own story, the Superman strutting the world's stage. This is the omnipotent, omniscient subject which the new atheism also claims to offer, with its faith in the power of science and reason to enable us to know and control the world.

Beyond the death of God

As creatures no longer conscious of being created, would we ourselves still be *homo creativus*, a creative ape after the murder of God? Might this mark another flashpoint in human evolution, another stage in the human story beyond God? Maybe there would in time be a *Mesozoic Symphony* or an *Evolution Oratorio*, or maybe there would be a different species altogether, a species no longer able to make music at all. This would be a rational species, a species capable of feats of science and technology beyond any we can yet imagine, a species which might indeed have pushed against 'the limits of understanding' and discovered 'that there are no limits'.[25] But would we still make music and art, poetry and sculpture, shaping our innermost mystery in the language of beauty and prayer? To quote Steiner again:

> where God's presence is no longer a tenable supposition and where His absence is no longer a felt, indeed overwhelming weight, certain dimensions of thought and creativity are no longer attainable … It is only when the question of the existence or non-existence of God will have lost all actuality, it is only when, as logical positivism teaches, it will have been recognized and felt to be strictly nonsensical, that we shall inhabit a scientific-secular world. Educated opinion has, to a greater or lesser degree, entered upon this new freedom. For it, emptiness is precisely and only that.[26]

For new atheists such as Dawkins, the emptiness is only a temporary gap in knowledge that will eventually be filled by science. To attempt to sculpt alternative, God-shaped meanings within that emptiness is to behave irrationally and to invite moral condemnation. But for most people in the world, the emptiness points beyond itself to something more mysterious, something that science will never explain. We are those who choose to remain in the mystery of the unfinished story, inhabitants of the 'immensity of waiting' which is Saturday.

For some, that waiting is a time of promise. There is sorrow but not futility in life. Love is stronger than death, and God does not abandon us to the sealed tomb and the eternal abyss. We are invited to look beyond the torture of Friday's cross, beyond the silence of Saturday's tomb, to the newness of life in the garden of Sunday. For others, Sunday will never compensate for Friday's horror. The story must end in desolation, for we cannot and will not forgive God. These are the questions which shape the forms of literary atheism which I considered in the last chapter, but they are, as Steiner suggests, quite different from the hubristic confidence of scientific rationalism. They are 'shadow-boxing' with God, a form of wrestling with God's absence which acknowledges that we must resist any explanation which would cover over that absence and render it meaningless. The abyss, like hope, bears the shape of God's absence.

Religious and atheist fundamentalisms refuse God's perceptible absence. For the religious fundamentalist, the certainty of God's presence crowds out every question and every doubt with the weight of an unbearable force. Because there is no freedom in such a God, there can be no freedom in the human either. The creativity of faith which is discovered in freedom is thus overwhelmed by destructive violence which feeds on the mind's captivity to the tyranny of a God made in the image of human power. But the new atheism also resists the creativity of freedom which is discovered in the haunting absence of God. In narrowing down the meaning of human life to the most reductive materialist criteria, it refuses any meaningful space to the diversity and plurality of stories by which humankind has shaped its meanings around the eloquent absence which surrounds us.

Contrary to the claims of atheists such as Dawkins and Dennett, faith goes hand in hand with a willingness to question, to challenge and to sift out genuine mystery from mystification, whether in the realm of science or art. At its most profound, faith is not an answer to life's questions but a willingness to inhabit the darkness of knowing that there are some things we cannot know. I always tell students beginning a degree in theology and religious studies, that if they graduate thinking that they know the answers, they have been badly taught. If they graduate with some understanding of the right questions to ask, they have been well taught.

Far from being a form of docile compliance in the face of divine omnipotence and priestly power, faith has the capacity to become a continuous confrontation between the human and the divine, in which we ourselves play judge and jury to God. In an extraordinary series of written responses to questions posed by an Italian journalist, Pope John Paul II acknowledged the questions which authors such as Dostoyevsky, Kafka and Camus posed with regard to the possible futility of faith. Here is what he went on to write:

> God created man as rational and free, thereby placing Himself under man's judgment. *The history of salvation is also the history of man's continual judgment of God.* Not only of man's questions and doubts but of his actual judgment of God.

He goes on to situate this judgement in the context of 'the scandal of the cross':

> Could it have been different? Could God have *justified Himself* before human history, so full of suffering, without placing Christ's Cross at the center of that history? Obviously, one response could be that God does not need to justify Himself to man. It is enough that He is omnipotent … But God, who besides being Omnipotence is Wisdom and – to repeat once again – Love, desires to justify Himself to mankind … God is not someone who remains only outside of the world, content to be in Himself all-knowing and omnipotent. *His wisdom and omnipotence are placed, by free choice, at the service of creation.* If suffering is present in the history of humanity, one understands why His omnipotence was manifested *in the omnipotence of humiliation on the Cross*. The scandal of the Cross remains the key to the interpretation of the great mystery of suffering, which is so much a part of the history of mankind.[27]

Pope John Paul II's words are unlikely to persuade those who are not already willing to entertain the possible truthfulness of the Christian story, but they surely cannot be dismissed as the rantings of a religious bigot committed to blind faith. They suggest a nuanced, attentive groping towards truth, by a man who was a philosopher as well as a pope, and who had experienced first-hand some of the greatest horrors of the twentieth century, first under Nazism and then under communism.

The creative imagination is the true home of faith. It occupies that furthest extreme where words creep to the very fringes of silence, and life tiptoes along the edges of death. In the darkest recesses of the imagination's cave, the human spirit shapes its questions about otherness, death and love in the delicate traceries of art, the haunted longings of music, the poetic shaping of silence.

Artistic and scientific knowledge, religion and rationality, are not competitors for the same space in the spectrum of human wisdom. Science cannot provide the answers to every human question, for scientific knowledge does not encompass all the ways of knowing that human consciousness is capable of. Art and beauty, creativity and imagination, provide a connecting narrative between the endeavours of science and the endeavours of religion. They invite us into conversations without violence, dialogue without closure.

The no-thinglyness of God

AC Grayling is a dedicated follower of the new atheism. I quoted Grayling's play, *On Religion*, in the Introduction, and I want to return to that now – to the idea that 'kindness, that's the big one, not love.'

In an interview prior to his co-writing of the play, Grayling said, 'I assumed we were going to slaughter the religious folk.' Then he admits, 'I quickly learned that good theatre needs to give both sides of the argument the best shot and trust the audience to make up their own minds.'[28] It is interesting that a self-confessed rationalist assumes that 'slaughter' is an appropriate way for a philosopher to deal with intellectual arguments, while giving both sides of the argument is the prerogative of the dramatist. It is an unintentional admission by Grayling of the extent to which the modern attack on religion by atheists has abandoned any pretence at reasoned argument and debate in going for the jugular every time.

There is a lesson to be learned from this. When Grayling was working on the play, he consulted religious as well as secular thinkers. As a result, the play offers a thought-provoking and by no means conclusive reflection on the relationship between scientific atheism, represented by a female Dawkins-figure called Grace, and liberal theology as represented by Grace's son, Tom. A sermon preached by Tom suggests the clear influence of theological consultants on the shaping of the script:

> For most religions the other is the god. But I think that we've got to stop thinking about God as a proper name, for a *thing*, as if the word God refers to some sort of object in the universe … God cannot be the creator of everything and something on the list of things being created … [T]he great story of what God is like in the Bible, it seems to me is the story of the Golden Calf and Moses going up the mountain. So you get the mountain, you get Moses going up the mountain – *this is the great story of religion I think* – Moses travels up the mountain. The higher he gets up the mountain, it gets cloudier and cloudier, so the nearer to God, the nearer to this other he gets less and less able to see less able to know his way about, okay, down below, okay, what's happening down below is that all of them are making God into this thing, a Golden Calf … So you've got this contrast, by the journey to the real divine which involves lostness, y'know, doubt, not being able to see, not being able to grasp this, this, this, y'know, this notion of God, no-thinglyness. And yet, at the bottom of the mountain there's this sort of real *thing* and they all bow down to it. But it's a con. And the whole story is saying that God isn't like any thing we expect. That's why it pisses me off when the atheists keep on trying to tell me what sort of God

I believe in … Because they want me to believe in a thing called God. But I don't. I don't believe God is a thing. I just believe in God.[29]

In this stumbling, hesitant monologue, there is a richer theology than one might discover by wading through any number of theological tomes. All theological language, all mysticism and prayer, all art, music and literature, are ways of trying – and failing – to express the 'no-thinglyness' of God.

Grayling's play shows us that, when we move beyond the sphere of polemics and conflict, we discover a space of encounter and engagement where both sides can speak and be heard. The imperative of art – of all art, including theatre – is not to defeat other ways of knowing but to explore the unknown, to spread the net of understanding a little wider. In this time when both religious and atheist extremists are seeking to close off these spaces of encounter, discovery and exploration with their conflicting versions of truth, we urgently need to rediscover the forgotten art of conversation, the quiet and courteous voice of wisdom, and the value of kindness in our dealings with one another.

There is a song which tells us, 'What the world needs now, is love sweet love', but perhaps Grayling's character, Ruth, is correct when she speaks of the dangerous power of love: 'I'm less sure about love these days, less sure that it's the most important thing because it's just too much sometimes. Just too unmanangeable.'[30] What the world needs now is not love but kindness, for there is a humility and modesty in kindness. It allows us to live and let live, not in an attitude of indifference but in an attitude of attentive concern for the needs of the other, and by an ethos which seeks to do no harm.

Arnold's poetic epitaph to religion can be a form of prayer, which invites atheists and believers alike to attend to the soft voice of reason, as we stand on the shore and listen fearfully to the long roar of an incoming tide bringing with it who knows what fearful flotsam and debris on its mighty wave? But as we stand waiting through this long Saturday, let us not forget the miracle and the mystery that we are here at all. Paul Davies writes:

> We, who are children of the universe – animated stardust –
> can nevertheless reflect on the nature of that same universe,
> even to the extent of glimpsing the rules on which it runs.
> How we have become linked into this cosmic dimension is a
> mystery. Yet the linkage cannot be denied … We are truly
> meant to be here.[31]

I began with a poem by Elizabeth Jennings, who writes of 'dust
with a living mind'. Beyond the confrontations of science and
religion, the Catholic poet and the agnostic cosmologist remind us
that we are motes of dust charged with mystery, and in con-
templating that mystery we discover the hope of our 'proud, torn
destinies'.

Bibliography

Ahmed, Akbar S., *Postmodernism and Islam: Predicament and Promise* (London and New York, Routledge, 2004)

Amis, Martin, 'The Voice of the Lonely Crowd', *The Guardian*, Saturday, 1 June 2002 at http://books.guardian.co.uk/review/story/0,12084,725608,00.html

Amis, Martin, 'The Age of Horrorism', *The Observer*, Sunday, 10 September 2006 at http://observer.guardian.co.uk/review/story/0,,1868732,00.html

Anderson, Pamela Sue, *A Feminist Philosophy of Religion* (Oxford, Blackwell, 1998)

Artigas, Mariano, Thomas F. Glick and Rafael A. Martinez, *Negotiating Darwin: The Vatican Confronts Evolution, 1877–1902* (Baltimore, John Hopkins University Press, 2006)

Augustine, *Confessions*, trans. Henry Chadwick (Oxford and New York, Oxford University Press, 1998)

Aunger, Robert (ed.), *Darwinizing Culture: The Status of Memetics as a Science* (Oxford, Oxford University Press, 2001)

Austin, Greg, Todd Kranock and Thom Oommen, *God and War: An Audit & An Explanation*, at http://news.bbc.co.uk/1/shared/spl/hi/world/04/war_audit_pdf/pdf/war_audit.pdf

Bainton, Roland H., 'The Early Church and War', *The Harvard Theological Review*, Vol. 39.3 (July 1946), pp. 189–212

Beattie, Tina, *Woman* (London and New York, Continuum, 2003)

Beauvoir, Simone de, *The Second Sex*, trans. H. M. Parshley (London, Penguin Books, 1972, first published 1949)

Behe, Michael, *Darwin's Black Box: The Biochemical Challenge to Evolution* (New York, The Free Press, 1996)

Bevan, Robert, *The Destruction of Memory: Architecture at War* (London, Reaktion Books, 2007, first published 2006)

Brainard, F. Samuel, *Reality and Religious Experience* (Pennsylvania, Pennsylvania State University Press, 2000)

Brock, Peter, *Varieties of Pacifism: A Survey from Antiquity to the Outset of the Twentieth Century* (Toronto, University of Toronto Press, 1998)

Broom, Neil, *How Blind is the Watchmaker?* (Downers Grove IL, InterVarsity Press, 2001)

Brown, Andrew, 'Dawkins the Dogmatist', *Prospect Magazine*, Issue 127, October 2006 at http://www.prospect-magazine.co.uk/article_details.php?id=7803

Bulkeley, Kelly, 'The Gospel According to Darwin: The Relevance of Cognitive Neuroscience to Religious Studies' at http://www.kellybulkeley.com/articles/article_RSR_cognitive_neurosci_review.htm

Burnham, John C., 'The Reception of Psychoanalysis in Western Cultures: An Afterword on Its Comparative History', *Comparative Studies in Society and History*, Vol. 24, No. 4, October 1982, pp. 603–10

Cahill, Lisa Sowle, *Love Your Enemies: Discipleship, Pacifism, and Just War Theory* (Minneapolis, Fortress Press, 1994)

Carroll, Lewis, *Alice's Adventures in Wonderland and Through the Looking Glass* (London, Penguin Classics, 2003, first published 1872)

Chadwick, Henry, *The Early Church*, Penguin History of the Church Vol. 1, revised edn (New York and London, Penguin Books, 1994)

Choi Hee An and Katheryn Pfisterer Darr (eds.), *Engaging the Bible: Critical Readings from Contemporary Women* (Philadelphia PA, Fortress Press, 2006)

Clayton, Philip (ed.), *The Oxford Handbook of Religion and Science* (Oxford, Oxford University Press, 2006)

Collins, Francis S., *The Language of God: A Scientist Presents Evidence for Belief* (New York and London, Free Press, 2006)

Cornwell, John, 'A Christmas thunderbolt for the arch-enemy of religion', *The Sunday Times*, 24 December 2006 at http://www.timesonline.co.uk/tol/news/article1264152.ece

Cornwell, John, *Darwin's Angel: A Seraphic Response to 'The God Delusion'* (London, Profile, 2007)

Cornwell, John, 'A Jaundiced Catalogue of Scandals', *The Tablet*, 16 June 2007

D'Aquili, E. G. and A. B. Newberg, 'The neuropsychological basis of religions, or why God won't go away', *Zygon* 33 (1998), pp. 187–201

Darwin, Charles, *The Origin of Species* (New York, Gramercy Books, 1979, first published 1859)

Darwin, Charles, *The Descent of Man and Selection in Relation to Sex* (London, John Murray, 1901, first published 1871)

Davies, Paul, *God & the New Physics* (London, Penguin Books, 1990, first published 1983)

Davies, Paul, *The Mind of God: Science and the Search for Ultimate Meaning* (London, Penguin Books, 2006, first published 1993)

Davis, Percival and Dean H. Kenyon, *Of Pandas and People: The Central Question of Biological Origins* (Richardson, TX, The Foundation for Thought and Ethics, 1989)

Dawkins, Richard, *The Selfish Gene*, 3rd edn (Oxford, Oxford University Press, 2006, first published 1976)

Dawkins, Richard, *The God Delusion* (London, Toronto, Sydney, Auckland, Johannesburg, Bantam Press, 2006)

Dawkins, Richard, 'Bible Belter', *The Times Literary Supplement,* September 5 2007 at http://tls.timesonline.co.uk/article/0,,25349-2649121,00.html

Dembski, William A., *Intelligent Design: The Bridge Between Science and Theology* (Downers Grove IL, InterVarsity Press, 1999)

Dembski, William A. and Michael Ruse (eds.), *Debating Design: From Darwin to*

DNA (Cambridge, Cambridge University Press, 2004)

Dembski, William A., 'Is Intelligent Design a Form of Natural Theology?' at http://www.designinference.com/documents/2001.03.ID_as_nat_theol.htm

Dembski, William A., 'Allen Orr in the *New Yorker* – A Response' at http://www.uncommondescent.com/evolution/allen-orr-in-the-new-yorker-a-brief-response/

Dennett, Daniel C., *Darwin's Dangerous Idea: Evolution and the Meanings of Life* (London and New York, Penguin Books, 1996, first published 1995)

Dennett, Daniel C., *Breaking the Spell: Religion as a Natural Phenomenon* (London, Allen Lane, 2006)

Derrida, Jacques, *Deconstruction in a Nutshell: A Conversation with Jacques Derrida*, edited with a commentary by John D. Caputo (New York, Fordham University Press, 1996)

Desmond, Adrian and James Moore, *Darwin: The Life of a Tormented Evolutionist* (New York and London, W. W. Norton & Company, 1994, first published 1991)

Donovan, Peter, *Interpreting Religious Experience* (London, Sheldon Press, 1979)

Dostoyevsky, Fyodor, *The Brothers Karamazov* (London and New York, Penguin Books, 2003, first published 1880)

Draper, John William, *History of the Conflict between Religion and Science* (Virginia, University of Virginia Library, Electronic Text Center, published 1874) at http://etext.virginia.edu/toc/modeng/public/DraHist.html

Eagleton, Terry, 'Lunging, Flailing, Mispunching', *The London Review of Books*, Vol. 28, No. 20, October 2006

Easlea, Brian, 'An Introduction to the History and Social Studies of Science: A Seminar Course for First-Year Science Students', *Science Studies*, Vol. 3, No. 2 (April 1973), pp. 185–209

Easlea, Brian, *Witch Hunting, Magic and the New Philosophy: An Introduction to Debates of the Scientific Revolution 1450–1750* Hemel Hempstead, Prentice Hall/Harvester Wheatsheaf, 1980)

Ehrenreich, Barbara and Deirdre English, *Complaints and Disorders: The Sexual Politics of Sickness* (New York, The Feminist Press, 1973)

Ellegard, Alvar, *Darwin and the General Reader: The Reception of Darwin's Theory of Evolution in the British Periodical Press, 1859–1872* (Chicago, University of Chicago Press, 1990, first published 1958)

Ellul, Jacques, *Violence: Reflections from a Christian Perspective* (London, Mowbrays, 1978)

Ellwood, Robert S., *Mysticism and Religion*, 2nd edn (New York and London, Seven Bridges Press, 1999, first published 1980)

Elshtain, Jean Bethke (ed.), *Just War Theory* (Oxford, Basil Blackwell, 1992)

Ferguson, John, *War and Peace in the World's Religions* (London, Sheldon Press, 1977)

Feuerbach, Ludwig, *The Essence of Christianity*, trans. George Eliot (London, Prometheus Books, 1989, first published 1854)

Fields, Jill, '"Fighting the Corsetless Evil": Shaping Corsets and Culture, 1900–1930', *Journal of Social History*, Vol. 33, No. 2 (Winter 1999), pp. 355–84

Fiorenza, Elisabeth Schüssler, *Bread Not Stone: The Challenge of Feminist Biblical Interpretation* (Boston, Beacon Press, 1995)

Fitzgerald, Timothy, *The Ideology of Religious Studies* (New York and Oxford, Oxford University Press, 2000)

Forman, Robert K. C. (ed.), *The Problem of Pure Consciousness: Mysticism and Philosophy* (Oxford, Oxford University Press, 1990)

Foucault, Michel, *Power/Knowledge: Selected Interviews & Other Writings 1972-1977*, ed. Colin Gordon (New York, Pantheon Books, 1980)

Foucault, Michel, *The Order of Things: An Archaeology of the Human Sciences*, trans. Alan Sheridan (London and New York, Routledge, 2001, first published 1966)

Frazer, James G., *The Golden Bough: The Magic Art and the Evolution of Kings*, 2 vols. (London, Macmillan and Co., 1911)

Frend, W. H. C., *The Rise of Christianity* (Philadelphia, Fortress Press, 1992, first published 1965)

Freud, Sigmund, 'The Future of an Illusion' in *Civilization, Society and Religion*, trans. James Strachey, ed. Albert Dickson, The Penguin Freud Library, Vol. 12 (London, Penguin Books, 1991, first published 1928)

Fyfe, Aileen, *Science and Salvation: Evangelical Popular Science Publishing in Victorian Britain* (Chicago and London, University of Chicago Press, 2004)

Garwood, Christine, *Flat Earth: The History of an Infamous Idea* (London, Macmillan, 2007)

Glick, Thomas F. (ed.), *The Comparative Reception of Darwinism* (Austin and London, University of Texas Press, 1975)

Goldacre, Ben, 'Opinions from the medical fringe should come with a health warning', *The Guardian,* Saturday, 24 February 2007 at http://www.guardian.co.uk/life/badscience/story/0,,2020306,00.html

Golden, Richard M., 'American Perspectives in the European Witch Hunts', *The History Teacher*, Vol. 30, No. 4 (August 1977), pp. 406–26

Gordon, Mike and A C Grayling, *On Religion* (London, Oberon Books, 2006)

Gould, Stephen Jay, *The Flamingo's Smile* (New York, W. W. Norton and Co., 1985)

Gould, Stephen Jay, *Wonderful Life: the Burgess Shale and the Nature of History* (London, Vintage, 2000)

Gould, Stephen Jay, *Rock of Ages: Science and Religion in the Fullness of Life* (London, Vintage, 2002, first published 2001)

Grand, Steve, *Creation: Life and How To Make It* (London: Weidenfield & Nicolson, 2000)

Gray, John, *Black Mass: Apocalyptic Religion and the Death of Utopia* (London, Allen Lane, 2007)

Grayling, A C, 'Through the Looking Glass', *The New Humanist*, Vol. 122, Issue 4 (July/August 2007) at http://newhumanist.org.uk/1423

Green, Toby, *Inquisition: The Reign of Fear* (London, Macmillan, 2007)

Hamer, Dean H., *The God Gene: How Faith is Hardwired into our Genes* (New York, Anchor, 2005)

Hannan, Patrick J., *Serendipity, Luck and Wisdom in Research* (Lincoln NE, iUniverse.com, 2006)

Harding, Sandra, *The Science Question in Feminism* (Milton Keynes, Open

University Press, 1986)

Harding, Sandra (ed.), *Is Science Multicultural? Postcolonialisms, Feminisms, and Epistemologies* (Bloomington and Indianapolis, Indiana University Press, 1998)

Hari, Johann, 'A battler beyond belief', *The Independent*, Friday, 15 June 2007

Harris, Sam, *The End of Faith: Religion, Terror, and the Future of Reason* (New York and London, W. W. Norton and Company, 2004)

Harris, Sam, *Letter to a Christian Nation* (New York, Alfred A. Knopf, 2006)

Hauerwas, Stanley, *Against the Nations: War and Survival in a Liberal Society* (Minneapolis, Winston Press, 1985)

Hauerwas, Stanley, *Dispatches from the Front: Theological Engagements with the Secular* (Durham North Carolina, Duke University Press, 1995)

Haught, J. F., *God After Darwin: A Theology of Evolution* (Westview, Colorado, Westview Press, 2000)

Hay, David, *Something There: The Biology of the Human Spirit* (London, Darton, Longman & Todd, 2006)

Hazlett, Ian, 'War and Peace in Christianity' in Perry Schmidt-Leukel (ed.), *War and Peace in the World Religions*, The Gerald Weisfeld Lectures 2003 (London, SCM Press, 2004), pp. 99–147

Hedges, Chris, 'False gods', *New Statesman*, 4 June 2007, at http://www.new statesman.com/200706040045

Hick, John, *The New Frontier of Religion and Science: Religious Experience, Neuroscience, and the Transcendent* (London, Palgrave Macmillan, 2006)

Himes, Kenneth R., Lisa Sowle Cahill, Charles E. Curran, David Hollenbach and Thomas A. Shannon (eds.), *Modern Catholic Social Teaching: Commentaries and Interpretations* (Washington DC, Georgetown University Press, 2005)

Hitchens, Christopher, 'Pious Nonsense: the Unholy "Christian" Case against War' at http://www.slate.com/id/2079860/

Hitchens, Christopher, *God Is Not Great: The Case Against Religion* (London, Atlantic Books, 2007); *God Is Not Great: How Religion Poisons Everything* (New York, Twelve Books, Hachette Book Group, 2007)

Holmes, Rachel, *The Hottentot Venus: The Life and Death of Saartjie Baartman (Born 1789 – Buried 2002)* (London, Bloomsbury Publishing, 2007)

Hrdy, Sarah Blaffer, *Mother Nature: Maternal Instincts & The Shaping of the Species* (London, Vintage, 2000, first published 1999)

Huxley, T. H., *Collected Essays*, Vol. II (London, Macmillan, 1894)

Idinopulos, Thomas A., 'The Mystery of Suffering in the Art of Dostoevsky, Camus, Wiesel, and Grünewald', *Journal of the American Academy of Religion*, Vol. XLIII (1) (1975), pp. 51–61

Irigaray, Luce, *Speculum of the Other Woman*, trans. Gillian C. Gill (Ithaca NY, Cornell University Press, 1985, first published 1974)

James, William, *The Varieties of Religious Experience*, ed. Martin Marty (New York, Penguin, 1982, first published 1902)

Jantzen, Grace, *Becoming Divine: Towards a Feminist Philosophy of Religion* (Manchester, Manchester University Press, 1988)

John Paul II, Pope, Message to Pontifical Academy of Sciences, 22 October 1996, available online at the website of the Catholic Information Network:

http://www.cin.org/jp2evolu.html

John Paul II, Pope, *Crossing the Threshold of Hope*, trans. Jenny and Martha McPhee (London, Jonathan Cape, 1994)

Johnson, Phillip E., *Darwin on Trial* (Downers Grove IL, InterVarsity Press, 1993)

Jones, James W., *Terror and Transformation: The Ambiguity of Religion in Psychoanalytic Perspective* (London and New York, Routledge, 2002)

Juergensmeyer, Mark, *Terror in the Mind of God* (Berkeley and Los Angeles CA and London, University of California Press, 2001, first published 2000)

Katz, Steven (ed.), *Mysticism and Language* (Oxford and New York, Oxford University Press, 1992)

Kaufmann, Walter, *Nietzsche: Philosopher, Psychologist, Antichrist*, revised edn (Princeton NJ, Chichester UK, Princeton University Press, 1975, first published 1950)

Kee, Howard Clark, *Understanding the New Testament*, 5th edn (Englewood Cliffs NJ, Prentice Hall, 1993, first published 1983)

Keller, Evelyn Fox, *Reflections on Gender and Science* (New Haven, Conn., Yale University Press, 1985)

Kuhn, Thomas S., *The Structure of Scientific Revolutions* 3rd edn (Chicago, University of Chicago Press, 1996, first published 1962)

Kukla, André, *Social Constructivism and the Philosophy of Science* (London and New York, Routledge, 2000)

Kundera, Milan, *The Curtain: An Essay in Seven Parts* (London, Faber and Faber, 2007)

Langley, Chris, *Soldiers in the Laboratory: Military involvement in science and technology – and some alternatives*, edited by Stuart Parkinson and Philip Webber, published by Scientists for Global Responsibility (SGR), January 2005, available to download at www.sgr.org.uk/ArmsControl/Soldiers_in_Lab_Report.pdf

Laqueur, Thomas, *Making Sex* (Cambridge MA, Harvard University Press, 1990)

Lash, Nicholas – details of essay from DLT

Lewis-Williams, David, *The Mind in the Cave* (London, Thames & Hudson, 2004, first published 2002)

Livingstone, David N., *Darwin's Forgotten Defenders: The Encounter Between Evangelical Theology and Evolutionary Thought* (Edinburgh, Scottish Academic Press and Grand Rapids MI, W. D. Eerdmans, 1987)

Lloyd, Genevieve, *The Man of Reason: Male and Female in Western Philosophy* (London and New York, Routledge, 1993, first published 1985)

Loughlin, Gerard, *Telling God's Story: Bible, Church and Narrative Theology* (Cambridge, Cambridge University Press, 1999, first published 1996)

Lucas, J. R., 'Wilberforce and Huxley: A Legendary Encounter', *The Historical Journal* 22, 2 (1979), pp. 313–30

Lyotard, Jean-François, *The Postmodern Condition: A Report on Knowledge* (Manchester, Manchester University Press, 1984, first published 1979)

MacIntyre, Alasdair, *Whose Justice? – Which Rationality?* (London, Gerald Duckworth & Co., 1996, first published 1988)

MacIntyre, Alasdair, *After Virtue*, new edn (London, Gerard Duckworth, 1997, first published 1981)

Maines, Rachel P., *The Technology of Orgasm: 'Hysteria,' the Vibrator, and Women's Sexual Satisfaction* (Baltimore, John Hopkins University Press, 1999)

Martin, David, *Does Christianity Cause War?* (Oxford, Clarendon Press, 1997)

Marx, Karl, *Marx: Early Political Writings*, edited and translated by Joseph O'Malley (Cambridge, Cambridge University Press, 1994)

McCutcheon, Russell T., *Manufacturing Religion: The Discourse on* Sui Generis *Religion and the Politics of Nostalgia* (Oxford and New York, Oxford University Press, 1997)

McEwan, Ian, *Saturday* (London, Jonathan Cape, 2005)

McGrath, Alister E., *Dawkins' God: Genes, Memes, and the Meaning of Life* (Oxford, Blackwell Publishing, 2004)

McGrath, Alister E. and Joanna Collicutt McGrath, *The Dawkins Delusion? Atheist Fundamentalism and the Denial of the Divine* (London, SPCK Publishing, 2007)

Merchant, Carolyn, *The Death of Nature: Women, Ecology and the Scientific Revolution* (San Francisco, HarperSanFrancisco, 1989, first published 1980)

Merritt, Stephanie, 'Have faith in the theatre', *The Observer*, Sunday, 3 December 2006, at http://arts.guardian.co.uk/features/story/0,,1962514,00.html

Midgley, Mary, *Science and Poetry* (London and New York, Routledge, 2001)

Midgley, Mary, *Evolution as a Religion: Strange Hopes and Stranger Fears* (London and New York, Routledge, 2002)

Midgley, Mary, *Myths We Live By* (London and New York, Routledge, 2003)

Milbank, John, *Theology and Social Theory: Beyond Secular Reason*, new edn (Oxford, Blackwell Publishers, 2005, first published 1990)

Miller, Kenneth, *Finding Darwin's God: A Scientist's Search for Common Ground between God and Evolution* (San Francisco, HarperCollins, 2001, first published 1999)

Moore, James R., *The Post-Darwinian Controversies: A Study of the Protestant Struggle to Come to Terms with Darwin in Great Britain and America, 1870–1900* (Cambridge and New York, Cambridge University Press, 1981, first published 1979)

Moreland, J. P. (ed.), *The Creation Hypothesis* (Downers Grove IL, InterVarsity Press, 1994)

Nietzsche, Friedrich, *The Portable Nietzsche*, edited and translated by Walter Kaufmann, new edn (London, Viking Portable Library, 1994, first published 1977)

O'Donovan, Oliver, *The Just War Revisited* (Cambridge, Cambridge University Press, 2003)

Orr, H. Allen, 'Devolution: Why intelligent design isn't', *The New Yorker*, 30 May 2005, available online at http://www.newyorker.com/archive/2005/05/30/050530fa_fact?currentPage=1

Pagels, Elaine, *Adam, Eve and the Serpent* (London, Vintage Books, 1989)

Peacocke, Arthur, *Theology for a Scientific Age*, enlarged edn (London, SCM Press, 1993, first published 1990)

Pennock, Robert T. (ed.), *Intelligent Design Creationism and Its Critics: Philosophical, Theological, and Scientific Perspectives* (Cambridge MA, MIT Press, 2001)

Petrella, Ivan (ed.), *Latin American Liberation Theology: The Next Generation*

(Maryknoll NY, Orbis Books, 2005)

Polkinghorne, John, *Belief in God in an Age of Science* (New Haven, Conn. and London, Yale University Press, 1998)

Porter, Jean, *Natural and Divine Law: Reclaiming the Tradition for Christian Ethics* (Grand Rapids, MI and Cambridge, UK, William B. Eerdmans, 1999)

Porter, Roy, 'The Body and the Mind, The Doctor and the Patient: Negotiating Hysteria', in Sander L. Gilman, Helen King, Roy Porter, G. S. Rousseau and Elaine Showalter (eds.), *Hysteria Beyond Freud* (Berkeley, Los Angeles and Oxford, University of California Press, 1993)

Ramadan, Tariq, *Western Muslims and the Future of Islam* (Oxford, Oxford University Press, 2005)

Reichbert, Gregory M., Henrik Syse and Endre Begby (eds.), *The Ethics of War: Classic and Contemporary Readings* (Oxford, Blackwell Publishing, 2006)

Rieger, Joerg, *Christ and Empire: From Paul to Postcolonial Times* (Philadelphia, Augsburg Fortress Press, 2007)

Ritvo, Lucille B., *Darwin's Influence on Freud: A Tale of Two Sciences* (New Haven, Conn. and London, Yale University Press, 1990)

Roberts, Royston M., *Serendipity: Accidental Discoveries in Science* (Chichester UK, John Wiley & Sons Inc., 1989)

Roughgarden, Joan, *Evolution's Rainbow: Diversity, Gender, and Sexuality in Nature and People* (Berkeley and Los Angeles, University of California Press, 2004)

Roughgarden, Joan, *Evolution and Christian Faith: Reflections of an Evolutionary Biologist* (Washington, Covelo and London, Island Press, 2006)

Rowland, Christopher (ed.), *The Cambridge Companion to Liberation Theology* (Cambridge, Cambridge University Press, 1999)

Rubenstein, Richard E., *Aristotle's Children: How Christians, Muslims, and Jews Rediscovered Ancient Wisdom and Illuminated the Dark Ages* (Orlando, Austin, New York, San Diego, Toronto, London, Harcourt Brace International, 2003)

Ruether, Rosemary Radford, *Sexism and God Talk*, new edn (London, SCM Press, 2002, first published 1983)

Ruse, Michael, *The Evolution-Creation Struggle* (Cambridge MA, Harvard University Press, 2005)

Russell, Letty M. (ed.), *Feminist Interpretation of the Bible* (Westminster, John Knox Press, 2004, first published 1985)

Ruthven, Malise, *Fundamentalism: The Search for Meaning* (Oxford, Oxford University Press, 2004)

Sallis, John (ed.), *Deconstruction and Philosophy: The Texts of Jacques Derrida* (Chicago, University of Chicago Press, 1987)

Spivey, Nigel, *How Art Made the World* (London, BBC Books, 2005)

Stark, Rodney, *One True God: Historical Consequences of Monotheism* (Princeton NJ, Princeton University Press, 2003, first published 2001)

Stark, Rodney, *For the Glory of God: How Monotheism Led to Reformations, Science, Witch-Hunts, and the End of Slavery* (Princeton NJ, Princeton University Press, 2004)

Stark, Rodney, *The Victory of Reason: How Christianity Led to Freedom, Capitalism, and Western Success* (New York, Random House, 2006)

Steiner, George, *Real Presences* (London and Boston, Faber and Faber, 1991, first published 1989)

Sugirtharajah, R. S., *The Bible and Empire: Postcolonial Explorations* (Cambridge, Cambridge University Press, 2005)

Sugirtharajah, R. S. (ed.), *Voices from the Margin: Interpreting the Bible in the Third World*, 3rd edn (Maryknoll NY, Orbis Books, 2006, first published 1991)

Switt, L. J., *The Early Fathers on War and Military Service*, Message of the Fathers of the Church, Vol. 19 (Wilmington DE, Glazier, 1983)

Toynbee, Polly, 'Behind the burka', *The Guardian*, Friday, 28 September 2001 at http://www.guardian.co.uk/religion/Story/0,,559537,00.html

Toynbee, Polly, 'Not in my name', *The Guardian*, Friday, 8 April 2005 at http://www.guardian.co.uk/comment/story/0,,1454850,00.html

Toynbee, Polly, 'We need to focus on this week's deaths in Iraq – they belong to us', *The Guardian*, Friday, 20 April 2007 at http://www.guardian.co.uk/commentisfree/story/0,,2061826,00.html.

Trible, Phyllis, *God and the Rhetoric of Sexuality*, new edn (London, SCM Press, 1992, first published 1978)

Trible, Phyllis, *Texts of Terror: Literary Feminist Readings of the Biblical Narratives* (Philadelphia, Augsburg Fortress Press, 1984)

Turner, Frank M., 'The Victorian Conflict Between Science and Religion: A Professional Dimension', *Isis*, 69 (3), 1978, pp. 356–76

Tylor, Edward B., *Primitive Culture: Researches into the Development of Mythology, Philosophy, Religion, Language, Art, and Custom*, 2 vols. (London, John Murray, 1920, first published 1871)

Walvin, James, *The Trader, the Owner, the Slave: Parallel Lives in the Age of Slavery* (London, Jonathan Cape, 2007)

Walzer, Michael, *Just and Unjust Wars: a Moral Argument with Historical Illustrations*, 2nd edn (New York, Basic Books, 1992, first published 1977)

Ward, Graham (ed.), *The Postmodern God: Theological Reader* (Oxford, Blackwell Publishers, 1997)

Ward, Keith, *Rational Theology and the Creativity of God* (Oxford, Basil Blackwell, 1982)

Ward, Keith, *God, Chance and Necessity* (Oxford, Oneworld Publications, 1996)

Ward, Keith, *Is Religion Dangerous?* (Oxford, Lion Hudson, 2006)

Ward, Keith, *Pascal's Fire: Scientific Faith and Religious Understanding* (Oxford, Oneworld Publications, 2006)

Wheen, Francis, *Karl Marx*, new edn (London, Fourth Estate, 2000, first published 1999)

White, Andrew Dixon, *A History of the Warfare of Science with Theology in Christendom*, 2 vols. (Kila MT, Kessinger Publishing, 2004, first published 1895)

Wicker, Brian (ed.), *Studying War – No More? From Just War to Just Peace* (Kampen, Kok Pharos, 1993)

Wiesel, Elie, *Night* (London and New York, Penguin Books, 1981, first published 1958)

Zwick, Mark and Louise, 'Pope John Paul II calls War a Defeat for Humanity: Neoconservative Iraq Just War Theories Rejected', *Houston Catholic Worker*,

Vol. XXIII, No. 4, July–August 2003, at http://www.cjd.org/paper/
jp2war.html

Notes

Introduction

1. Richard Dawkins, *The God Delusion* (London, Toronto, Sydney, Auckland, Johannesburg, Bantam Press, 2006).

2. Christopher Hitchens, *God Is Not Great: The Case Against Religion* (London, Atlantic Books, 2007). Also published as *God Is Not Great: How Religion Poisons Everything* (New York, Twelve Books, Hachette Book Group, 2007).

3. Daniel C. Dennett, *Breaking the Spell: Religion as a Natural Phenomenon* (London *et al.*, Allen Lane, 2006); Sam Harris, *The End of Faith: Religion, Terror, and the Future of Reason* (New York and London, W. W. Norton and Company, 2004) and *Letter to a Christian Nation* (New York, Alfred A. Knopf, 2006).

4. Francis S. Collins, *The Language of God: A Scientist Presents Evidence for Belief* (New York and London, Free Press, 2006); Alister E. McGrath and Joanna Collicutt McGrath, *The Dawkins Delusion? Atheist Fundamentalism and the Denial of the Divine* (London, SPCK Publishing, 2007).

5. Martin Amis, 'The Voice of the Lonely Crowd', *The Guardian*, Saturday, 1 June 2002 at http://books.guardian.co.uk/review/story/0,12084,725608,00.html.

6. Dawkins, *The God Delusion*, op. cit., p. 3.

7. Ibid., p. 6.

8. Andrew Brown, 'Dawkins the Dogmatist', *Prospect Magazine*, Issue 127, October 2006 at http://www.prospect-magazine.co.uk/article_details.php?id=7803.

9. Richard Dawkins, 'Bible Belter', *The Times Literary Supplement*, September 5 2007 at http://tls.timesonline.co.uk/article/0,,253492649121,00.html.

10. John Gray, *Black Mass: Apocalyptic Religion and the Death of Utopia* (London, Allen Lane, 2007), p. 189.

11. Hitchens, *God is Not Great*, op. cit., p. 11.

12. Terry Eagleton, 'Lunging, Flailing, Mispunching', *The London Review of Books*, Vol. 28, No. 20, October 2006.

13. For an analysis of this confrontation and the dogmatism involved on both sides of the debate, see Michael Ruse, *The Evolution-Creation Struggle* (Cambridge MA, Harvard University Press, 2005).

14. See the news report dated 28 March 2006 at the University of Minnesota website – http://www.ur.umn.edu/FMPro?-db=releases&-lay=web&-format=umnnewsreleases/releasesdetail.html&ID=2816&-Find.

15. Dennett, *Breaking the Spell*, op. cit., pp. 14–15.

16. Ibid., p. 32.

17. Ibid., p. 31.

18. Martin Amis, 'The Age of Horrorism', *The Observer*, Sunday, 10 September 2006 at http://observer.guardian.co.uk/review/story/0,,1868732,00.html.

19. See Alister E. McGrath, *Dawkins' God: Genes, Memes, and the Meaning of Life* (Oxford, Blackwell Publishing, 2004); McGrath and McGrath, *The Dawkins Delusion*, op. cit.; Keith Ward, *God, Chance and Necessity* (Oxford, Oneworld Publications, 1996); *Is Religion Dangerous?* (Oxford, Lion Hudson, 2006); *Pascal's Fire: Scientific Faith and Religious Understanding* (Oxford, Oneworld Publications, 2006).

20. Dawkins, *The God Delusion*, op. cit., p. 36.

21. John Cornwell, 'A Christmas thunderbolt for the arch-enemy of religion', *The Sunday Times*, 24 December 2006 at *Timesonline*, http://www.timesonline.co.uk/tol/news/article1264152.ece.

22. Johann Hari, 'A battler beyond belief', *The Independent*, Friday, 15 June 2007, p. 24.

23. Collins, *The Language of God*, op. cit., p. 229.

24. Mary Midgley, *Evolution as a Religion: Strange Hopes and Stranger Fears* (London and New York, Routledge, 2002), p. 34. See also Midgley, *Science and Poetry* (London and New York, Routledge, 2001); *Myths We Live By* (London and New York, Routledge, 2003).

25. Midgley, *Evolution as a Religion*, op. cit., p. 1. For a similar argument, see also John Gray, *Black Mass*, op. cit. I discuss Gray's ideas further in Chapter 6.

26. Joan Roughgarden, *Evolution and Christian Faith: Reflections of an Evolutionary Biologist* (Washington, Covelo and London, Island Press, 2006), p. 9.

27. See Thomas S. Kuhn, *The Structure of Scientific Revolutions*, 3rd edn (Chicago, University of Chicago Press, 1996, first published 1962).

28. Dawkins popularised the term 'meme' in his book *The Selfish Gene*, 3rd edn (Oxford, Oxford University Press, 2006, first published 1976). For different scholarly views on the scientific credibility of the theory of memes, see Robert Aunger (ed.), *Darwinizing Culture: The Status of Memetics as a Science* (Oxford, Oxford University Press, 2001). See also Midgley's critique of the concept of memes in *Myths We Live By*, op. cit.

29. AC Grayling, 'Through the Looking Glass', *The New Humanist*, Vol. 122, Issue 4 (July/August 2007) at http://newhumanist.org.uk/1423.

30. Hitchens used this metaphor during a public conversation with Ian McEwan at the Garrick Theatre, London, on 19 June 2007.

31. Mike Gordon and AC Grayling, *On Religion* (London, Oberon Books, 2006), p. 79.

Chapter 1: The Invention of Science

1. For an interesting study of this struggle, see Frank M. Turner, 'The Victorian Conflict Between Science and Religion: A Professional Dimension', *Isis*, 69 (3), 1978, pp. 356–76.

2. James R. Moore, *The Post-Darwinian Controversies: A Study of the Protestant Struggle to Come to Terms with Darwin in Great Britain and America, 1870–1900* (Cambridge and New York, Cambridge University Press, 1981, first published 1979), p. 121.

3. T. H. Huxley, *Collected Essays*, Vol. II (London, Macmillan, 1894), p. 149, quoted in Turner, 'The Victorian Conflict Between Science and Religion', op. cit., p. 370.

4. Huxley, *Collected Essays*, Vol. II, op. cit., p. 52, quoted in Turner, 'The Victorian Conflict Between Science and Religion', op. cit., p. 358.

5. Moore, *The Post-Darwinian Controversies*, op. cit., p. 58.

6. Others included John William Draper, whose best-selling *History of the Conflict between Religion and Science* (1874) directly targeted the Catholic Church, and Andrew Dixon White, whose *History of the Warfare of Science with Theology in Christendom* (1895), although less polemical than Draper's, perpetuated the notion of a war of ideas.

7. See Christine Garwood, *Flat Earth: The History of an Infamous Idea* (London, Macmillan, 2007).

8. Stephen Jay Gould, *Rock of Ages: Science and Religion in the Fullness of Life* (London, Vintage, 2002, first published 2001), p. 117.

9. Moore, *The Post-Darwinian Controversies*, op. cit., p. 99.

10. Ibid., pp. 99–100.

11. Charles Darwin, *The Origin of Species* (New York, Gramercy Books, 1979, first published 1859), pp. 459–60.

12. Mrs Isabella Sidgwick, 'A Grandmother's tales', *Macmillan's Magazine*, LXXVIII, no. 468, October 1898, pp. 433–4, quoted in J. R. Lucas, 'Wilberforce and Huxley: A Legendary Encounter', *The Historical Journal* 22, 2 (1979), pp. 313–30, p. 314.

13. For studies of Darwin's reception and the impact of the theory of evolution, see Mariano Artigas, Thomas F. Glick and Rafael A. Martinez, *Negotiating Darwin: The Vatican Confronts Evolution, 1877–1902* (Baltimore, John Hopkins University Press, 2006); Alvar Ellegard, *Darwin and the General Reader: The Reception of Darwin's Theory of Evolution in the British Periodical Press, 1859–1872* (Chicago, University of Chicago Press, 1990, first published 1958); Aileen Fyfe, *Science and Salvation: Evangelical Popular Science Publishing in Victorian Britain* (Chicago and London, University of Chicago Press, 2004); Thomas F. Glick (ed.), *The Comparative Reception of Darwinism* (Austin and London, University of Texas Press, 1975); David N. Livingstone, *Darwin's Forgotten Defenders: The Encounter Between Evangelical Theology and Evolutionary Thought* (Edinburgh, Scottish Academic Press and Grand Rapids MI, W. D. Eerdmans, 1987).

14. Adrian Desmond and James Moore, *Darwin: The Life of a Tormented Evolutionist* (New York and London, W. W. Norton & Co., 1994. first published

1991), p. xxi.

15. Charles Darwin, *The Descent of Man and Selection in Relation to Sex* (London, John Murray, 1901, first published 1871), p. 857.

16. Ibid., p. 858.

17. Ibid., p. 860.

18. Ibid.

19. Sarah Blaffer Hrdy, *Mother Nature: Maternal Instincts & The Shaping of the Species* (London, Vintage, 2000, first published 1999), p. xiv.

20. Joan Roughgarden, *Evolution's Rainbow: Diversity, Gender, and Sexuality in Nature and People* (Berkeley and Los Angeles, University of California Press, 2004), p. 167.

21. See Francis Wheen, *Karl Marx* new edn (London, Fourth Estate, 2000, first published 1999).

22. Karl Marx, 'A Contribution to the Critique of Hegel's Philosophy of Right: Introduction' in *Marx: Early Political Writings*, edited and translated by Joseph O'Malley (Cambridge, Cambridge University Press, 1994), p. 57. Italics as given.

23. Ibid.

24. Cf. Jean Porter, *Natural and Divine Law: Reclaiming the Tradition for Christian Ethics* (Grand Rapids, MI and Cambridge, UK, William B. Eerdmans, 1999).

25. Cf. Kenneth R. Himes, Lisa Sowle Cahill, Charles E. Curran, David Hollenbach and Thomas A. Shannon (eds.), *Modern Catholic Social Teaching: Commentaries and Interpretations* (Washington DC, Georgetown University Press, 2005).

26. There is an extensive range of literature on liberation theology in different contexts, but for a good overview see Ivan Petrella (ed.), *Latin American Liberation Theology: The Next Generation* (Maryknoll NY, Orbis Books, 2005); Christopher Rowland (ed.), *The Cambridge Companion to Liberation Theology* (Cambridge, Cambridge University Press, 1999).

27. See Lucille B. Ritvo, *Darwin's Influence on Freud: A Tale of Two Sciences* (New Haven, Conn. and London, Yale University Press, 1990).

28. Sigmund Freud, 'The Future of an Illusion' in *Civilization, Society and Religion*, trans. James Strachey, ed. Albert Dickson, The Penguin Freud Library, Vol. 12 (London, Penguin Books, 1991), p. 241.

29. For different cultural responses to Freud, see John C. Burnham, 'The Reception of Psychoanalysis in Western Cultures: An Afterword on Its Comparative History', *Comparative Studies in Society and History*, Vol. 24, No. 4, October 1982, pp. 603–10.

30. See Stephen Jay Gould, *Wonderful Life: the Burgess Shale and the Nature of History* (London, Vintage, 2000).

31. For a more detailed account of the Scopes trial and its aftermath, see Gould, *Rock of Ages*, op. cit., pp. 133–50. See also the website http://www.law.umkc.edu/faculty/projects/ftrials/scopes/scopes.htm.

32. For the text of the letter and the list of signatories, see the website of the British Humanist Association, http://www.humanism.org.uk/site/cms/contentviewarticle.asp?article=1348.

33. See the British Humanist Association website at http://www. humanism.org.uk/site/cms/.

34. Polly Toynbee, quoted at http://www.humanism.org.uk/site/cms/news articleview.asp?article=2382.

Chapter 2: The Man of Science and His Religious Others

1. Cf. Timothy Fitzgerald, *The Ideology of Religious Studies* (New York and Oxford, Oxford University Press, 2000); Russell T. McCutcheon, *Manufacturing Religion: The Discourse on Sui Generis Religion and the Politics of Nostalgia* (Oxford and New York, Oxford University Press, 1997).

2. These ideas were first explored in the pioneering work of Simone de Beauvoir, *The Second Sex*, trans. H. M. Parshley (London, Penguin Books, 1972, first published 1949). More recently, they have been associated with the work of Luce Irigaray. Cf. Luce Irigaray, *Speculum of the Other Woman*, trans. Gillian C. Gill (Ithaca NY, Cornell University Press, 1985, first published 1974).

3. Cf. Jacques Derrida, *Deconstruction in a Nutshell: A Conversation with Jacques Derrida*, edited with a commentary by John D. Caputo (New York, Fordham University Press, 1996); John Sallis (ed.), *Deconstruction and Philosophy: The Texts of Jacques Derrida* (Chicago, University of Chicago Press, 1987).

4. William James, *The Varieties of Religious Experience*, ed. Martin Marty (New York, Penguin, 1982, first published 1902), p. 31, quoted in Daniel C. Dennett, *Breaking the Spell: Religion as a Natural Phenomenon* (London, Allen Lane, 2006), p. 11.

5. Akbar S. Ahmed, *Postmodernism and Islam: Predicament and Promise* (London and New York, Routledge, 2004), p. 223.

6. Edward B. Tylor, *Primitive Culture: Researches into the Development of Mythology, Philosophy, Religion, Language, Art, and Custom*, 2 vols. (London, John Murray, 1920, first published 1871), Vol. 1, p. 26.

7. Ibid., Vol. 2, p. 453.

8. James G. Frazer, *The Golden Bough: The Magic Art and the Evolution of Kings*, 2 vols. (London, Macmillan and Co., 1911), 'Preface to the Second Edition', Vol. 1, p. xxv.

9. Ibid., pp. xxv–xxvi.

10. Ibid., p. xxvi.

11. Richard Dawkins, *The God Delusion* (London, Toronto, Sydney, Auckland, Johannesburg, Bantam Press, 2006), p. 156.

12. Cf. John Gray, *Black Mass: Apocalyptic Religion and the Death of Utopia* (London and New York, Allen Lane, 2007).

13. Christopher Hitchens, *God Is Not Great: The Case Against Religion* (London, Atlantic Books, 2007), p. 64.

14. Ibid., p. 65.

15. Quoted in Dawkins, *The God Delusion*, op. cit., p. 14.

16. Dennett, *Breaking the Spell*, op. cit., p. 9.

17. Census results on religion can be found at the National Statistics website: http://www.statistics.gov.uk/cci/nugget.asp?id=293. For the *Financial Times*/Harris Poll on belief in God in the USA and five European countries in 2006, see www.prnewswire.com. For links to a range of statistical surveys, see the website 'Bane of Monotheism', http://www.vexen.co.uk/religion/rib.html#18.

18. Dawkins, *The God Delusion*, op. cit., p. 18.

19. Ibid.

20. Ibid., p. 19.

21. Ibid.

22. Ibid.

23. Ibid.

24. Lewis Carroll, *Alice's Adventures in Wonderland and Through the Looking Glass* (London, Penguin Classics, 2003, first published 1872), p. 186.

25. Hitchens, *God Is Not Great*, op. cit., p. 7.

26. Ibid., p. 175.

27. Ibid., p. 176.

28. Ibid., p. 241.

29. Arthur Peacocke, *Theology for a Scientific Age*, enlarged edn (London, SCM Press, 1993, first published 1990), pp. 5–6.

30. Dawkins, *The God Delusion*, op. cit., p. 374.

Chapter 3: The Enlightenment and Its Aftermath

1. For readers who would like to undertake a more extensive introductory study of the debates and issues explored here, I would recommend Brian Easlea's excellent seminar series, 'An Introduction to the History and Social Studies of Science: A Seminar Course for First-Year Science Students', *Science Studies*, Vol. 3, No. 2 (April 1973), pp. 185–209. Although not quite up to date, this article provides discussion points and bibliographies for a range of topics relevant to the issues I raise here.

2. Modern studies about the relationship between knowledge and power owe much to the ideas of the French philosopher Michel Foucault, who explored these themes extensively in his writings. Cf. Michel Foucault, *The Order of Things: An Archaeology of the Human Sciences*, trans. Alan Sheridan (London and New York, Routledge, 2001, first published 1966); Michel Foucault, *Power/Knowledge: Selected Interviews & Other Writings 1972-1977*, ed. Colin Gordon (New York, Pantheon Books, 1980).

3. See Brian Easlea, *Witch Hunting, Magic and the New Philosophy: An Introduction to Debates of the Scientific Revolution 1450–1750* (Hemel Hempstead, Prentice Hall/Harvester Wheatsheaf, 1980); Evelyn Fox Keller, *Reflections on Gender and Science* (New Haven, Conn., Yale University Press, 1985); Carolyn Merchant, *The Death of Nature: Women, Ecology and the Scientific Revolution* (San Francisco, HarperSanFrancisco, 1989, first published 1980).

4. There is still a lack of reliable scholarship about the witch-hunts, despite

considerable popular interest in the subject which has spawned a very wide range of theories, some more respectable than others. Cf. the critical essay by Richard M. Golden, 'American Perspectives in the European Witch Hunts', *The History Teacher*, Vol. 30, No. 4 (August 1977), pp. 406–26. Books which explore the relationship between the rise of science and the witch-hunts include Easlea, *Witch Hunting, Magic and the New Philosophy*, op. cit., and Merchant, *The Death of Nature*, op. cit.

5. Francis Bacon, '*De Dignitate et Augmentis Scientiarum*' (written 1623), in *Works*, James Spedding, Robert Leslie Ellis and Douglas Devon Heath (eds.), 14 vols. (London, Longmans Green, 1870), Vol. 4, p. 296, quoted in Merchant, *The Death of Nature*, op. cit., p. 168.

6. James Walvin, *The Trader, the Owner, the Slave: Parallel Lives in the Age of Slavery* (London, Jonathan Cape, 2007), p. xv.

7. Ibid., p. xvi.

8. Roy Porter, 'The Body and the Mind, The Doctor and the Patient: Negotiating Hysteria', in Sander L. Gilman, Helen King, Roy Porter, G. S. Rousseau and Elaine Showalter (eds.), *Hysteria Beyond Freud* (Berkeley, Los Angeles and Oxford, University of California Press, 1993), p. 249. This book is available for free download at http://content.cdlib.org/xtf/view?docId=ft0p3003d3&brand=eschol. See also Thomas Laqueur, *Making Sex* (Cambridge MA, Harvard University Press, 1990).

9. See Rachel P. Maines, *The Technology of Orgasm: 'Hysteria,' the Vibrator, and Women's Sexual Satisfaction* (Baltimore, John Hopkins University Press, 1999).

10. See Jill Fields, '"Fighting the Corsetless Evil": Shaping Corsets and Culture, 1900–1930', *Journal of Social History*, Vol. 33, No. 2 (Winter 1999), pp. 355–84 available on-line at Http://findarticles.com/p/articles/mi_m2005/is_2_33/ai_58675450.

11. Lucien Warner, *A popular Treatise on the Functions and Diseases of Women* (New York, Manhattan Publishing, 1874), quoted in Barbara Ehrenreich and Deirdre English, *Complaints and Disorders: The Sexual Politics of Sickness* (New York, The Feminist Press, 1973), pp. 12–13.

12. See Stephen Jay Gould, 'The Hottentot Venus' in *The Flamingo's Smile* (New York, W. W. Norton and Co., 1985), pp. 291–305; Rachel Holmes, *The Hottentot Venus: The Life and Death of Saartjie Baartman (Born 1789 – Buried 2002)* (London, Bloomsbury Publishing, 2007).

13. Richard Dawkins, *The God Delusion* (London, Toronto, Sydney, Auckland, Johannesburg, Bantam Press, 2006), p. 363.

14. Ibid., p. 362.

15. Polly Toynbee, 'Behind the burka', *The Guardian*, Friday, 28 September 2001, available on the *Guardian Unlimited* website: http://www.guardian.co.uk/religion/Story/0,,559537,00.html.

16. Ibid.

17. See *The World Health Report 2005* at the website: http://www.who.int/whr/2005/en/.

18. Polly Toynbee, 'Not in my name', *The Guardian*, Friday, 8 April 2005, at http://www.guardian.co.uk/comment/story/0,,1454850,00.html.

19. For a critical evaluation of social constructivism and its impact on the under-standing of science, see André Kukla, *Social Constructivism and the Philosophy of Science* (London and New York, Routledge, 2000). See also Sandra Harding, *The Science Question in Feminism* (Milton Keynes, Open University Press, 1986), and Harding (ed.), *Is Science Multicultural? Postcolonialisms, Feminisms, and Epistemologies* (Bloomington and Indianapolis, Indiana University Press, 1998).

20. Thomas S. Kuhn, *The Structure of Scientific Revolutions* 3rd edn (Chicago, University of Chicago Press, 1996, first published 1962), p. 4.

21. Cf. Patrick J. Hannan, *Serendipity, Luck and Wisdom in Research* (Lincoln, Nebraska, iUniverse.com, 2006); Royston M. Roberts, *Serendipity: Accidental Discoveries in Science* (Chichester, UK, John Wiley & Sons Inc., 1989).

22. See 'Fraud Scientist made Unwitting Discovery, say Researchers', *The Guardian*, Friday, 3 August 2007, at http://www.guardian.co.uk/science/2007/aug/03/stemcells?gusrc=rss&feed=11.

23. See Ben Goldacre, 'Opinions from the medical fringe should come with a health warning', *The Guardian,* Saturday, 24 February 2007. This and other articles referred to can be found on *The Guardian* website: http://www.guardian.co.uk/life/badscience/story/0,,2020306,00.html.

Chapter 4: Science, Religion and War

1. Christopher Hitchens, *God Is Not Great: The Case Against Religion* (London, Atlantic Books, 2007), p. 13.

2. Richard Dawkins, *The God Delusion* (London, Toronto, Sydney, Auckland, Johannesburg, Bantam Press, 2006), pp. 1–2.

3. Sam Harris, *The End of Faith: Religion, Terror, and the Future of Reason* (New York and London, W. W. Norton and Co., 2004).

4. Dawkins, *The God Delusion*, op. cit., p. 278.

5. Ibid., p. 249.

6. Robert Bevan, *The Destruction of Memory: Architecture at War* (London, Reaktion Books, 2005).

7. Greg Austin, Todd Kranock and Thom Oommen, *God and War: An Audit & An Explanation*, at http://news.bbc.co.uk/1/shared/spl/hi/world/04/war_audit_pdf/pdf/war_audit.pdf.

8. Ibid., p. 16.

9. Ibid., p. 14.

10. Ibid., pp. 24–5.

11. For estimated numbers of war casualties, see *Historical Atlas of the Twentieth Century* at the website: http://users.erols.com/mwhite28/warstat1.htm.

12. Austin, Kranock and Oommen, *God and War*, op. cit., p. 17. For a provocative but challenging analysis of the extreme forms of violence associated with post-Enlightenment political utopias, see John Gray, *Black Mass: Apocalyptic Religion and the Death of Utopia* (London and New York, Allen Lane, 2007).

13. John Ferguson, *War and Peace in the World's Religions* (London, Sheldon Press,

1977), p. 122. See also David Martin, *Does Christianity Cause War?* (Oxford, Clarendon Press, 1997).

14. Cf. Ian Hazlett, 'War and Peace in Christianity' in Perry Schmidt-Leukel (ed.), *War and Peace in the World Religions*, The Gerald Weisfeld Lectures 2003 (London, SCM Press, 2004), pp. 99–147.

15. Ibid., p. 248.

16. Ibid.

17. Cf. Phyllis Trible, *Texts of Terror: Literary Feminist Readings of the Biblical Narratives* (Philadelphia, Augsburg Fortress Press, 1984).

18. See 'First video game banned in Britain puts player in role of sadistic killer', *The Times Online*, 20 June 2007, available at the website: http://technology. timesonline.co.uk/tol/news/tech_and_web/gadgets_and_gaming/ article1957433.ece.

19. Cf. Howard Clark Kee, *Understanding the New Testament*, 5th edn (Englewood Cliffs NJ, Prentice Hall, 1993).

20. There is scholarly debate as to the actual extent of early Christian pacifism in practice. For a good overview of these different debates, see 'Christian Pacifism: Early Christian Views of War', *Crusades Encyclopedia* at http://www.crusades-encyclopedia.com/christianpacifism.html. One of the most widely cited sources is Roland H. Bainton, 'The Early Church and War', *The Harvard Theological Review*, Vol. 39.3 (July 1946), pp. 189–212. For more recent sources, see Peter Brock, *Varieties of Pacifism: A Survey from Antiquity to the Outset of the Twentieth Century* (Toronto, University of Toronto Press, 1998); Lisa Sowle Cahill, *Love Your Enemies: Discipleship, Pacifism, and Just War Theory* (Minneapolis, Fortress Press, 1994); L. J. Switt, *The Early Fathers on War and Military Service*, Message of the Fathers of the Church, Vol. 19 (Wilmington DE, Glazier, 1983).

21. See Elaine Pagels, *Adam, Eve and the Serpent* (London, Vintage Books, 1989), in which she explores the earliest Christian understanding of freedom and its gradual decline.

22. See Jacques Ellul, *Violence: Reflections from a Christian Perspective* (London, Mowbrays, 1978); Stanley Hauerwas, *Against the Nations: War and Survival in a Liberal Society* (Minneapolis, Winston Press, 1985); Brian Wicker (ed.), *Studying War – No More? From Just War to Just Peace* (Kampen, Kok Pharos, 1993).

23. For the just war tradition, see Jean Bethke Elshtain (ed.), *Just War Theory* (Oxford, Basil Blackwell, 1992); Oliver O'Donovan, *The Just War Revisited* (Cambridge, Cambridge University Press, 2003); Gregory M. Reichbert, Henrik Syse and Endre Begby (eds.), *The Ethics of War: Classic and Contemporary Readings* (Oxford, Blackwell Publishing, 2006); Michael Walzer, *Just and Unjust Wars: a Moral Argument with Historical Illustrations*, 2nd edn (New York, Basic Books, 1992).

24. Christopher Hitchens, 'Pious Nonsense: the Unholy "Christian" Case against War' at http://www.slate.com/id/2079860/.

25. See Johann Hari's website, JohannHari.com, at http://www.johannhari. com/archive/article.php?id=309.

26. Polly Toynbee, 'We need to focus on this week's deaths in Iraq – they belong to us', *The Guardian*, Friday, 20 April 2007, available at the website: http://www.guardian.co.uk/commentisfree/story/0,,2061826,00.html.

27. Ibid.

28. Polly Toynbee, 'Behind the burka', *The Guardian*, Friday, 28 September 2001, available on the *Guardian Unlimited* website: http://www.guardian.co.uk/religion/Story/0,,559537,00.html.

29. See Mark and Louise Zwick, 'Pope John Paul II calls War a Defeat for Humanity: Neoconservative Iraq Just War Theories Rejected', *Houston Catholic Worker*, Vol. XXIII, No. 4, July–August 2003, at http://www.cjd.org/paper/jp2war.html.

30. Sam Harris, *The End of Faith: Religion, Terror, and the Future of Reason* (New York and London, W. W. Norton and Company, 2004), p. 145.

31. Ibid., p. 53.

32. Ibid., p. 199.

33. Ibid., p. 203.

34. Ibid., p. 143.

35. Ibid., p. 144.

36. See the weblog at http://www.amptoons.com/blog/archives/2006/07/13/american-soldiers-arrested-for-rapeexecution-of-14-year-old-girl-and-her-family/.

37. Dawkins, *The God Delusion*, op. cit., p. 252.

38. Dawkins, *The God Delusion*, op. cit., p. 278.

39. Ibid., p. 302.

40. Ibid., p. 303.

41. Richard Dawkins, 'Bible Belter', *The Times Literary Supplement*, 5 September 2007, at http://tls.timesonline.co.uk/article/0,,253492649121,00.html.

42. Chris Hedges, 'False Gods', *New Statesman*, 4 June 2007, at http://www.newstatesman.com/200706040045.html.

43. Chris Langley, *Soldiers in the Laboratory: Military involvement in science and technology – and some alternatives*, edited by Stuart Parkinson and Philip Webber, published by Scientists for Global Responsibility (SGR), January 2005, available to download at the website: www.sgr.org.uk/ArmsControl/Soldiers_in_Lab_Report.pdf.

44. Ibid., p. 10.

45. Ibid., p. 11.

46. Ibid.

47. Ibid., p. 12.

48. For examples of scientists committed to working in the public interest, see the websites of AAAS (The American Association for the Advancement of Science) at http://www.aaas.org/; FAS (The Federation of American Scientists) at http://www.fas.org/main/home.jsp; CSPI (The Center for Science in the Public Interest) at http://www.cspinet.org/. See also the report by The Royal Society, 'Science and the Public Interest', available to download from the Society's website at http://www.royalsoc.ac.uk/page.asp?id=4686.

Chapter 5: Science, Theology and Politics

1. For a more wide-ranging engagement with perspectives from different religious traditions, see Philip Clayton (ed.), *The Oxford Handbook of Religion and Science* (Oxford, Oxford University Press, 2006).

2. John Polkinghorne, *Belief in God in an Age of Science* (New Haven, Conn. and London, Yale University Press, 1998), p. 76.

3. Keith Ward, *God, Chance and Necessity* (Oxford, Oneworld Publications, 1996).

4. Keith Ward, *Is Religion Dangerous?* (Oxford, Lion Hudson, 2006).

5. Keith Ward, *Pascal's Fire: Scientific Faith and Religious Understanding* (Oxford, Oneworld Publications, 2006).

6. Alister E. McGrath, *Dawkins' God: Genes, Memes, and the Meaning of Life* (Oxford, Blackwell Publishing, 2004).

7. Alister McGrath and Joanna Collicutt McGrath, *The Dawkins Delusion?* (London, SPCK Publishing, 2007).

8. Nicholas Lash, *Theology on Pilgrimage* (London, Darton, Longman & Todd, 2008 (forthcoming)).

9. John Cornwell, *Darwin's Angel: A Seraphic Response to 'The God Delusion'* (London, Profile, 2007).

10. Paul Davies, *The Mind of God: Science and the Search for Ultimate Meaning* (London, Penguin Books, 2006, first published 1993), p. 20.

11. Paul Davies, *God & the New Physics* (London, Penguin Books, 1990, first published 1983), p. 217.

12. Ibid., p. 216.

13. Ibid., p. 229.

14. See Edward Babinski's website of Christian evolutionist resources at http://www.edwardtbabinski.us/evolution/christian_evolutionists.html.

15. Pope John Paul II, Message to Pontifical Academy of Sciences, 22 October 1996, available online at the website of the Catholic Information Network: http://www.cin.org/jp2evolu.html.

16. Polkinghorne, *Belief in God in an Age of Science*, op. cit., p. 50.

17. For an exploration of different meanings of the anthropic principle, see Davies, *The Mind of God*, op. cit., ch. 8.

18. Ibid., p. 24.

19. Richard Dawkins, *The God Delusion* (London, Toronto, Sydney, Auckland, Johannesburg, Bantam Press, 2006), p. 100.

20. See Dawkins, *The God Delusion*, op. cit., pp. 153–7.

21. Ibid., p. 368.

22. Ibid., p. 370.

23. Ibid., p. 371.

24. Steve Grand, *Creation: Life and How To Make It* (London, Weidenfeld & Nicolson, 2000), quoted in Dawkins, *The God Delusion*, op. cit., p. 371.

25. Dawkins, *The God Delusion*, op. cit., p. 371.

26. See Michael Behe, *Darwin's Black Box: The Biochemical Challenge to Evolution* (New York, The Free Press, 1996); Neil Broom, *How Blind is the Watchmaker?* (Downers Grove IL, InterVarsity Press, 2001); William Dembski, *Intelligent Design: The Bridge Between Science and Theology* (Downers Grove IL, InterVarsity Press, 1999); Phillip E. Johnson, *Darwin on Trial* (Downers Grove IL, InterVarsity Press, 1993). For an anthology of different writers supporting the theory, see J. P. Moreland (ed.), *The Creation Hypothesis* (Downers Grove IL, InterVarsity Press, 1994). For a wider range of perspectives and critiques, see Robert T. Pennock (ed.), *Intelligent Design Creationism and Its Critics: Philosophical, Theological, and Scientific Perspectives* (Cambridge MA, MIT Press, 2001).

27. See James R. Moore, *The Post-Darwinian Controversies: A Study of the Protestant Struggle to Come to Terms with Darwin in Great Britain and America, 1870–1900* (Cambridge and New York, Cambridge University Press, 1981, first published 1979), pp. 309–11.

28. See Edwards v. Aguillard, US Supreme Court Decision, at http://www.talkorigins.org/faqs/edwards-v-aguillard.html.

29. Percival Davis and Dean H. Kenyon, *Of Pandas and People: The Central Question of Biological Origins* (Richardson TX, The Foundation for Thought and Ethics, 1989).

30. See the Discovery Institute website at http://www.discovery.org/ (last accessed 19 May 2007).

31. William A. Dembski, 'Is Intelligent Design a Form of Natural Theology?' at http://www.designinference.com/documents/2001.03.ID_as_nat_theol.htm (last accessed 19 May 2007). A wide range of Dembski's writing is available through links from this website.

32. Quoted in Willam A. Dembski, 'The Logical Underpinnings of Intelligent Design', in Dembski and Michael Ruse (eds.), *Debating Design: From Darwin to DNA* (Cambridge, Cambridge University Press, 2004), p. 324.

33. Michael Behe, *Darwin's Black Box* (New York, Free Press, 1996).

34. William A. Dembski, *Intelligent Design: The Bridge Between Science and Theology* (Downers Grove IL, InterVarsity Press, 1999), p. 47.

35. Lash, *Theology on Pilgrimage*, op. cit.

36. Lash, *Theology on Pilgrimage*, op. cit.

37. Richard Dawkins, *The God Delusion*, op. cit., p. 113.

38. See Daniel C. Dennett, *Darwin's Dangerous Idea: Evolution and the Meanings of Life* (London and New York, Penguin Books, 1996, first published 1995).

39. For a readable summary of scientific arguments against intelligent design theory, see H. Allen Orr, 'Devolution: Why intelligent design isn't', *The New Yorker*, 30 May 2005, at http://www.newyorker.com/archive/2005/05/30/050530fa_fact?currentPage=1. See also William A. Dembski, 'Allen Orr in the *New Yorker* – A Response' on Dembski's weblog: http://www.uncommondescent.com/evolution/allen-orr-in-the-new-yorker-a-brief-response/. Dembski's website gives extensive coverage to intelligent design theorists and their critics. For theological criticisms of intelligent design theory, see J. F. Haught, *God After Darwin: A Theology of Evolution* (Westview, Colorado,

Westview Press, 2000); Kenneth Miller, *Finding Darwin's God: A Scientist's Search for Common Ground between God and Evolution* (San Francisco, HarperCollins, 2001, first published 1999).

40. There are no references to the Wedge document on the Discovery Institute's website, but it can be accessed at http://www.antievolution.org/features/wedge.pdf.

41. Daniel C. Dennett, *Breaking the Spell: Religion as a Natural Phenomenon* (London *et al.*, Allen Lane, 2006), p. 295.

42. Dawkins, *The God Delusion*, op. cit., p. 199.

43. Christopher Hitchens, *God Is Not Great: The Case Against Religion* (London, Atlantic Books, 2007), p. 286.

Chapter 6: History, Faith and Reason

1. AC Grayling, 'Through the Looking Glass', *The New Humanist*, Vol. 122, Issue 4 (July/August 2007), at http://newhumanist.org.uk/1423.

2. Among the many studies available on the early Church, good introductions can be found in Henry Chadwick, *The Early Church*, Penguin History of the Church Vol. 1, revised edn (New York and London, Penguin Books, 1994); W. H. C. Frend, *The Rise of Christianity* (Philadelphia, Fortress Press, 1992, first published 1965).

3. Richard E. Rubenstein, *Aristotle's Children: How Christians, Muslims, and Jews Rediscovered Ancient Wisdom and Illuminated the Dark Ages* (Orlando, Austin, New York, San Diego, Toronto, London, Harcourt Brace International, 2003), p. 3.

4. Ibid., p. 5.

5. Ibid., p. 6.

6. See Rodney Stark, *One True God: Historical Consequences of Monotheism* (Princeton NJ, Princeton University Press, 2003, first published 2001); *For the Glory of God: How Monotheism Led to Reformations, Science, Witch-Hunts, and the End of Slavery* (Princeton NJ, Princeton University Press, 2004); *The Victory of Reason: How Christianity Led to Freedom, Capitalism, and Western Success* (New York, Random House, 2006).

7. See Tariq Ramadan, *Western Muslims and the Future of Islam* (Oxford, Oxford University Press, 2005).

8. Richard Dawkins, *The God Delusion* (London, Toronto, Sydney, Auckland, Johannesburg, Bantam Press, 2006), p. 303.

9. Sam Harris, *The End of Faith: Religion, Terror and the Future of Reason*, (New York and London, W. W. Norton and Co., 2004) pp. 14–15.

10. Christopher Hitchens, *God Is Not Great: The Case Against Religion* (London, Atlantic Books, 2007), p. 64.

11. Bertrand Russell, quoted in Dawkins, *The God Delusion*, op. cit., p. 52.

12. Dawkins, *The God Delusion*, op. cit., p. 53.

13. Ibid.

14. Terry Eagleton, 'Lunging, Flailing, Mispunching', *London Review of Books*,

Vol. 28, No. 20, 19 October 2006.

15. John Gray, *Black Mass: Apocalyptic Religion and the Death of Utopia* (London and New York, Allen Lane, 2007).

16. Ibid., p. 230.

17. Ibid., p. 73.

18. Grayling, 'Through the Looking Glass', op. cit.

19. Cf. Toby Green, *Inquisition: The Reign of Fear* (London, Macmillan, 2007).

20. Cf. Alasdair MacIntyre, *Whose Justice? – Which Rationality?* (London, Gerald Duckworth & Co., 1996, first published 1981).

21. See Genevieve Lloyd, *The Man of Reason: Male and Female in Western Philosophy* (London and New York, Routledge, 1993, first published 1985).

22. See Tina Beattie, *Woman* (London and New York, Continuum, 2003); Joerg Rieger, *Christ and Empire: From Paul to Postcolonial Times* (Philadelphia, Augsburg Fortress Press, 2007); Rosemary Radford Ruether, *Sexism and God Talk*, new edn (London, SCM Press, 2002, first published 1983); R. S. Sugirtharajah, *The Bible and Empire: Postcolonial Explorations* (Cambridge, Cambridge University Press, 2005); Sugirtharajah (ed.), *Voices from the Margin: Interpreting the Bible in the Third World*, 3rd edn (Maryknoll NY, Orbis Books, 2006, first published 1991).

23. Cf. Pamela Sue Anderson, *A Feminist Philosophy of Religion* (Oxford, Blackwell, 1998).

24. Cf. Choi Hee An and Katheryn Pfisterer Darr (eds.), *Engaging the Bible: Critical Readings from Contemporary Women* (Philadelphia PA, Fortress Press, 2006); Elisabeth Schussler Fiorenza, *Bread Not Stone: The Challenge of Feminist Biblical Interpretation* (Boston, Beacon Press, 1995); Letty M. Russell (ed.), *Feminist Interpretation of the Bible* (Westminster, John Knox Press, 2004, first published 1985); Phyllis Trible, *God and the Rhetoric of Sexuality*, new edn (London, SCM Press, 1992, first published 1978).

25. See Ludwig Feuerbach, *The Essence of Christianity*, trans. George Eliot (London, Prometheus Books, 1989, first published 1854).

26. Grace Jantzen, *Becoming Divine: Towards a Feminist Philosophy of Religion* (Manchester, Manchester University Press, 1988), p. 28.

27. Dawkins, *The God Delusion*, op. cit., p. 31.

28. Ibid.

29. Hitchens, *God Is Not Great*, op. cit., p. 175.

30. 'Kingdoms of this world, and otherwise' in *The Economist*, 25 January 2007, available at http://www.economist.com/world/international/displaystory.cfm?story_id=8602944&CFID=4902544&CFTOKEN=88886800.

Chapter 7: Kitsch, Terror and the Postmodern Condition

1. Jean-François Lyotard, *The Postmodern Condition: A Report on Knowledge* (Manchester, Manchester University Press, 1984, first published 1979).

2. Malise Ruthven, *Fundamentalism: The Search for Meaning* (Oxford, Oxford

University Press, 2004), p. 198.

3. Ibid., pp. 201–2.

4. Mark Juergensmeyer, *Terror in the Mind of God* (Berkeley and Los Angeles CA and London, University of California Press, 2001).

5. Ibid., p. 232.

6. Ibid., p. 229.

7. Ibid., p. xiii.

8. Ibid., p. xiv. John Gray does not refer to Juergensmeyer's book in *Black Mass*, which I discussed in Chapter 6. However, there are interesting resonances between the two.

9. Sam Harris, *The End of Faith: Religion, Terror, and the Future of Reason* (New York and London, W. W. Norton and Company, 2004), p. 16.

10. Ibid., p. 221.

11. For scholarly debates on the relationship between religious doctrines and mystical experiences, see F. Samuel Brainard, *Reality and Religious Experience* (Pennsylvania, Pennsylvania State University Press, 2000); Peter Donovan, *Interpreting Religious Experience* (London, Sheldon Press, 1979); Robert S. Ellwood, *Mysticism and Religion*, 2nd edn (New York and London, Seven Bridges Press, 1999, first published 1980); Robert K. C. Forman (ed.), *The Problem of Pure Consciousness: Mysticism and Philosophy* (Oxford, Oxford University Press, 1990); Steven Katz (ed.), *Mysticism and Language* (Oxford and New York, Oxford University Press, 1992).

12. Harris, *The End of Faith*, op. cit., p. 79.

13. Cf. James W. Jones, *Terror and Transformation: The Ambiguity of Religion in Psychoanalytic Perspective* (London and New York, Routledge, 2002).

14. John Gray, *Black Mass: Apocalyptic Religion and the Death of Utopia* (London and New York, Allen Lane, 2007), p. 209.

15. Christopher Hitchens, *God Is Not Great: The Case Against Religion* (London, Atlantic Books, 2007), p. 283.

16. Cf. Stanley Hauerwas, *Dispatches from the Front: Theological Engagements with the Secular*, new edn (Durham, North Carolina, Duke University Press, 1995); Alasdair MacIntyre, *Whose Justice? Which Rationality?* (London, Gerald Duckworth & Co., 1996, first published 1988) and *After Virtue*, new edn (London, Duckworth, 1997, first published 1981); John Milbank, *Theology and Social Theory: Beyond Secular Reason*, new edn (Oxford, Blackwell Publishers, 2005). See also Graham Ward (ed.), *The Postmodern God: Theological Reader* (Oxford, Blackwell Publishers, 1997).

17. See Richard Dawkins, *The God Delusion* (London, Toronto, Sydney, Auckland, Johannesburg, Bantam Press, 2006), p. 64.

18. For a good selection of Nietzsche's writings, see *The Portable Nietzsche*, edited and translated by Walter Kaufmann, new edn (London, Viking Portable Library, 1994, first published 1977). See also Water Kaufmann, *Nietzsche: Philosopher, Psychologist, Antichrist*, revised edn (Princeton NJ, Princeton University Press, 1975, first published 1950).

19. Fyodor Dostoyevsky, *The Brothers Karamazov* (London and New York, Penguin Books, 2003, first published 1880), p. 320.

20. Hitchens, *God Is Not Great*, op. cit., p. 5.

21. Ibid., p. 230.

22. See John Cornwell's critique of Hitchens' reading of *The Brothers Karamazov* in John Cornwell, 'A Jaundiced Catalogue of Scandals', *The Tablet*, 16 June 2007, p. 19.

23. Elie Wiesel, *Night* (London and New York, Penguin Books, 1981, first published 1958), p. 45.

24. Quoted in Thomas A. Idinopulos, 'The Mystery of Suffering in the Art of Dostoevsky, Camus, Wiesel, and Grünewald', *Journal of the American Academy of Religion*, Vol. XLIII (1) (1975), pp. 51–61, pp. 51–2.

Chapter 8: Creativity and the Story of God

1. For an exploration of the theological significance of story-telling and narrative, see Gerard Loughlin, *Telling God's Story: Bible, Church and Narrative Theology* (Cambridge, Cambridge University Press, 1999, first published 1996).

2. See Mary Midgley, *Science and Poetry* (London and New York, Routledge, 2001).

3. This was a series of talks and debates organised by the Science Network in association with the Crick-Jacobs Center at the Salk Institute, La Jolla, California, 5–7 November 2006. Visual recordings of the proceedings can be found at the website, beyondbelief2006.org. The Dawkins talk I am referring to was in Session 3, where he shared a platform with the Christian evolutionary biologist Joan Roughgarden.

4. See also Richard Dawkins, *The God Delusion* (London, Toronto, Sydney, Auckland, Johannesburg, Bantam Press, 2006), p. 86.

5. Ibid., pp. 86–7.

6. Christopher Hitchens, *God Is Not Great: The Case Against Religion* (London, Atlantic Books, 2007), p. 286.

7. Ian McEwan, *Saturday* (London, Jonathan Cape, 2005), p. 279.

8. Ibid., p. 55.

9. Ibid., p. 5.

10. Ibid.

11. Terry Eagleton, 'Lunging, Flailing, Mispunching', *The London Review of Books*, Vol. 28, No. 20, October 2006.

12. Dawkins, *The God Delusion*, op. cit., p. 347.

13. McEwan, *Saturday*, op. cit., p. 26.

14. Ibid., p. 4.

15. George Steiner, *Real Presences* (London and Boston, Faber and Faber, 1991, first published 1989), pp. 231–2.

16. Ibid., p. 214.

17. Ibid., p. 216.

18. Ibid., p. 229.

19. Milan Kundera, *The Curtain: An Essay in Seven Parts* (London, Faber and

Faber, 2007), p. 15.

20. Cf. Keith Ward, *Rational Theology and the Creativity of God* (Oxford, Basil Blackwell, 1982).

21. Cf. David Lewis-Williams, *The Mind in the Cave* (London, Thames & Hudson, 2004, first published 2002); Nivel Spivey, *How Art Made the World* (London, BBC Books, 2005).

22. Lewis-Williams cites the work of E. G. D'Aquili and A. B. Newberg, 'The neuropsychological basis of religions, or why God won't go away', *Zygon* 33 (1998), pp. 187–201. See Lewis-Williams, *The Mind in the Cave*, op. cit., pp. 290–91. See also Dean H. Hamer, *The God Gene: How Faith is Hardwired into our Genes* (New York, Anchor, 2005); David Hay, *Something There: The Biology of the Human Spirit* (London, Darton, Longman & Todd, 2006); John Hick, *The New Frontier of Religion and Science: Religious Experience, Neuroscience, and the Transcendent* (London, Palgrave Macmillan, 2006). See also the review essay by Kelly Bulkeley, 'The Gospel According to Darwin: The Relevance of Cognitive Neuroscience to Religious Studies' at http://www.kellybulkeley.com/articles/article_RSR_cognitive_neurosci_review.htm.

23. Lewis-Williams, *The Mind in the Cave*, op. cit.

24. Augustine, *Confessions* X.xxvii (37), trans. Henry Chadwick, (Oxford and New York, Oxford University Press, 1998), 10.27–38.

25. Dawkins, *The God Delusion*, op. cit., p. 374.

26. Steiner, *Real Presences*, op. cit., p. 230.

27. Pope John Paul II, *Crossing the Threshold of Hope*, trans. Jenny and Martha McPhee (London, Jonathan Cape, 1994), pp. 62–3. Italics as given.

28. AC Grayling, quoted in Stephanie Merritt, 'Have faith in the theatre', *The Observer*, Sunday, 3 December 2006, available at http://arts.guardian.co.uk/features/story/0,,1962514,00.

29. Mick Gordon and AC Grayling, *On Religion* (London, Oberon Books, 2006), pp. 75–6.

30. Ibid., p. 78.

31. Paul Davies, *The Mind of God: Science and the Search for Ultimate Meaning* (London, Penguin Books, 1993, first published 1992), p. 232.

Index